WITHDRAWAL

Leading and Managing Teaching Assistants

There are more than 200,000 teaching assistants (TAs) in the UK. This comprehensive, practical book deals with how to make use of them effectively. Written by a recognised authority on TAs, the book investigates

◆ the roles of leadership and management
◆ the various roles of TAs and what distinguishes them from other support staff
◆ the whole-school learning environment
◆ the needs of the school and the needs of the TAs
◆ good practice in appointing and developing TAs – giving examples and outlining the technicalities
◆ the uses of a TA in the classroom – giving guidance for teachers
◆ methodologies in leading a team of TAs.

This supportive and stimulating book is balanced with practical and effective strategies for managing TAs. TAs can contribute to higher standards for pupils, better curriculum delivery, improved work–life balance and effectiveness for teachers and the enrichment of whole-school policies.

Including examples of good practice, real-life accounts, research evidence, sources of help and suggestions for further reading, this book provides all the guidance a manager will need to help them make the best use of their TAs.

Anne Watkinson is a former teacher, headteacher of two schools and an LEA senior adviser. She has written books for TAs following her own research. She is now a freelance educational consultant and has worked with the DfES and the TDA.

Leading and Managing Teaching Assistants

A practical guide for school leaders, managers, teachers and higher level teaching assistants

Anne Watkinson

Routledge
Taylor & Francis Group

LONDON AND NEW YORK

First published 2008
by Routledge
2 Park Square, Milton Park, Abingdon, Oxon OX14 4RN

Simultaneously published in the USA and Canada
by Routledge
270 Madison Ave, New York, NY 10016

*Routledge is an imprint of the Taylor & Francis Group,
an informa business*

© 2008 Anne Watkinson

Typeset in Garamond and Gill Sans by
Florence Production Ltd, Stoodleigh, Devon
Printed and bound in Great Britain by
TJ International, Padstow, Cornwall

British Library Cataloguing in Publication Data
A catalogue record for this book is available from the British Library

Library of Congress Cataloging in Publication Data
Watkinson, Anne.
  Leading and managing teaching assistants: a practical guide for
  school leaders, managers, teachers, and higher-level teaching
  assistants/Anne Watkinson.
      p. cm.
    Includes bibliographical references and index.
  1. Teachers' assistant – Great Britain – Handbooks, manuals, etc.
  2. School personnel management – Great Britain – Handbooks,
  manuals, etc.   I. Title.
  LB2844.1.A8W38 2008
  371.14'124—dc22   2007027718

ISBN10: 0–415–45306–2 (pbk)
ISBN10: 0–203–93305–2 (ebk)

ISBN13: 978–0–415–45306–6 (pbk)
ISBN13: 978–0–203–93305–3 (ebk)

For Mark and his Devon HLTAs
without whom this book would not have been written

Contents

Illustrations

Figures

Tables

Boxes

Preface

As a teacher and a headteacher, I was privileged to work with some amazing people who were not qualified teachers, teaching assistants (TAs), on whose expertise, cheerful personality, knowledge and understanding I, other teaching staff and pupils depended. The variety of jobs which they willingly undertook appeared never ending. They supported us as people emotionally as well as with teaching and learning tasks. They initiated things, brought in skills they had learnt outside and asked to go on courses. Later, when I became an adviser and started to run courses for them I found there was little known about them. They were 'historically invisible', 'the forgotten staff'. Ever since, I have been researching their role, listening to them and their managers, watching them and writing for and about them.

The spur to writing this book came from an invitation to work in Devon with a group of Higher Level TAs (HLTAs) and their Support Staff Adviser, Mark Freeman, to explore their leadership and management role with them and some of their senior managers. This work was to enable the HLTAs to research their own role and develop it in their own schools. It has resulted in some rich first-hand accounts from the schools which are available on the Devon Local Authority website. Discussions with those staff and Mark made me realise that some more written guidance for leaders and managers of other schools might be useful.

I have visited schools in Devon, Suffolk, Essex and Thurrock over the last few months, talked with TAs, HLTAs, their managers and leaders and advisers. TAs from across the country have sent me accounts of their experiences and I have discussed many of the issues with advisers from other authorities. The photographs and materials shown throughout the book are from these schools and show examples of real work in progress. None of the schools claim to have the final answer, all say they need to be flexible, able to change according to changes in circumstances, and their strategies are developing all the time.

I hope that all those leading and managing TAs, headteachers, senior leadership or management team members, line managers, class teachers and the TAs themselves, now often in leadership capacities, will find something useful in these pages.

Acknowledgements

I would like to thank:

◆ Mark Freeman, Support Staff Adviser of Devon County Council for his support, interest and endless source of up-to-date, useful information; also his hospitality and friendship.
◆ The Devon HLTAs, whose intelligence, expertise and enthusiasm has made this book such a joy to research and write; particularly
  – Ann Melhuish, Tina Casson and Tracey Brighton for allowing me to quote from their case studies
  – Ann, Tina, Tracey, Gillian Watkins, Liz Chisholm, Sarah Webber and Susette Barrett for their documentation.
◆ The staff of schools who have been so willing to share their experiences with me, telling me about what works for them, spending time discussing the issues, giving so freely of their own documentation for the book and allowing me to photograph freely; particularly
  – Bishops Park College, Essex
  – Broadhembury CE Primary School, Devon
  – Carlton Colville Primary School, Suffolk
  – Clacton County High School, Essex
  – Courtney Senior of Harris Middle School, Lowestoft, Suffolk
  – Deneholm Primary School, Thurrock
  – Feniton CofE Primary School, Devon
  – King Edward VI Community College, Totnes, Devon
  – Lakenheath Community Primary School, Suffolk
  – Margaret Miller of Roebuck Primary School, Stevenage, Hertfordshire
  – Market Field School, Elmstead Market, Essex
  – Oaklands Infant School, Chelmsford, Essex
  – Piper's Vale Community Primary School, Ipswich, Suffolk
  – Queen Elizabeth's Community College, Crediton, Devon
  – Runwell Community Primary School, Essex
  – Stifford Clays Junior School, Thurrock
  – Whipton Barton Junior School, Exeter, Devon

◆ The pupils of the schools who never seem to mind yet another inquisitive visitor;

◆ The many schools, Local Authority advisers and colleagues with whom I have been able to discuss the diverse issues that this subject raises; particularly Nicki Harris of Essex Human Resources.

◆ And my husband Frank, for his encouragement, endless patience, domestic help and constant support of my ICT systems.

Abbreviations

ALS	additional literacy support
CPD	continuous professional development
CRB	Criminal Records Bureau
DCSF	Department for Children, Schools and Families
DFE	Department for Education
DfES	Department for Education and Skills
EAL	English as an additional language
EBD	emotionally and behaviourally disturbed
ECM	Every Child Matters
EO	equal opportunities
EP	educational psychologist
FE	Further Education
FHEQ	Framework for Higher Education Qualifications
FTE	full-time equivalent
GCSE	General Certificate of Secondary Education
GTP	graduate training route
HE	Higher Education
HLTA	higher level teaching assistant
HMI	Her Majesty's Inspectorate
ICT	information and communications technology
IEP	individual education plan
IiP	Investors in People
INSET	in-service education for teachers
IoE	Institute of Education, University of London
ITT	initial teacher training
JD	job description
LA	local authority
LEA	Local Education Authority
LGA	Local Government Association
LNS	Literacy and Numeracy Strategies
LSA	learning support assistant
LSC	Learning and Skills Council

MDA	mid-day assistant
NC	National Curriculum
NLS	National Literacy Strategy
NNS	National Numeracy Strategy
NOS	National Occupational Standards
NQF	National Qualification Framework
NTO	National Training Organisation
NVQ	National Vocational Qualification
Ofsted	Office for standards in education
PA	personal assistant
PGCE	Postgraduate Certificate of Teaching
PPA	planning, preparation and assessment
PwC	PricewaterhouseCoopers
QCA	Qualifications and Curriculum Authority
QTS	Qualified Teacher Status
RPA	regional provider of assessment
SCITT	school-centred initial teacher training
SDP	School Development Plan
SEAL	social and emotional attitudes to learning
SEF	Self-evaluation Form
SEN	special educational needs
SENCO	special educational needs coordinator
SIP	School Improvement Plan
SLT	Senior Leadership Team
SMT	Senior Management Team
STAC	Specialist Teacher Assistant Certificate
SWDB	School Workforce Development Board
SWOT	strengths, weaknesses, opportunities and threats
TA	teaching assistant
TDA	Training and Development Agency
TES	Times Educational Supplement
TTA	Teacher Training Agency
WAMG	Workforce Agreement Monitoring Group
WR	Workforce Remodelling

Chapter 1

Introduction

Teachers or instructors of children and young people have always had their assistants. The Greeks, teaching in the open air did. The Victorians are well documented for using the older pupils as pupil teachers. During the 1960s, the teacher unions were struggling, first to ensure that all teachers were qualified, and then to gain graduate status for qualified teachers. Largely because of this, 'unqualified' ancillaries were derided as usurping the teachers' place. However, many schools employed welfare assistants to help with first aid, caring tasks and menial classroom tasks such as paper cutting or paint pot washing. The early 1990s saw the beginnings of serious research into staff supporting in the classroom, and women were seen as a possible 'Mum's army' to support those teaching children under eight years old. The first qualifications for assistants started to appear, although many concentrated on provisions in the early years of education.

Following the general election of 1997, government initiatives have ensured an exponential growth of the number of teaching assistants (TAs) in schools. By 2000 a five-pronged strategy was developed with money and projects behind their words:

◆ recruitment money was distributed to schools via Local Education Authorities (LEAs);
◆ induction materials were prepared to be rolled out to school via the LEAs;
◆ a career ladder for TAs was developed with the writing of National Occupational Standards (NOS) at levels 2 and 3 leading to nationally recognised qualifications;
◆ advice on management was published which is still a seminal text recommended by the Department for Children, Schools and Families (DCSF) and the Training and Development Agency (TDA); and
◆ pathways to teaching were made easier with workplace routes.

There must now be well over 200,000 people employed in this capacity, if government statistics quote 150,000+ full-time equivalents (FTEs). There are very few schools without TAs yet few TAs have full-time contracts. More people cannot just be tacked on to an existing group without consideration of their conditions of service and the impact on the leadership and management of the school. It was recognised some years ago that: 'The substantial increase in the number of teaching assistants in schools and the corresponding increase in our expectations of what they do, not surprisingly has made the management of teaching assistants more complex' (Ofsted 2002: 18). Even now some TAs are still not fully included into whole-school activities

Since local management of schools was introduced in the late 1980s, heads have been able to staff their schools according to need rather than take the allocations handed to them by their local authority (LA). Many schools have stayed with the traditional one teacher per class of 30 in primary, and one teacher for 20 to 30 in secondary, with fewer in practical classes, specialised sixth form or special educational needs (SEN) groupings.

With the establishment of the national curriculum (NC), there has been even more emphasis on year grouping in primary schools; nationally produced schemes of work reinforce this. The Literacy and Numeracy Strategies (LNS) of the last ten years have reinforced this structure bringing an almost wholesale return to class teaching in primary schools. Parental pressure also supports the concept and seems to influence headteachers and governors more in their staffing structure than any other issue. The NC and its associated testing culture and published league tables has even brought about the demise of the middle school systems in some authorities. It is believed that this year grouping structure has raised standards. Class-based staffing and the consequent financing of such a straitjacketing concept has dominated many schools, to the detriment of allowing pupil needs, people potential and initiative possibilities to be thought through effectively.

The LNS undoubtedly brought about needed changes in lesson planning and execution for some teachers and a considerable increase in the use of TAs for curriculum work as distinct from their SEN, welfare and more menial roles. This was not only to support individuals or small groups with extraction or catch-up agendas, but also to support groups in whole classes.

The major initiative that has affected the employment of TAs in the last 20 years, one that has affected secondary schools and primary in equal measure, is that of inclusion. This has also accelerated in the last ten years.

Complaints about teacher workload, reported in some depth in a Pricewaterhouse Coopers (PwC) report (PricewaterhouseCoopers 2001), the introduction of the LNS dependent on additional adult support and an increasing emphasis on the inclusion of pupils with SEN in mainstream schools led to the ideas of Workforce Remodelling (WR) introduced to schools in 2003. WR was an attempt to encourage schools to think more innovatively about their staff, especially their support staff, in managing the needs of the curriculum and pupils and coping with the ever increasing initiatives. The proposals were outlined in documents headed 'Time for standards: reforming the school workforce' (DfES 2002). The unions, with one exception, signed up to an agreement for implementation (ATL *et al.* 2003). Part of the agenda of the WR was to utilise staff most effectively to increase standards. A lot of guidance was published to support schools, a three-year funded project with local and national advisers accompanied the proposals.

Schools have been encouraged to consider the employment of support staff by looking at their staffing structure and management as a more holistic exercise. Historically, most schools had used rather ad hoc employment strategies to appoint assistants. The idea was to take a fresh look at the needs of the school, the pupils, the curriculum and their local circumstances to decide what combination of teachers and support staff best fitted these needs. The TDA has become the disseminator of all the WR material since the project's completion. Their website states:

> The remodelling change process enables and encourages schools and their partners to:
>
> ◆ identify and agree where change is necessary
> ◆ facilitate a vision of the future shared across the whole-school and stakeholder communities
> ◆ collaborate internally and externally, with other schools, organisations and agencies, in an effective and productive way
> ◆ create and implement plans for 'tailored change in an atmosphere of consensus
> ◆ embed an inclusive and proactive culture of long term progress, and improve standards for staff, stakeholders and pupils.
>
> (TDA 2007b)

A new status, that of higher level TAs (HLTAs) has also been introduced to enable experienced TAs, who did not wish to be teachers, yet are of high calibre, to be recognised. Foundation degrees, work-based routes to teaching and apprenticeships have all added to a scene of complex employment structure possibilities for TAs. A national pay and conditions structure for TAs is at last being considered (TES 2007a). The TDA now has overall responsibility for TA matters, enabling joined-up thinking to take place at government level. Previously, the Teacher Training Agency (TTA) was responsible for teachers and the Employers Organisation (EO) for support staff as local government employees.

Three years later, when earmarked standards funds have been exhausted for WR, it is suggested that whole-school budgets should be sufficient to enable managers to fund staffing according to their local needs, not those of government or historical perceptions. However, this is not so evident at school level. Also, employment of TAs is not just a matter of structure. It is evident from personal observation, discussion with advisers across the country and assessing and moderating the HLTA applications, that there is still considerable misunderstanding of the potential of TAs, their best use and deployment and how the day-to-day matters of school life can best be facilitated for the good of the pupils and the TAs themselves. TAs of all descriptions and levels raise serious issues, most of which could be resolved by better management practice, whole-school vision and a sense of collegiate responsibility for the learning, health and welfare of the pupils within a school.

There are further government initiatives coming on stream which will influence schools' use of TAs. The Every Child Matters (ECM) agenda permeates everything from the schools' inspection framework to all the local agencies concerned with children. Extended schools, where school buildings and communities encompass far more than educating children from 9 a.m. to 3 p.m., personalised learning, assessment for learning, are just a few of the buzzwords echoing round staffrooms along with major changes in the 14 to 19 agenda and the imminent revision of the NC.

Maggie Miller's story exemplifies how the changes in the national scene have brought about change in her personal life and the potential growth of TAs' usefulness given supportive management.

School example

Maggie left school with five 'O' levels and an 'OA' level and went to work in a bank, then a computer firm and then for her husband's firm, only leaving at the birth of her son. She then took what is a common route, first becoming a school volunteer in her son's school, later becoming employed as a special needs welfare helper. She then went back to college, and after teaching adults basic literacy skills for a while, went back to a part-time post in a junior school. She is now the TA team coordinator, leading a team of 11 TAs, as well as being the behaviour support coordinator. She liaises with both the head and the SEN coordinator (SENCO), and also with teachers, social workers and parents, and runs weekly meetings for the TAs. Her team leadership role includes performance management and her now HLTA role includes covering for teacher absence and planning, preparation and assessment (PPA) time. She undertakes other school administrative tasks and a lunchtime information and communication technology (ICT) club. She has her National Vocational Qualification (NVQ) assessor's award and so can assess in-house TAs at level 3 NVQ where they wish to achieve it.

A further Cambridge University course in counselling skills has brought her in touch with a much wider group of educationalists. She now has the expertise and confidence to address conferences and run workshops. She has developed a county-wide role as TA consultant for Hertfordshire LA, including profiling the training needs of TAs using the NAPTA/Pearson Educational tools.

The potential of appropriate leadership and management

TAs' development is a process during which adults who have outward-going, caring personalities, a commitment to education and are prepared to develop and undergo training of a variety of kinds can provide responsive, sensitive and knowledgeable aides to the teaching and learning process. WR was an opportunity to rethink, but it also opened up further problems for leaders and managers to deal with, such as the support that TAs need to fulfil a larger role. Also, what teachers might need to work effectively with the additional adults. The issue of dealing with yet more staff was not new.

> Why bother? In this instance, we believe there are good reasons, both educational and financial for bothering. We believe it is time to look again at the traditional patterns of staffing in schools. Over the years, teachers' roles have become unnecessarily rigid . . . We think there is much scope yet to be explored and we are sure that there will be benefits not only to associate staff and their teacher colleagues able to focus more properly on pedagogy, but also to individual pupils and to the school as a whole. It is right they should be staffed by colleagues from a variety of backgrounds, bringing appropriate skills to the corporate life of the institution.
>
> (Mortimore et al. 1994: 222)

It is a common experience with training institutions and LAs that unfunded courses for senior staff about managing TAs collapse from lack of support. Whether this is because of other priorities or a sense that managers know all they need to know is impossible to say. If you have read this far, you are clearly not one of those who feel they know all about the subject, and you are willing to think about your practice. Managers and leaders are not just 'those at the top'. Teachers lead and manage TAs, but still have very little guidance despite this becoming part of the standards for Qualified Teacher Status (QTS) in 2001. With the acceptance of HLTA status in schools, job evaluation and various grades with concomitant job descriptions (JDs), TAs themselves have also become managers and leaders of teams of TAs.

THINKING POINTS

How well do you know your team of TAs? Figure 1.1 shows how training and personality can combine to produce a professional TA. Consider your TA team and try to place them on the diagram as a series of crosses. Hopefully they are well into the upper right hand quartile?

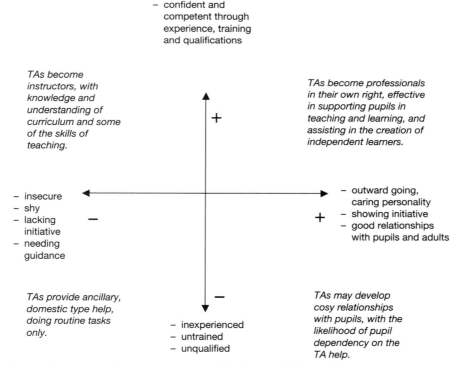

Figure 1.1 Looking at the TAs by themselves (Watkinson 2003: 166)

The usefulness of a TA is only as good as their management and deployment. It is up to you, the leaders and managers to maximise the use you make of the skills, knowledge and understanding developed by TAs that will create support for pupils, teachers and the school to provide a consistent high standard of professional practice and improve standards for staff and pupils. Whatever your rationale for employing them, you want them, as with any resource, to be effective. A simple list of factors for effective working by teaching assistants was given in Lee's survey in 2002. The presence of this book seems to indicate that there is still a need for leaders and managers to consider some of these. To start you off you could check what you have in place against this list:

- clarity of role
- accurate and updated job description
- thorough induction and support structures
- clear line management
- consideration of most appropriate deployment of teaching assistants
- time for teaching assistants and teaching staff to collaborate
- guidance and support for teaching assistants on strategies to use with pupils
- support and, where required, training for teaching staff on the most effective ways of managing and working with teaching assistants
- communication strategies which ensure that teaching assistants are fully informed both on aspects of school life directly relevant to their work and more broadly
- paid time for teaching assistants to participate in meetings and whole-school activities
- paid time for teaching assistants to participate in relevant training and development opportunities
- appropriate accreditation and career structures for teaching assistants
- salary levels and structures which recognise teaching assistants' skills and expertise and reward them appropriately for their contribution

(Lee 2002: vii)

THINKING POINTS

Now look at Figure 1.2. You aim to place your own school in the upper right hand quartile of the diagram. Can you?

Maybe you will have to consider what the DfES refer to as:

levers that need to be in place to ensure schools and settings benefit fully from the contribution of teaching assistants.

- Effective leadership and management
- Continuing professional development

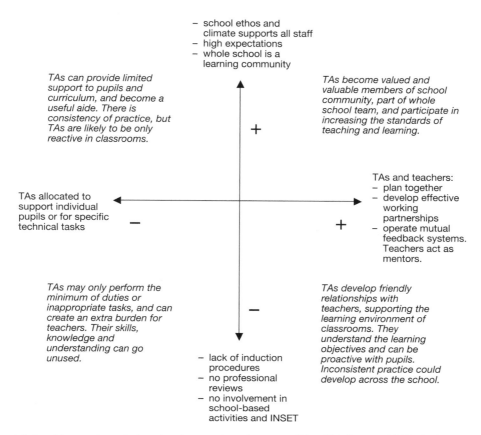

- school ethos and
  climate supports all staff
- high expectations
- whole school is a
  learning community

TAs can provide limited
support to pupils and
curriculum, and become a
useful aide. There is
consistency of practice, but
TAs are likely to be only
reactive in classrooms.

TAs become valued and
valuable members of school
community, part of whole
school team, and participate in
increasing the standards of
teaching and learning.

TAs and teachers:
- plan together
- develop effective
  working
  partnerships
- operate mutual
  feedback systems.
  Teachers act as
  mentors.

TAs allocated to
support individual
pupils or for specific
technical tasks

TAs may only perform the
minimum of duties or
inappropriate tasks, and can
create an extra burden for
teachers. Their skills,
knowledge and
understanding can go
unused.

TAs develop friendly
relationships with
teachers, supporting the
learning environment of
classrooms. They
understand the learning
objectives and can be
proactive with pupils.
Inconsistent practice could
develop across the school.

- lack of induction
  procedures
- no professional
  reviews
- no involvement in
  school-based
  activities and INSET

Figure 1.2 Looking at the whole-school scene in relation to TAs (Watkinson 2003: 167)

◆ Focused support for children and the use of evidence-based intervention
  programmes
◆ Joint planning and reviewing progress
◆ Monitoring impact
◆ Performance management.

(DfES 2005b)

Help and support for leaders and managers

Help is already available. A volume of DfEE (later DfES, now DCSF) guidance on
the employment and deployment of TAs was published in 2000 (DfES 2000). This
has not been updated because it is still relevant. Despite being available for seven
years, few schools seem to have a copy. The DfES produced guidance on management
for TAs involved with the LNS but, again, no school has referred to this in discussion
(DfES 2005b). The Workforce Agreement Monitoring Group (WAMG) have issued
guidance in notes from time to time and LA advisory groups helped state schools
for three years and some of these advisers still exist. WAMG still meets. Yet,
money, resourcing diverse people, still sometimes seems to be thrown at problems,
without in-depth consideration of what would be the best strategies to support
pupils, teachers, the school and the curriculum. Cost effectiveness is rarely evaluated.

TAs are often still seen as a cheaper option to employing teachers and, thus, assumed to be value for money.

WR has brought in more suggestions of what can enhance the work of support staff, not least that managers should introduce performance management strategies for all staff. Headteachers and senior managers went to the courses when the WR ideas were introduced. The WR ideas appear to have made little impact on the structure, deployment and management of TAs in many schools. Issues of complying with the regulations concerning the 10 per cent non-contact (PPA) time for teachers, along with the need for administrative support in 25 named areas rather took precedence in a list of priorities for using staff, along with the apparent increasing numbers of children with anti-social behaviour, deprived backgrounds of one sort or another and more severe physical needs in mainstream schools.

Managing Teaching Assistants was published in 2003, based on a lot of the research which I undertook while still an adviser (Watkinson 2003a). While that book received an excellent review in the TES, and still sells, it takes no account of WR, the HLTA initiative, the massive increase in numbers of TAs with the concomitant initiatives and publicity about the role, so it is now out of date. I hope that this book will prove an updated and more accessible version of the previous title. The original book is still relevant, containing as it does some original Ph.D. research, survey and case study material. This book uses some material from the previous one, but refers to the state in schools in 2007.

The term TA is used throughout to cover those support staff who assist closely the teaching and learning of pupils. Schools use various terms but TA is the preferred generic term of the DfES. LSA (learning support assistant) is often used where schools have used it or to DCFC/TDA denote specific assistance to pupils with SEN.

How to use the book

You can read it from cover to cover, but you will probably dip in and find what you want from the index or list of contents. Read the text accompanying figures to find how the materials are suggested to be used, or how they originated. All the suggested formats are from schools. Examples from schools appear in bold or as figures. Some suggestions for simple thought-provoking exercises for you appear in shaded boxes. Most of the references come from books or reports that could prove interesting for further reading, and there are further lists of useful books at the end of Chapters 4 and 8. However senior there is still need to develop professionally, be reflective practitioners and be a role model for the learners in your care. Schools that have become learning communities, where all the staff are participating in continuous exploration of new ideas and sharing them with colleagues, are lively places, always on the look out for improvement. When dealing with human beings, especially children and young people, no two days are the same. The hope is that the book stimulates thought and perhaps changes in action which go on to increase opportunities for pupils' learning and TAs' progression in their chosen careers.

After this introductory chapter, Chapter 2 discusses the issues of leadership and management that underpin the operation of our schools, with a particular emphasis on the need for distributed leadership to include that by the TAs themselves. Recognising that teachers and TAs may be trained to manage learning, resources or finances but rarely people, Chapter 3 looks particularly at these issues.

Chapter 4 describes the various things that TAs can, and have been known to do in schools across all phases and types of school, and thus the potential of this section of support staff. Chapter 5 develops the view that until schools see their staff and pupils as a whole, supported by the school community of parents and carers, governors, agencies and interested parties in their localities, the full potential of human resource has not been tapped. This chapter also recognises the impact the various externally imposed initiatives may make. Given the variety of schools, needs of pupils and talents of TAs, Chapter 6 explores how a school can best investigate their human resources through formal or informal audits.

Chapter 7 contains materials and ideas for senior managers to consider when reviewing the performance of existing TAs. Reviewing performance is only the start of a process, Chapter 8 describes the various ways of developing the effectiveness of TAs once their needs have been determined. At some point, you will employ new staff so Chapter 9 gives advice and ideas to use when appointing and inducting your TAs.

Chapter 10 considers the issues of teacher–TA relationships in order to optimise their joint work in the classroom. Managers and leaders also need to recognise how to support teachers in making the best use of any other adult working in their classroom, be it paid TA or volunteer. TAs complain of differing practice by different teachers in the same school where use has not been considered as well as deployment.

Chapter 11 sums up the various themes developed throughout the book. We are in advance of many countries in developing a paraprofessional workforce to support teaching and learning, but we still have much to learn about the best use of human resources.

Chapter 2

Leadership and management

Leadership or management?

It is important to consider these two together. Just give a few minutes thought to the following exercise.

THINKING POINTS

Who do you see as the leaders in your school?

Do you have a senior leadership team or a senior management team? Of whom does it consist? (The size of school will probably influence your answer.) Are they all qualified teachers? Does this matter?

Who in your school leads/manages a team?

Consider the site manager – or caretaker. Does he/she have responsibility for: a team of workers, a budget, a resource/work area?

Consider the bursar/finance assistant. What are their responsibilities?

Consider your team of teaching assistants:

◆ What is the rationale for membership of the TA team in your school?
◆ Has it always been like that?
◆ What is the area or importance or size of a team leader's/manager's responsibility (budget – team of people – curriculum/pastoral area – salary)?
◆ What is their feedback into school decision making?
◆ Are they managers or leaders – or both?

The distinctions between leadership and management are blurred and both are necessary. It is the balance that matters and being in the right role at the right time. When are you a leader in your school and when a manager? You will be both at times.

Consider the following:

LEADING is concerned with:
♦ vision
♦ strategic issues
♦ transformation
♦ ends
♦ people
♦ doing right things

MANAGING is concerned with:
♦ implementation
♦ operational issues
♦ transaction
♦ means
♦ systems
♦ doing things right
(West-Burnham 1997 quoted in Collarbone and Billingham 1998: 1)

Because you are in a school, dealing with people rather than machines or goods, you do not just deal with implementation and operational issues, the means and the systems. You will have a vision of what you want to do, and what the school wants you to do, you will think strategically, discuss ideas, consider change and changes. You deal with people, and are concerned with achieving an end – the development and achievement of pupils and staff, possibly also parents and governors, not just the processes which lead to that end.

West-Burnham also considers the links between leading and managing and administration.

Leadership	Management	Administration
doing the right things	doing things right	doing things
path making	path following	path tidying
complexity	clarity	consistency
		(West-Burnham 2004: 3)

Generally, the roles and responsibilities of school leaders cover a range of strategic and operational areas including: setting the strategic direction and ethos of the school; managing teaching and learning; developing and managing people; and dealing with the requirements of the accountability regime.

(PricewaterhouseCoopers 2007: v)

Any member of staff at any time could be leading or managing. Consider Figure 2.1 without thinking of individuals. What are the lines of responsibilities?

There are some findings from this recent PwC report which it would be useful to consider.

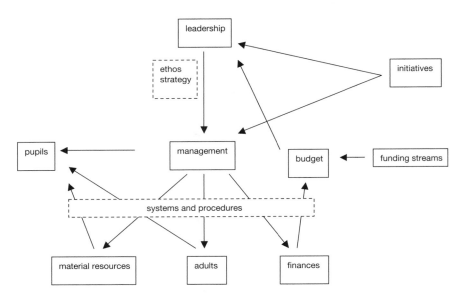

Figure 2.1 Some of the routes of effective leadership and management

THINKING POINTS

Do any of the following apply to you?
Some school leaders:
'were more comfortable with an operational role rather than a strategic one'
'expressed their frustration that the current environment does not allow them to be as involved in this area (teaching and learning) as they would like'
think 'developing people and nurturing talent is a key strategic issue'
think 'priorities and future skills' needs . . . staff management, recruitment and retention appeared quite far down the list'
'may not have embraced the people agenda as fully as in . . . other sectors (e.g. the private sector)'
think 'collaboration and networking . . . ought to become the rule'
advocate 'including professionals from other agencies on the leadership teams'
'now have to be much more outward looking then they used to be'
think there is a 'need for a range of "softer" inter-personal skills relating to networking and communication'
get 'too involved in operational and delivery matters . . . at the expense of embracing their more strategic imperatives'
'wish for a stability and consistency which cannot be delivered and which is not enjoyed by any other organisation in the public or private sector'
(PricewaterhouseCoopers 2007: vi, vii)

The PwC research into school leadership in state schools found that although structures and models matter, the behaviour of the leaders of an organisation has a greater influence on pupil performance. When looking at the leadership and management of TAs this finding is very apparent. It is the people who lead, run and organise the school who make the difference; it is the way leaders behave at every level. Some schools have gone down the paper-based route with formal policies and procedures, and it works; others have put similar structures in place but it doesn't. Some of the more haphazard schemes, where nothing is written down, work because the people make them work. They say they would find structures put in place for their TAs oppressive and time consuming. The best schools have both – clear procedures, but a culture of collaboration and a climate of consultation and implementation which makes all the difference. There is no one model that will fit all schools, even though the characteristics of the TAs are similar. The quality of people employed to do the TA job is important, but it is the way in which they are deployed, used, developed and supported that can make the difference. TAs can enhance the teaching and learning experience for pupils and other staff, and also, in fact, for parents, families and other people linked with the school.

Roles and responsibilities of leadership

The key role and responsibilities of school leadership categorised by the PwC report from their research were:

◆ accountability: fulfilling legal and other responsibilities;
◆ strategy: setting the strategies ethos and improvement planning;
◆ teaching and learning;
◆ staffing: recruitment and professional development;
◆ networking: establishing effective relationships with colleagues or organisations;
◆ operations: day-to-day management.

These categories do not necessarily represent what actually happens. Despite the best laid plans, any leader, including the head, might have emergencies to deal with; they might get diverted by administrative or other duties because of circumstances. The headteacher of a three-teacher rural primary school will have a different balance of time allocations to that of a head of an 1,800-pupil urban secondary school. Some heads are increasingly having extra roles outside their schools, maybe as some sort of adviser.

Leadership by headteachers

Mortimore *et al.* (1988) established that the purposeful leadership of the staff by the headteacher was one of the key factors in a successful school and 'all the research confirmed by HMI and more recently Ofsted, suggests that leadership in schools is the key factor in improvement and success' (Brighouse and Woods 1999: 45). Brighouse and Woods went on to recognise the complexity of schools and that leadership of all who work in the school is important. Ethos and culture stem from the influence of the headteacher. About eight years ago, a group of TAs in a school gave me the following on a piece of paper.

School example

Why it works so well in our school:

Teaching assistants are given planning time to get resources and ideas for the right approach ready for lessons to come that week.

We are treated as part of the (school) team and we all support each other.

We know each other (the whole school) [their brackets] socially.

The teaching assistants are encouraged to go on courses and use training schemes.

We are included on the progression of IEPs [individual education plans] and forward our comments and ideas.

The teaching assistants who have achieved their STAC [Specialist Teacher Assistaant Certificate] course would love to go further.

We work with outside agencies i.e. speech therapists on behalf of the child's teacher and report back to the teacher with progress and ideas.

I went back to that school a few years later and the head had changed. So had they. The tales they then told me were of how dissatisfied they were, how it did not work well any more, how they had all joined a union and called the local representative in to discuss the changes the new head wanted to make. The leadership had become top-down and the ethos and culture had changed.

The current initiatives are likely to bring about changes in emphasis of current school heads' roles. The PwC report indicates that in order to operate more effectively in the current climate of initiatives they will have to:

◆ dedicate more time to the strategic vision . . .
◆ keep up to date with classroom practice . . .
◆ be actively involved in promoting a CPD [continuous professional development] culture throughout the school . . .
◆ implement and promote effective performance arrangements for the entire workforce . . .
◆ consider the appropriateness of external roles in the context of the school both in terms of the benefits and to the grades of person undertaking the role.

(They also give a list of areas where heads should not be spending significant amounts of time.)

(PricewaterhouseCoopers 2007: 32, 33)

All of these have considerable significance to the employment of support staff, especially teaching assistants. Below, I take each of these areas and give an indication of where TAs could fit into the PwC scheme of things for headteachers.

Vision: As a head you need to see where teaching assistants best fit into the needs of the school and pupils and not just rely on a historical way of solving problems.

It appears that few heads have used WR to do this; maybe the ECM agenda or extended schools will nudge a few more of you in that direction.

Classroom practice: You need to consider whether one-to-one pupil support is the best way to tackle individual needs. The personalised learning agenda promotes the idea that all children need consideration not just those with SEN or who have been recognised as gifted and talented. Do all the classes need literacy or numeracy support – maybe technical and practical subjects have more need for an extra pair of hands? What are the best arrangements for supporting the Early Years or good assessment practice?

CPD culture for all: There are still people working in schools who see CPD as going on courses. Some, generally support staff now it must be said, see no need for further training. But CPD is much more than training or external courses. The culture of CPD is about all members of a school community being learners, about adults being lifelong learners; it is about listening, watching, questioning, challenging and reflecting.

Implement and promote effective performance management for the entire workforce: It is clear, talking with TAs of all descriptions in all shapes and sizes of schools that this process is very supportive for them. For some it is only a 10-minute chat while for others it is a full blown, formalised system with observations and paperwork.

School example

Two heads of schools visited, both considered outstanding in their recent Ofsted inspections, had both sent a simple questionnaire to their TAs in the preceding weeks. They thought they knew them well, relationships were excellent but just asking questions such as: 'What do you enjoy most?' and 'What could make your job better or easier?' threw up ideas and items for consideration that they had not considered.

Networking: Is it good practice to support the most challenging children with the least trained staff, or pay the staff associated with the most difficult problems, the least? Might it not be better practice and more cost effective, for instance, to employ trained counsellors, behaviour management experts or other external agents for a short time at a high rate rather than seek palliative care arrangements? Many of these issues are raised in the ECM agenda.

Areas where heads should not be spending considerable time: These are often areas which support staff can carry out quite adequately if not better than the heads. One thing that has been striking in my recent visits to schools is where TAs have been allowed or encouraged to take on the most interesting and diverse roles within the school.

Distributed leadership

The PwC leadership report does give some models of leadership, from the traditional top-down approach through 'distributed leadership' models to models where outside agencies are included in school leadership teams, federations of schools and what they call a systems leadership model where leaders are not tied to one school or even one set of schools but their expertise is shared nationally. They make it clear that one size does not fit all. This is certainly true of leadership and management models for teaching assistants. Every school has its own history, needs and people available to take responsibility.

One of the strongest themes to come out of the PwC research was the importance of 'developing staff, nurturing talent and, related to this, "distributing" leadership throughout the organisation'.

> Distributed leadership is much more than just sharing out tasks. Rather, it also encompasses a shared approach to strategic leadership in which professionals throughout the organisation are genuinely engaged and can influence its culture, ethos and strategic direction, albeit to an extent that is commensurate with their position.
>
> (PricewaterhouseCoopers 2007: viii)

This is not new. A case study presented at a conference in 2003 reported on distributed leadership using support staff started after an Ofsted report on adults in the school in 1997 (DfES 2004). The strategies used were ones that make up much of the substance of this book.

TAs themselves can also lead, especially those who have been encouraged or supported. However, it is more usual for a senior TA to be included in teaching staff meetings to recognise their seniority than to be included in senior leadership or management teams. The PwC report indicates that where the culture of the remodelling agenda was implemented wholeheartedly, many more support staff were brought in to share responsibilities. The categories: head, SENCO, line manager, teacher and lead TA, make useful ones under which to look at the various leadership roles in a school and how they relate to the work of TAs. Table 2.1 is a summary table of the possibilities in an imaginary school.

THINKING POINTS

Try taking a blank of the table (Table 2.2) and fill it in for yourself.

Senior TA and HLTA leadership

If you are an HLTA reader, you might have found that suggestions of TA team leadership or management could just cause a bit of friction with your colleague TAs, but with sensitivity you should be able to recognise this, understand it, and

Table 2.1 Looking at leadership responsibilities with regard to TAs

PWC categories	Headteacher	SENCO	Line manager (DH, HoD or other)	Teacher	Lead TA/HLTA
Accountability	Total but can delegate	For SEN provision	For a particular team or group	For any work done by TAs with children in their class; Sharing planning and arranging feedback	Responsibilities defined in job description
Strategy	Decision re use of additional adults – LSA/TA; Individual/class/school/curriculum responsibilities	Ideas on use of LSAs to support SEN	Possibly little	Regarding ways of working in a particular classroom, within policies of school	Developing the way the team works
Teaching and learning	Oversight, maybe some 'hands on'	Progress of SEN students supported by LSAs	Possibly little	Leading and managing the teaching and learning in the classroom	Possibly little
Staffing	Budget allocation with governors	Appointment, CPD, welfare, performance management of team of LSAs	Appointment, CPD, welfare, performance management of particular team	May have some say and involvement in appointment; Mentoring	May have some say and involvement in appointment, CPD, welfare, performance management; Mentoring
Networking	With other agencies and heads	Liaison with class teachers or HoDs, SENCO groups	Liaison with other staff in similar role and SENCO support groups	Close relationship with TA, staffroom, corridor chats, interest groups	Staffroom and meetings
Operations	Actual day-to-day contact will vary with size of school	Resource provision for use by LSAs, meeting content and logistics	May meet with team	Day-to-day contact vital; Some resource provision	Meetings and possibly timetabling

Table 2.2 What are the leadership responsibilities regarding TAs in your school?

PWC categories	Headteacher	SENCO	Line manager (DH, HoD or other)	Teacher	Lead TA/HLTA
Accountability					
Strategy					
Teaching and learning					
Staffing					
Networking					
Operations					

deal with it. One or two of your colleagues may have wished to be assessed instead of you. They could see you as 'getting too big for your boots' or 'above' them. If you are a non HLTA reader, you must try to understand the dynamics and feelings of your TA team when considering appointments. You can go through a proper process of selection and appointment for different posts and training opportunities. HLTAs can look for the positive characteristics in your colleagues, emphasise those, maintain your friendships and support.

School example

Some years ago, a large secondary school with 1,800 pupils, 90+ teachers and 30+ TAs, organised their TA teams into two strands: one of LSAs managed by the SENCO and one of TAs to become curriculum, class-based support. One of these TAs in the science department went for the HLTA status and the plan was to have another HLTA in the English and one in the mathematics department. The HLTAs would be responsible for line managing a curriculum-based team of TAs and providing planned cover for classes. Over time this has not worked out. The needs of the schools were for an HLTA to support English but a third to support behaviour management. This third was not so much a line management role but a liaison one between departments and the SENCO to ensure behaviour management needs were covered. The first science-based HLTA changed her role over time. Leadership and management of the other TAs was not appropriate to the relationships of the TAs or the needs of the science department. The Key Stage 3 leader now organises all the cover of groups and classes, having a much better overview of the curriculum demands and pupil needs being a senior teacher. The HLTA was wasted as teacher emergency cover having greater skills with small groups of students. She is now line managed by one of the assistant heads although she still works with the science team of TAs as she has curriculum knowledge in the area. She now has other responsibilities and instead of line managing the science TAs she works with them.

Figure 2.2 An HLTA and TAs conferring during their mid-morning break

School example

One primary school has a team of seven TAs, largely allocated as one TA per class, and one LSA shadowing a child with a statement for severe behaviour problems. The members of the team were long established before the WR initiative appeared. One TA, however, had used her own initiative to undertake the NVQ Level 2 training at a local college. When the HLTA assessment procedure was mooted, she was an obvious candidate. She had to undertake the Numeracy level 2 qualification essential for attaining the HLTA status but did this and was successfully assessed. She then undertook PPA cover with planning time built in and ICT coordination. She started attending teaching staff meetings and even became a governor. But, despite acting as liaison after these meetings and effectively operating as a leader, she declined to be labelled 'The leader' – she felt it would be divisive in her group of colleagues and she would lose friendships.

The 'Guidance to the standards' (TTA 2004) clearly states that management responsibility is not a requirement for HLTA standards, although guiding the work of other adults is (3.3.6). The new draft standards also include '29. direct the work of other adults who support teaching and learning' (TDA 2007a). It will be interesting to look more closely at the language used: 'guide' and 'direct' when the new guidance to the new standards is published.

Some schools are using a senior TA as a team leader to ease the workload of the SEN coordinator (SENCO) or deputy head or whoever managed the team in the past. One or two schools have even developed senior management teams which consist of senior teachers, the senior TA, mid-day supervisor, bursar and site manager, recognising the pivotal part such support teams play in the running of the school.

One interesting aspect of the PwC research was to ask schools in their surveys how many included support staff themselves in their senior leadership team. Only 13 per cent of primary schools responding included one such team member, 60 per cent of secondary schools have one or more and 24 per cent of special schools have at least two. However, these were most often finance staff. No figures were given for the inclusion of teaching assistants. I have come across some cases but it is rare.

> There was evidence from responses relating to the future of school leadership that a cultural divide between teaching and support staff was hindering the effective working of the school and that support staff in terms of career progression could receive greater emphasis.
>
> (PricewaterhouseCoopers 2007: 103)

This is partly due, the report suggests, to a perception that non-teaching staff are lesser, they are not professionals. There are also concerns that pay scales and conditions of service (for example, term time only contracts) for support staff are different to those for teachers, so rewarding support staff for leadership activities might be problematic. This should not be insurmountable given a bit of imagination and creative accounting.

Developing models

The changes in leadership and management teams and cultures which will be needed under the ECM agenda, with extended schools and interagency working is, as yet, untried by most schools. It could mean significant changes. The PwC report explores further models beyond that of distributed leadership. It is possible that in big schools, a chief executive (non-teaching) could coordinate the work of a headteacher (teaching and learning), a social worker/health worker (managing a centre supporting problems of care), an Early Years professional and a geriatric specialist alongside financial and buildings managers on one site. Some schools are already working towards federation for instance, although the most senior person there is usually the head 'teacher'. A few schools are already tackling social problems within their current management structure.

School example

A new secondary school in a deprived area has established a Multi Agency Professional Support Team, led by a non-teacher. In this department there are social workers and health professionals, both nurses and mental health workers. There are educational psychologists (EPs), Connexions workers and links with the family liaison workers in nearby primary schools. The learning mentors are based here. Incorporated in the design of the school were areas for a community/school library, a mother/carer and toddler group and accommodation for retired people. The school-based department for support however was not in the original architectural plan, but has proved its worth already in supporting some very vulnerable young people. Of the 800–900 students, apart from those with a statement of SEN, 20 are looked-after children. The team work with all the school in their delivery group and some funding is shared. The LSAs are appointed to classes not to individual children, because 'the LSA is not there to contain the child'. There is a very close relationship between the learning mentors who do work more one-to-one with children, the LSAs in the MAPS team and the LSAs managed by the teachers and line managed by the Inclusion coordinator.

Qualities of leadership

If leadership is to be distributed to other staff to be most effective, then other issues follow – training for the job, retention of trained and experienced staff, appointments for potential leadership roles as well as the obvious skills for the job. The effect of appointments on other members of staff may be an issue. 'Effective leadership is not just a job, it is a complex interaction between a range of personal and professional qualities and experiences' (West-Burnham and Ireson 2006: 5).

Skills required for good leadership are soft skills – the ability to build relationships and teams. The traditional view of leadership is that of power through hierarchical control. The following phrases are taken from various sources and my own observations. Good leadership appears to be much more about style and behaviour than knowledge and particular strategies.

THINKING POINTS

Just jot down what you think your style and behaviour is as a leader in the school then look at your list in relation to the following lists of phrases.

Leadership is not about:

◆ control, ensuring that you 'win' arguments;
◆ taking advantage of the position;
◆ suppressing any negative feelings so that you always look 'in charge';
◆ being negative or overly critical of others;
◆ showing that you know better because you have been better educated or have a higher status, avoiding embarrassment, feeling vulnerable or incompetent.

It is about:

◆ engagement
  – the ability to mobilise people to tackle tough problems;
  – being personable, approachable and accessible;
◆ being aware of the dynamics of your organisation, its systems and relationships;
◆ motivating and empowering others;
◆ being flexible rather than dogmatic;
◆ role modelling, of being a lead learner professionally and personally;
◆ allowing yourself to show ignorance, or incompetence or vulnerability at times;
◆ being able to stand back, reflect and learn from experience;
◆ being self-aware – reflecting on what you do and sharing those reflections with others;
◆ having core values which you act out in practice rather than imposing on others;
◆ seeing the bigger picture;
◆ being decisive if necessary, consultative where possible;
◆ being able to pay attention to detail, including maintenance and development;
◆ being optimistic, enthusiastic and resilient;
◆ retaining confidence and maintaining calmness;
◆ encouraging a climate of trust;
◆ having vision and communicating it to others.

Good leaders are people who communicate through:

◆ what they say;
◆ their example and action;
◆ policies, programmes and practice that enable other people to be able, responsible and worthwhile;
◆ motivating other people even by the way they listen.

Support staff interviewed for the PwC report viewed the important characteristics of leaders to be that they should:

◆ Recognise and value the work of others
◆ Communicate effectively with all staff
◆ Provide development opportunities
◆ Adopt an open consultative approach
◆ Be visible
◆ Have a constructive approach to performance management
◆ Act and feedback on concerns raised.

(PricewaterhouseCoopers 2007: 52)

A softer, perceptive style of leader not only sees the qualities of TAs, appreciates them and manages them but sees beyond to the potential of using such talent most creatively.

The above lists look at the personal traits which support good leadership, now think about what you do in your leadership role within the school. How does it compare with the following list?

Effective school leadership – overview of findings from research evidence

◆ school leadership is second only to classroom teaching as an influence on pupil learning;
◆ almost all successful leaders draw on the same basic repertoire of leadership practices (the main elements are: building vision, developing people, redesigning the organisation, managing teaching and learning);
◆ the ways in which leaders apply these basic leadership practices, not the practices themselves, demonstrate responsiveness to the contexts in which they work;
◆ school leaders improve teaching and learning indirectly through their influence on staff motivation, commitment and working conditions;
◆ school leadership has a greater influence on schools and students when it is widely distributed;
◆ some patterns of distribution are more effective than others; and
◆ a small handful of personal traits explain a high proportion of the variation in leadership effectiveness.

(Source: Leithwood *et al.* (2006) 'Seven strong claims about effective school leadership', National College of School Leadership – (PricewaterhouseCoopers 2007: viii))

If you are interested in following these ideas of developing your own personal effectiveness as a leader, there is a useful paper which contains sets of questions to ask yourself (West-Burnham and Ireson 2006). It takes you through five steps: looking at your ideal self, but then recognising your real self. From this it takes you through a learning agenda, looking at your own learning styles, experimenting with ways of doing things to developing trusting relationships from which strong leadership can grow.

How organisations work

The matters discussed so far have concentrated on personal effectiveness as a leader or manager. Leading or managing what? Schools are organisations, institutions, buildings, collections of people and children engaged in a common pursuit, that of learning. Watkins and Mortimore (1999) warned against considering schools as learning factories rather than learning organisations. While schools are not factories making a product, or a business setting out with the main aim of making a profit, there is much to learn from studying some of the management literature that has developed. Senge, an American management expert, has been a great influence to those leaders and managers interested in some of the less mechanistic ways of approaching organising a business or industry. He published a seminal text on how organisations work in 1990 which has had such resonance in schools that he went on to investigate their running in particular and work with school leaders (Senge 1990; Senge *et al.* 2000). His ideas were based round five disciplines which, if followed and developed, can transform the ways in which any organisation, industry, business or school works. His basic tenet is that successful organisations are learning organisations where all who work there need to participate in the way they operate. Distributed leadership enables the whole school to operate as a learning community, not a fragmented set of individuals pursuing their own effectiveness. Individual people matter, but what all the people in the organisation can do together is greater than the sum of all the individuals.

Senge describes five disciplines of organisations: personal mastery, shared vision, team working, mental models and systems thinking. He reckons that systems thinking is the most important but the others are needed in order to provide the context. Flood (1999) has incorporated a much wider body of work in his revisit of the Fifth Discipline and found the results not only enriching but potentially empowering.

This chapter has dealt with the importance of vision and personal mastery for the leader or manager. Senge's premise is that any leader or manager has also to consider these disciplines in relation to each individual in the establishment. All members of the organisation need personal mastery. The next chapter will discuss how people work together, the characteristics of team working. The chapters on TAs' potential and the school context look at the variety of models and systems which have developed so that you can form some ideas of models and systems you might wish to use in your school.

This chapter has concentrated on qualities of leadership, but without the more organisational and management strategies the school will operate on ephemeral qualities, dependent on charismatic 'hero' headship. As you read further into the more bureaucratic systems and strategies suggested in later chapters, it is possible to get buried in the safety blanket of organisation. The emphasis in recent years has been on leadership, because it is so important. The nitty gritty of management is considered easier but without the vision it is empty bureaucracy. Schools need good leadership, management and administration.

Chapter 3

Managing people

Schools are about people. While we often talk about human resources; managing these resources is not the same as managing material resources or equipment. People have feelings, a life outside the school and can initiate action or inaction. Relationships between the people of an organisation are crucial to the success of that organisation.

Teachers are not often trained to manage people. It is largely assumed that if you can manage children you can manage people. The new national QTS standards include 'working as a team member' and also 'ensuring colleagues working with them are appropriately involved in supporting learning and understand the roles they are expected to fulfil' (Q32, and 33). Post threshold teachers are required to 'promote collaboration' and to 'contribute to the professional development of colleagues through coaching and mentoring' and advanced skills teachers should 'possess the analytical, interpersonal and organisational skills necessary to work with staff and leadership teams beyond their own school'. How much training is available to develop such skill? HLTAs and senior TAs also seem to be expected just to be able to do it.

The Total Quality Management school of thought believes that all can be controlled through quality assurance and quality control systems but these have not found much support or favour in school circles. Schools are about human beings not production lines. It is still the actual face-to-face stuff that many of us fall down on. We resort to paper systems and policies, and hope that these direct people. Or we bring in external advisers to sort out problems rather than talk about issues to the people concerned directly. Certainly with TAs, the move to making the implicit explicit makes the difference. It makes instinctive, imitative behaviour purposeful and more effective. When things go wrong, often, all it actually needs is someone to have a quiet word at an early stage to point out what is astray. Even if things get to a difficult stage, talking it through has to happen at some point.

Responsibility posts are now given for teaching and learning rather than resource management and this often means managing a team of people. Those thrown in at the deep end of management, like some HLTAs, may well need some help in some of the 'managing people' issues as well as ideas of systems. Management is linked to leadership and those of you reading this book need to put some thought into which bits of each are part of your role. For those of you new to running meetings, carrying out appointment procedures and reviewing performance this chapter will talk through the people management bits of those tasks.

> Educational organisations depend for their success on the quality, commitment and performance of the people who work there.
>
> (O'Neill and Glover 1994: 1)

Building relationships – working with other adults

Some people appear to have inborn skills in relating to people, what Gardner (he of the Multiple Intelligences theories) would call interpersonal skills (Gardner 1983). These people appear to make friends easily, get on well with strangers, mix with all sorts. Others are shyer and hold back in company. Interestingly, where managing people is concerned, the 'friendly' types might not be the best managers – they like to keep things easy going; the HLTAs who would rather keep their friendships than become their managers may be like this. Friendship may come later, but is not the essence of good management. Intrapersonal skills are as important in management as the interpersonal ones, requiring the ability to know oneself and analyse why things are as they are. Goleman has suggested combining the two personal attributes in an 'emotional intelligence'. This concept has proved very useful when considering relationships. He defines five domains:

1. Knowing one's emotions
2. Managing emotions
3. Motivating oneself
4. Recognising emotions in others
5. Handling relationships

> (Goleman 1996)

Looking at that list you can see immediately how being competent in these five areas would help in managing people. If you know yourself and what makes you happy or sad, what things upset you and what you find difficult to control, you can then manage your emotions. Getting angry when dealing with people does not help, calmness is much more effective. There are times when you have to put on a show. There is the once a year type of major 'telling off' for a class that has gone over the top when a display of anger (acted and totally under your control) can be very effective because you do not do it the rest of the year. When managing staff, there may be very infrequent times when you need to 'read the riot act' but again, you must be in control of your anger or you are lost. If you are going to have to deal with a member of staff who has done something they should not have done, you want to be able to listen to their side of the story, not just go at it head on.

The third point of motivation is also interesting. There is a school of thought that you cannot motivate anyone else, only yourself; you can only find out what motivates other people and respond to it. Dealing with difficult disciplinary or new situations such as running a meeting, might need you to look at your motivation. Are you looking for personal praise from others, dealing with a person you do not like at last, or thinking of what is right for the school?

You need to understand what motivates staff to get the best out of them. Good leaders influence motivation in others. It is not about bullying. It is interesting to find out what motivates your TAs despite the low pay. Why are they in the job? Most people go to work to earn money to pay for living. The lucky ones are those who enjoy their jobs, for whom their hobby is their job or vice versa. TAs are largely a group of more mature women who have another source of income, although this is sometimes a second job and sometimes income support. This enables them to do a poorly paid job for the satisfaction they get. You need to understand people's learning styles to understand how best to support them, find out what they are good at and use it to develop them. 'Catch them being good' is a catch phrase for dealing with recalcitrant children, but it is a maxim that helps management of people.

When dealing with individuals or groups of people the ability to recognise emotions in others is a most useful skill. There are usually tell-tale physical signs of emotion: sweating when you talk to them, tears welling in the eyes, lack of eye contact, nervous fiddling with hands, excuses to get away. If you can be sufficiently in control of yourself to be able to watch the other person or a group in a meeting for their reactions to what you have to say, you will know when you have said enough. Being able to handle relationships – personal or professional – can be worked at. If you are nervous of confrontation or conflict it is more likely that you will handle it sensitively and well, rather than trample all over other people's feelings.

Hayes recognises how important relationships are for the classroom teacher and suggests an audit for looking at your relationship with other adults:

Exercise 9.1 Audit of your relationships with other adults

Use the following criteria to carry out a regular audit of your relationships with other adults. Use the bullet points beneath each criterion to guide your thinking.

Developing a right attitude by . . .

Being positive about life in general

◆ see situations in terms of 'half full' rather than 'half empty'
◆ look beyond the immediate problem at the end product
◆ keep failure and difficulties in perspective
◆ resist the temptation to moan about trivial matters

Giving other people's ideas a chance

◆ take a keen interest in what people say
◆ stay open to new possibilities
◆ adopt a neutral stance until the situation is clear
◆ take time to reflect upon the merit of new ideas

Showing the right body language

◆ maintain good eye contact
◆ incline the head to indicate understanding
◆ smile or look serious according to the issue
◆ face the person directly

Expressing your viewpoint with tact

◆ speak openly but courteously
◆ acknowledge the merit of different opinions
◆ allow for the fact that you may be mistaken
◆ show that you are willing to learn from others

Empathising with colleagues

◆ demonstrate genuine care by word and action
◆ try hard to understand their position
◆ ask sensitive questions to help unlock uncertainty
◆ listen more than advise.

(Hayes 2000: 159)

If you can operate like this with colleagues you should not find managing them difficult.

The tasks of management

Just as leadership is not about control, management is not about power; it is about getting things done in the organisation. The principles are similar to those of behaviour management of children: respect, rights, responsibilities and rules. Many schools have a mission statement that mentions everyone in the school having or showing respect for each other. It is not just about children respecting each other and the adults, but everyone behaving in that way. The rights and responsibilities should be spelt out at induction and then reviewed with the annual review. The 'rules' for the adults in the school are the legal framework, the policies and procedures of the school. However you want to manage other people in your job you must stay within that guidance. This means that if you want to call a meeting of the TAs you must know whether that is in paid time or not. If you want to change current practice in such matters there will be procedures to do this. You consult your line manager in the first instance, and if you are the head, you might have to consult the governors.

Even organising a one-off occasion will call for a whole gamut of individual tasks, each one involving dealing with people as well as paperwork. It will involve delegation and deploying, joint planning, directing and briefing the other adults, explaining roles, contexts, objectives, methods and outcomes. You need sensitivity and tact, good planning with a well thought out programme, and the ability to give clear advice and consider the team members' personal needs. Whatever the situation is for you, whether short or longer term leadership is envisaged, whether you are working with a group of volunteer mums or leading the senior management team, you still need to use similar strategies – those of good relationships. Consider the following situation which is only partly fictional.

School example

A possible example of team organisation by a TA: a trip to a nature reserve
The TA told the teacher in charge of the Y6 class, when they were planning during the summer holidays, that she had enjoyed a recent visit to a reserve with her young

family. She suggested that such a visit might fit in with the long-term planning that they were doing for the year ahead. The teacher welcomed this and later made the booking for May the following year directly after SATs week. She talked through the objectives and plan for the day with the reserve Education Officer. As the TA had experience of the site, the teacher asked her to organise the group of volunteer adults to accompany them on their visit. As the year progressed, a wheelchair-bound child joined the class and another TA became attached to the class to attend to the physical needs of the child, which were considerable. Further joint planning now occasionally involved the second TA at the first TA's suggestion. This second TA had contacts among the parent group, so the two TAs drew up a list of who they might ask to accompany them on the trip. They also asked some of the people who met the children from school. They found they could draw upon a variety of people with different talents. One was the parent of one of the children who spoke Italian at home, one a fireman who did shift work, another was looked after by their grandmother and the last member of their team was a young single mother. All were rather diffident when approached but agreed.

The TA decided that this group should meet before the trip and made arrangements, making a cup of tea for them after school and provided some limited activities for their children while they met. With the agreement of the teacher, she shared the plans for the day, the expectations the teacher and school had regarding behaviour, and asked for ideas. She made sure the appropriate checks of the adults were done in the office and that all the other families were aware of who would be helping on the day, particularly the parents of the disabled child. On reaching the reserve the TA had a quick word with the Reserve Officer and explained the needs of several of the children, particularly the toilet access. The officer was able to provide her with a small walkie-talkie for the support TA in case she got left behind at any point.

The pre-meeting not only ensured the day's visit went smoothly, but proved to be the beginning of a summer's team of help for the class and school. The Italian speaker, who had never visited the school before offered some picture books with photographs of animals and Italian text. Later in the term she came into class and showed them how to make real pizza dough. The fireman, used to lifting, solved all the coach travelling problems for the support TA and arranged a visit of the fire engine to the school fete. The grandmother asked to come in to help with reading in the infant classes, while the young mother proved to relate really well to a couple of disenchanted boys and became friends with their mothers. The TA arranged with a group of the Y6 to set up a small tea party at the end of term for the helpers, to say thank you. The pupils were then able to show off some of the work that had resulted from the visit.

(Watkinson 2005: 47, 48)

As you read the story you can find:

◆ clear objectives;
◆ consultation with all levels of people in the team;
◆ health and safety considerations;
◆ SEN consideration;

◆ using other people's talents and knowledge;
◆ careful planning and preparation;
◆ getting through diffidence barriers;
◆ high expectations;
◆ following up ideas;
◆ celebration and valuing.

The Ofsted report on managing the school workforce summarised their findings:

Schools that manage their workforce effectively to help raise standards are those that actively:

◆ **manage the culture** by creating a climate in which staff can work together productively
◆ **manage the staff** by implementing effective policies and procedures which ensure that highly competent people are recruited, deployed and trained and developed further
◆ **manage the working** environment by investing in it to make it a place where staff and pupils feel able to work hard and are motivated to do so
◆ **manage change by** harnessing the energies of the workforce to plan for and introduce changes that lead to better teaching and higher standards.

(Ofsted 2003b: 2)

The team approach

One of Senge's five disciplines is team working. As we have gained more and more TAs, they are less and less individuals who support individual children, or individual teachers, they have become a team of their own. The teacher has a host of adults with whom he or she forms a team – TAs, volunteers, parents and perhaps a governor can also form a class team. Subject faculties form teams; key stages, separate buildings or houses may constitute a team.

Look at the following list and consider the various teams in your school.

Teams are working well when:

◆ members are clear what needs to be done, the time-scale involved and who is to do what;
◆ members feel they have a unique contribution to make to the work of the team;
◆ mutual respect prevails among members;
◆ a climate of trust encourages the free expression of ideas, suggestions, doubts, reservations and fears;
◆ individual talents and skills are used effectively;
◆ members are able to discuss alternative approaches and solutions before taking decisions;
◆ there are established ways of working together which are supportive and efficient in the use of time;
◆ progress is checked regularly and members are clear about who they report to and when.

(Hargreaves and Hopkins 1991: 137)

In school teams, clarity of purpose is required. It would be helpful, at the beginning of taking up any such role that you clarified with the rest of the members:

◆ the objectives of the team;
◆ what commitment will be required;
◆ the purpose and timing of meetings;
◆ clear roles for members of the group known to all members;
◆ relationship to other groups and to the whole-school team;
◆ an understanding of any accountability procedures;
◆ whether working practices of the team will be monitored, mentored or directed from outside;
◆ what constraints or boundaries the team will be operating within;
◆ how you all will judge whether the team is successful.

Teams don't just happen by chance. They may have recognised structures set up by themselves or other people, but basically they will be a group of people with feelings, whose contribution needs to be valued. It is a balance between:

◆ attending to the culture of the group and the structure and organisation;
◆ enabling continuity yet ensuring appropriate change;
◆ maintenance and innovation;
◆ openness and trust;
◆ individual strengths and cooperation;
◆ cohesiveness and freedom to disagree;
◆ cooperation and argument.

(Watkinson 2005: 45, 46)

Teams depend on the variety of contributions of their members: you need thinkers and workers, innovators and those who are more cautious. The whole is greater than the parts and balanced teams of different types of people get results more quickly than teams of similar people. If you are asked for advice, remember others may have experience in other directions and can helpfully contribute. If you are asked an opinion about members of the team or its work by anyone outside the team, remain non-judgemental about other team members and again refer to other team members if it is about their particular role. You are not the sole source of information.

Team building

Some schools have tried the team-building techniques, rather favoured in some industries and businesses, to assist the building of the team. On the whole, these are considered a bit false by school staff, although some aspects as part of a whole-school in-service education for teachers (INSET) day may create some light relief and fun. I heard of a school where all the staff went on the local abseiling wall, but generally the more practical school-based activities work just as well. Turning out the classroom of a teacher who has left but also left an incredible heap of tat can be fun, especially when long lost resources are found buried in the depths.

Figure 3.1 Two HLTAs try out a team-building exercise with their TAs

Be cheerful and optimistic, welcoming to new members and show genuine enthusiasm for what the team achieves. Be considerate, people are not automata. Simple things like cups of tea or buns do help relationships especially at the end of the day. 'Thank yous' are important, a sign of valuing an individual's contribution. Don't gossip about team members or others when in a team meeting. Seek the help of others outside the team if you need it, you are not on your own in a school, and people like to feel they have a contribution to make.

(Watkinson 2005: 46)

The whole-school INSET day can be a powerful way of indicating that policies and practice within the school are for everybody, that there is only one philosophy for all. It is where leadership and management should meet. INSET days or meetings which are all vision with no practical outcomes are soon forgotten and viewed as a waste of time – leadership without management. If all sectors of those going to attend are consulted on the agenda beforehand it shows that all views are valued. Clearly the larger the school the more difficult such an exercise becomes. If the teaching staff is 100 strong it is likely that the support staff is even larger, and the INSET day becomes a fully fledged conference – and why not, if only once a year or even once in three years? Groups of primary schools, sometimes with their associated secondary school, set up conference days with national speakers for all attendees, followed by specific workshops for teachers, TAs, midday assistants (MDAs) and administrative and caretaking staff. It takes some organising but can be very worthwhile and promote some powerful messages.

Some schools regularly begin the academic year with such a day or half day, beginning the year as they mean to go on. Some hold a whole-school day or conference, off site, every three years as part of a triennial review of the school aims and objectives, and a major revamp to the school development/improvement plan (SDP/SIP). If the SDP is merely a tool, documenting change, sometimes seemingly for change's sake, it becomes yet another piece of paper, however worthy or useful – bureaucracy without management or leadership. Priorities, strategic policies and procedures can be discussed openly. Task groups can be formed with representatives of all sections who can spend time actually putting action plans with dates together.

> Governors, heads and staff have all reported how development planning encourages collaboration, and how this makes implementing the plan both more enjoyable and more effective. The school's partners often want to help but do not know how to do so: development planning provides genuine opportunities for harnessing this goodwill and support. *Collaboration:*
>
> ◆ creates a commitment to a common purpose among governors, head and staff and the school's partners;
> ◆ improves communication and reduces misunderstanding;
> ◆ fosters creativity in finding solutions when problems are discussed;
> ◆ enhances motivation;
> ◆ prevents individuals from becoming isolated;
> ◆ generates a sense of collective achievement;
> ◆ supports teamwork.
>
> (Hargreaves and Hopkins 1991: 137).

Kerry (2001) gives the characteristics of what he refers to as 'superteams' which promote 'creative dissatisfaction' as teams who:

> ◆ constantly re-visit what they are trying to achieve;
> ◆ are persistent;
> ◆ set high expectations and standards;
> ◆ are highly committed to each other and to the task;
> ◆ communicate effectively with others;
> ◆ are proactive;
> ◆ bring in others to help the work of the team;
> ◆ prioritise and hit their targets;
> ◆ are never fully satisfied.
>
> (pp. 60, 61)

Relationships within and between the school teams

Teacher and TAs

Most of the instances in The Good Practice Guidance, which was based on research by Farrell and colleagues (1999) refer to TAs working with other people. Indicator 3.1 is about teachers and TAs working cooperatively and gives specific instances of activities that show cooperation. Most of these need time outside contact time with the pupils in the classroom, so it is obvious that your decisions about paying for and timetabling such opportunities will encourage cooperative working. Indicator 3.2 talks about learning together, which requires meeting together, joint commitment and partnership. Indicator 4 looks at TAs' attendance at functions, the involvement of governors, parents and visiting advisers in liaising and linking with TAs and liaison within the schools of relevant senior staff and TAs. Indicator 5 also talks of meetings, liaisons and communication.

TAs and teachers alike need to feel confident that time spent on such joint activities is worthwhile, not just to themselves but to the way the school operates as a whole; they certainly like to feel trusted. Some schools talk about this kind of thing explicitly. Rose (2001) describes working in a 'failing' school, where some teams had excellent communication but not all.

> You cannot work as a team if some people will not let others have responsibilities or ideas on how to help . . . A strong headteacher and senior teachers were needed to show a direction for the school . . . people who are willing to listen to others and accept their views but also have a clear view of where the school is going and a good knowledge of the children.
>
> (pp. 77, 78)

The school later got a strong leader with 'a new approach to communication between staff so that everyone was involved. There was a new sense of trust – this is really important for support assistants as it shows them respect' (p. 78).

MacBeath and colleagues (1996) give the five key features of good relationships as:

◆ There is a shared sense of teamwork among all staff
◆ Older pupils help younger ones
◆ Bullying is not tolerated
◆ Parents and governors feel welcomed and valued in the school
◆ People address one another in ways which confirm their value as individuals.

(p. 36)

How does your school measure up?

Meetings: relating to a group of adults in public

Working alongside someone in a team or considering personal relationships within the team are on a different level from actually running a meeting or even taking a training session. These are much more like being the teacher in a class situation. Similar strategies apply.

THINKING POINTS

You need:

Clear aims – write them down and refer to them before and afterwards

Good planning

- write down lists, or even write out your speech
- prepare an agenda or a programme and circulate it in good time even if it is not very formal
- be sure how you want to deal with any other business
- have an idea of how long each item will take
- how do you want people to sit – in a circle or rows, or armchairs in the staffroom or round tables in a classroom?

Prepared resources such as PowerPoint slides or artefacts – you can use these for your notes for your talk if you like

- Do you need spare sheets of paper or spare pencils?
- Will you have handouts?

To decide on how formal you want to be – will you take questions, are you just leading a discussion?

- Will there be decisions?
- Do you need someone to take minutes?
- Depending on how public the occasion is you may even want to consider what you will wear. Will you get very hot and bothered for instance?
- Think how you will deal with inappropriate behaviour – people who talk all through what you are trying to say.

To be at the venue before the start so that all is ready

- Make sure refreshments are organised if you are having them – biscuits or mints or water on tables, a hot water urn and tea and coffee for help yourself or whatever

Practised performance – voice volume control, eye contact, gestures

Some kind of participation

Some sort of feedback – ask a friend in the group to comment afterwards, or have a sheet for ideas to follow up if it is a training session

Follow up any ideas, suggestions or agree action

The more prepared you are the better will be your confidence and therefore the better your performance and the more effective the session. The first time is the worst.

If you are going to chair a formal meeting you need to consider things such as:

◆ Making sure people know each other, where the toilets and fire exits are
◆ Ensuring everybody knows the purpose of the meeting, its length and how you are going to run it
◆ How decisions will be made – will voting be needed and if so who is eligible to vote?
◆ How matters will be recorded and taken forward.

If this is to be a really formal meeting then make sure you are familiar with the sort of ways in which things should go and the ways in which agenda are formulated. The role of the chair is an enabler, a listener allowing each to contribute, encouraging the reticent to comment and keeping the garrulous or dominant person under a bit of control.

Some really useful thoughts on how to actually deal with people in such public situations are given below.

Dealing with the people
Watch for the people who are more reflective/quieter and invite them to speak without putting too much pressure on them.

When people are having side conversations bring them back into line by:

◆ politely asking them to save their conversations until the end of the meeting
◆ giving them the opportunity to speak to the whole group, although this needs to be done without sarcasm or hostility
◆ stopping talking and establishing dead silence
◆ making clear eye contact with the guilty parties.

If people interrupt each other, challenge them politely 'Hold on, Sweep, let Soo finish what she was saying.'

The person who talks too much needs stopping. Try phrases like these:

◆ 'Can you summarise your main points briefly for us?'
◆ 'I know you have a lot of knowledge on this subject and I appreciate your comments, but we do need to hear from other people too.'

The person who goes off on digressions also needs challenging.

◆ 'That's an interesting point. Can you help me understand how it relates to this item?'
◆ 'I know you have a real interest in this subject, but we don't have time to discuss it here. Can you take it off-line, please?'

Negative people also need managing – the kind who always know that nothing suggested will work. Try:

- 'I can see your point, but can you suggest how we can make it work this time?'
- 'You may be right, but let's look at the evidence before we decide.'

Check how others really feel.

Repetition wastes time, so again you need to bring people into line: 'That's an important point, Florence, but Dougal has already gone over the ground thoroughly.'

(Johnson 2007: 8)

Interviews and one-to-ones: relating to individuals on formal or public occasions

This section is about how you deal with candidates when you are interviewing or how you treat people when doing performance reviews. Some of you will be able to have training in this area which is really helpful. Often the training involves role play which some people hate, just because it means having to put on a public face, no longer being able to hide in anonymity, but this is precisely why such training techniques are used. Interviewing for a job and for performance reviews is going to have an effect on the recipient for their future. You do, in fact, for a short time, have their life in your hands. It is a responsibility, and should be taken very seriously.

The main thoughts to hold onto are:

- How would you like to be treated in such circumstances?
- When people are put at their ease you are more likely to get truthful and productive answers to questions.
- Preparation is key.
- There will be some legal obligations of which you should be aware.
- There will be some policies regarding your school's procedures in such matters.
- Confidentiality is important.

The issues in these circumstances are very important and the potential for things going wrong fairly high, so if you are asked to undertake either of these for the first time do ask for guidance, support and, if possible, training. Such interviews or meetings are probably the most important of their kind to take place for the future of the individual concerned and the school itself. This is one reason why it is advisable not to interview for jobs alone. The processes for performance review and interviewing are relatively easily described and guidance is available. Face-to-face ways of behaving need practice.

Dealing with issues: dealing with difficult people and difficult situations

The best advice for the immediate difficult situation is to remember any behaviour management strategies you have learnt when dealing with children.

THINKING POINTS

When it happens:

◆ Be calm.
◆ If possible let the angry person have time and space to calm down – offer a cup of tea, a quiet place and wait a bit.
◆ Don't interview them alone if there is any possibility of violence.
◆ Let the angry person have their say.
◆ Listen to what is not said or what might be behind any tirade.
◆ Do not commit yourself to any action immediately – say 'things can be considered', 'you will need to consult others'.
◆ Make notes of the problem and take it seriously.
◆ Have a box of tissues handy in case the difficulty becomes emotional.
◆ Don't take the problem personally – be professional.
◆ Keep your own emotions in check as far as possible, two angry people will not help – but recognise that you do have an emotional reaction.
◆ Keep your distance but keep eye contact.
◆ Do not get into a win or lose situation.
◆ Focus on the problem not the participants.
◆ Talk through possible resolutions.
◆ Check through with them before they leave the essence of the problem and how you will get back to them.

Afterwards:

◆ Investigate the problem and listen to other points of view.
◆ Refer to your line manager, if they are not involved, for advice or someone senior or in an advisory capacity in the LA.
◆ Ensure you do get back to the complainer later.
◆ Do something personally satisfying or enjoyable to relax.

I have seen underperforming TAs, TAs who, differently deployed or managed, could do better. The difficulties of grasping the nettle of people management have prevented many schools not only from radical change but also small improvements in practice. The secret is to speak when issues are small, to deal with the issues in private, but keep a record for your own good. One HLTA said to me, 'If I am a team leader I must speak if I see them (the other TAs) do something that I know is wrong. That is part of my responsibility isn't it?' It is part of leading and managing. An early small word can save a lot of aggravation at a later date. Poor performance while a TA is on probation should be dealt with when it occurs, not at the end of the probationary period. If 'the word' takes place in private, no face is lost, support can be put in place unobtrusively and standards will rise. The main problem with managing TAs has been lack of explicit instructions, the assumption that they will know implicitly what to do. They don't always know and would welcome being told.

Even if heads and governors are persuaded of the educational benefits from reorganising, dealing with any possibility of redundancy proceedings often puts leaders and managers off. Working in education has been a 'soft option' in employment terms compared with most of industry and business, where the talk can be of 'people shedding'. Despite research into how organisations best manage such situations, school leaders lack experience in the skills required. School staff work closely together and any hint of disturbing the status quo is just that, disturbing. Many heads hope and wait for voluntary staff change – a retirement of a teacher or a deputy say, before implementing structural change. Some take the opportunity of imposed change, such as rebuilding, to take the blame rather than themselves. It can be done, humanely and happily, but despite the advice and funding, WR has not brought about widespread significant change.

The difficulties faced in people management are twofold – how to finance any changes and the reactions of the people concerned. The two are connected. Models that incur any threat of demotion or redundancy carry with them atmospheres of demoralisation and even despair, something that makes leaders think twice about dealing with them. With limited resources, significant change is likely to mean, at the least, reconsideration of JDs, and thus unsettling times. The recent job evaluation in some authorities, with single status agreements being made for all non-teaching staff across the board, has, in itself, been a traumatic time for schools. Do take advice if you feel redundancy is possible. Early consultation and openness about things such as declining budgets can make a lot of difference to morale and success.

Chapter 4

Why employ TAs?

The rationale of having TAs in the first place

Schools in other countries often do not have assistants to teaching and learning as we have, and in some countries do not even have administrative support. It largely appears to have come about as the result of seeing the potential of individuals by advisers, headteachers and teachers of having that extra pair of hands. I fear though, in many instances, the growth in range of jobs done by TAs has been the result of available, cheap, intelligent people who fill gaps that are seen by them and by the leaders in the school. If vision and strategic planning are the foremost qualities of good leadership, the rationale for the employment of a considerable number of people must reside with the leaders. You may need to stand back and just rethink that group of people. Consider the range of possibilities, then look at the current and possibly future needs of the school – its pupils, its other staff, the parent and governing bodies and the community. In Senge's terms, make 'mental models' of the possibilities, then look at the strategies for developing and appointing the right people to fulfil your vision.

If you are not the senior leader, this should not stop you having a picture of what a team of TAs or an individual TA could do. However, you then have to share your ideas with the head so that it can become part of the school vision, not just remain in your team, classroom or department. Senior TAs are, themselves, proving good leaders, not always by design, but by default. This should be recognised by their line managers, so any lead TAs reading this, make sure you have the right discussions upwards as well as with your team.

From welfare to teaching

Forty years on from the publication of the Plowden report, as it was known, we are again in a time of impending teacher and, more particularly, headteacher shortage. The average age of teachers and heads is high and fewer younger people make teaching their life's work. Career patterns have changed globally, the idea of a lifelong vocation is rarer. Reorganisation and change is the name of the game we are all required to play. Few people remember the Plowden report for its contribution about assistants, but even then, the writers saw one of the ways forward in mainstream schools as expansion in ancillaries as they called them. Only 22 per cent of schools had welfare assistants to 'relieve teachers in caring for the needs of young children' (Plowden 1967: 318). There was 'little logical pattern' in the employment of assistants. For some, class size was the rationale, some the experience (or lack of it) of the class teacher, and for some a definition of function. Unfortunately, little has changed here either. The rationale for employment is as varied as the variation in schools.

However, the nature of the tasks undertaken by TAs, and their recognised competence and capabilities have changed beyond recognition. Then, the help given by assistants was seen as generally of a welfare-care nature.

> There is no reason why they should not prepare materials for art and craft, look after plants and animals, help with displays and exhibitions, and record school broadcasts. The combination of role with the school secretary is seen as helpful, although the 'all rounders' are unlikely to be able to also help with musical or mechanical equipment.
>
> (Plowden 1967)

An article in the TES caught the mood of change with its title *To boldly go beyond washing paint-pots* (Haigh 1996). TAs can do much more but the paint-pots have to be washed. Unfortunately, there does seem to be less use of paint-pots currently; changes in the curriculum, with its accompanying strategies have reduced the opportunities for messy and creative activities as well as physical ones. There are still TAs whose jobs are to clear up after small children and perform menial tasks, but they also carry out almost any support role that is possible in schools. Trying to categorise these is the difficulty.

Workforce remodelling

In order to look more clearly at the current roles of TAs one needs to look in several dimensions: the activities or tasks they undertake; the levels of skill, knowledge and understanding they bring to the tasks; and the kind of structures, JDs, pay scales and contracts which are used. Standards have defined levels helpfully and WR has brought in national agreement of clear descriptors of levels. The support staff framework is in Table 4.1, to be found on the www.tda.gov.uk website.

Table 4.1 The support staff framework as seen by the TDA

Administration	Learning support	Pupil support	Site staff	Specialist & technical
Exam officer Finance General administration	Cover supervision Early Years Special needs Sports coach Teaching assistant/ bilingual support	Behaviour/ guidance/ support Care staff Mid-day supervisor/ playworker	Catering staff Premises staff	ICT Librarian Science/design and technology

An analysis of the varied roles of support staff as seen at the beginning of WR is to be found in the first report on an investigation into support staff roles being made at the Institute of Education (IoE). However, their classification is not part of the general language of employment to be found in schools. They suggested seven groups:

1   TA equivalent (TA, LSA (SEN pupils), nursery nurse, therapist).
2   Pupil Welfare (Connexions personal adviser, education welfare officer, home–school liaison officer, learning mentor, nurse and welfare assistant).
3   Technical and specialist staff (ICT network manager, ICT technician, librarian, science technician and technology technician).
4   Other pupil support (bilingual support officer, cover supervisor, escort, exam invigilator, language assistant, MDA and mid-day supervisor).
5   Facilities staff (cleaner, cook and other catering staff).
6   Administrative Staff (administrator/clerk, bursar, finance officer, office manager, secretary, attendance officer, data manager, examination officer and PA [personal assistant] to the headteacher).
7   Site staff (caretaker and premises manager).

(Blatchford *et al.* 2006)

Despite the claims of the authors of the report that the above classification was a best fit both on task description and school experience, my own experience does not totally conform to this classification. Largely the differences are in primary schools, where with fewer people doing everything that has to be done, individual people undertake a range of roles of a similar nature. Also, line management within the school, where contract staff have been returned to the control of the school itself, tends to fall in a different direction to that indicated by the classification. For the sake of this book I intend to limit myself to TA equivalent, excluding therapists as they are usually employed outside the school except in the few, newer, larger schools already going down the ECM agenda route. Many TAs also perform one or more of these roles, and not only in primary schools. What this whole debate does do, is recognise the complexity of the support staff roles.

THINKING POINTS

You need to think clearly about:
What needs to be done in this school?
What kind of people are already working in the school?
What do they do?
What could they do given encouragement, training and appropriate reward?
What are the best kind of posts to support this?
How do I match posts to people to needs?

Whether the IoE classification will form part of the current investigation by the DfES into pay and conditions of service of support staff this summer, or become generally accepted, remains to be seen (TES 2007a). While different local authorities are free to set their own criteria for job evaluation, the variation across England, let alone the other countries of the United Kingdom will not give helpful categorisation either.

The main way of describing TAs' work in the literature is by case study. Some of these are listed at the end of the chapter along with references to various surveys and books describing TA work. This chapter will use the categorisation most generally used, also found in 'School support staff: the way forward' (NJC 2003). That is, to look at how TAs support pupils, the curriculum, teachers and the school and then look at some of the qualities, skills and levels of understanding which they bring to the job.

It is not really possible to separate the work of TAs into these separate strands, because their role is complex and varied. A TA supporting pupils in a lesson is helping the aims of the teacher and being an extra pair of eyes and ears, using the curriculum, formal or informal and carrying out school policies. The role of a TA that differentiates them from other kinds of assistant (such as administrative or lunchtime assistants), is their direct involvement in the teaching and learning processes of the classroom. Over recent years the relative emphasis put on using TAs in each area has changed considerably.

The four strands of TA work

Supporting pupils

TAs usually describe their own role as supporting pupils and it is this area of their work that brings them the most job satisfaction. The support of SEN children, with help paid for by what was then the LEA, initiated after the Warnock report (DES 1978) was the beginning of the national recognition of the role of assistants in the classroom to support pupils. Schools do often distinguish general class support TAs from their SEN support by calling the latter LSAs and some use their senior TA to coordinate the SEN support work. Some HLTAs are assistant SENCOs.

School example

In both a secondary school and a primary that I visited, the schools had developed a senior TA role as an LSA coordinator. For both, their role first thing in the morning was to ensure coverage of all the students with SEN by checking the absence list of TAs and the timetables. In the secondary school, with 35 LSAs, the HLTA has instituted her own notice board in the staffroom to deal with the daily changes.

TAs used to talk rather diffidently of carrying out the IEPs, developing fine motor skills, or life skills, of problems such as autism, complex learning difficulties, Down's Syndrome, poor language skills, or social awareness. Now, they can be the school expert in these areas, providing advice to teachers whose experience of a condition might be much less. TAs have become trained in speech and language issues, for instance, and go to specific training in this area. Others might visit

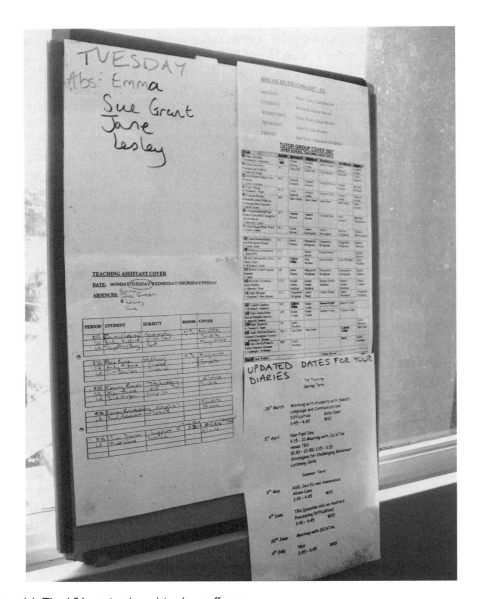

Figure 4.1 The LSA notice board in the staffroom

specialist schools such as those for autism and develop relationships and liaison mechanisms. They become the contact person for visiting advisers such as occupational or physiotherapists. They often attend IEP annual reviews, as the person who has worked most closely with the child. They write reports for the SENCO to include in submissions for statementing. 'Successful ideas very often come from non-teaching staff as they are at the chalk face and are often involved in a personalised approach to children' (Anon. 2007a).

Despite some dissenting voices at that time, Farrell *et al.* (1999) indicated that TAs can contribute to the teacher's understanding of pupils' needs from their observations. Given training and guidance, they now carry out assessments for teachers on a regular basis. Frequently TAs will participate in reading assessments, Standard Assessment Tasks/Tests (SATs) practices and end of unit test situations. But more generally, their daily assessments of achievements, understanding or skills acquisition is now a valued part of the TA role. The feedback at the end of a lesson, the report for a visiting therapist or specialist, the presence at an IEP review meeting have become vital parts of the TA role. The teacher alone cannot make such close assessments of individual progress as the TA who has fewer pupils to consider and regular close contact.

What assistants do when they are with individual pupils varies with the nature of the condition, the age and stage of the pupil but also the policies of the school. It is still common, but thankfully decreasing, to find what has been called the 'velcro' approach to helping individual pupils with SEN. This is where the assistant shadows or 'sticks' to the pupil with SEN. This is, of course, necessary in certain cases of physical need, but the aim of schooling is to create independent learners not dependent ones. The aim of inclusion is to include, not label and publicly identify a need for support. The increased inclusion in mainstream school has largely been managed by increasing the availability of individual attention, but it needs to be managed by the deployment and classroom strategies allowing the TA to support as and when appropriate rather than fulfilling an allocated number of hours of personal attention. This support is what Balshaw, as long ago as 1991, called a 'child deficit' model of employment (Balshaw 1991).

While TAs often know less of learning theories than newly qualified teachers, they do show a great deal of interest in them, they do understand about the individual differences between children. It is still true that the vast majority of TAs are female, and have their own families; that is why they do the job – it fits in with looking after their own children. This experience gives them an experiential and instinctive understanding of children's development. In secondary schools, the mothers of teenage children are able to talk with recalcitrant teenagers in a way some teachers, concentrating on their subject matter find difficult or too time consuming.

Balshaw has a useful page where she categorises child/student contact activities: curriculum and learning related, pastoral care related and aspects of physical support; and non contact activities: preparation tasks, liaison and coordination tasks. Evaluating such support is very difficult. If the presence of the children with SEN is dependent on additional support, who says how much, for how long and of what nature is best? Blatchford *et al.* (2002) tried in their KS1 study but the variability in quality of provision prevented them from making firm conclusions.

TAs supporting learning is observable more as process than in its outcomes. The Ofsted report regarding TAs gave a list of strategies HMI (Her Majesty's Inspectorate) observed where TAs help pupils to learn better. Ofsted (2002) found 'teachers value highly the support provided by teaching assistants and the benefits of having another skilled adult in the classroom' (p. 4). The report also quoted Ofsted Section 10 reports where it had been found that the quality of teaching in lessons with TAs is better than without them.

O'Brien and Garner (2001) were convinced that the accounts of LSAs themselves showed that they could enable 'children to think in a more focused way about their learning . . . by: modelling positive behaviour, establishing and developing relationships, increasing learner confidence and self-belief, encouraging risk taking – in fact empowering the learner' (p. 3).

Farrell *et al.* (1999) suggested the key to creating independent learning for pupils is for TAs to have flexibility in the way they work, to be clear about when to intervene and when to become a general resource. Lacey (1999) spoke of 'just the right amount and type of support for individual pupils' (p. 33). Children need to learn to think, become independent learners and understand their own learning styles.

> The job of the school is to motivate the learner; to encourage her or him to want to learn; to help the learner understand how to learn; and to believe that it is possible to do so . . . This will also be dependent on the way she is being taught.
>
> (MacGilchrist *et al.* 1997)

The Code of Practice is quite clear:

> There is sometimes an expectation that this help will take the form of the deployment of extra staff to enable one-to-one tuition to be given to the child. However, this may not be the most appropriate way of helping the child. A more appropriate approach might be to provide different learning materials or special equipment; to introduce some group or individual support; to devote extra adult time to devising the nature of the planned intervention and to monitoring its effectiveness; or to undertake staff development and training to introduce more effective strategies.
>
> (DfES 2001)

School policies and senior managers do need to recognise how TAs are allocated, and what work they are actually doing in order to communicate with budget managers, governors and parents. Secondary schools are increasingly employing class-based TAs to prevent the stigma attached to getting help from a TA (Davey 2007). There are stories of parents demanding their five hours a week personal support because they know money for this support has been allocated to the school after the provision of a statement.

There has also been a growth in the use of TAs for counselling purposes, again, some going on to serious training in the field. Use of counselling methods in behaviour management, if backed up by consistent availability of help, has achieved success in many schools in dealing with issues such as bereavement, family breakdown and conflict resolution. Such is the success of such methods, that the role of learning mentor has been developed where individual pupils have an allocated, trained and available adult who can support their needs – not only in counselling situations but for their learning needs. The functional map (Sauvé *et al.* 2003) for learning mentors identifies the role as supporting and mentoring individual educational needs, developing one-to-one relationships. It includes various professional aspects of the role, including liaising with agencies and networking, and developing professional expertise, but the role is also to support participation and encourage social inclusion. It is a specific role for working out of the classroom to support pupils, hoping to get them back into the classroom as soon as appropriate.

TAs are used in test and examination conditions as readers, prompters and scribes. This all has to be done under controlled conditions, and by arrangement with the

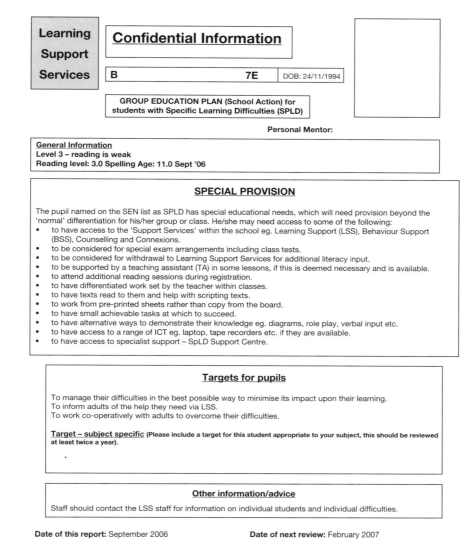

Learning Support Services

Confidential Information

| B | 7E | DOB: 24/11/1994 |

GROUP EDUCATION PLAN (School Action) for students with Specific Learning Difficulties (SPLD)

Personal Mentor:

General Information
Level 3 – reading is weak
Reading level: 3.0 Spelling Age: 11.0 Sept '06

SPECIAL PROVISION

The pupil named on the SEN list as SPLD has special educational needs, which will need provision beyond the 'normal' differentiation for his/her group or class. He/she may need access to some of the following:
- to have access to the 'Support Services' within the school eg. Learning Support (LSS), Behaviour Support (BSS), Counselling and Connexions.
- to be considered for special exam arrangements including class tests.
- to be considered for withdrawal to Learning Support Services for additional literacy input.
- to be supported by a teaching assistant (TA) in some lessons, if this is deemed necessary and is available.
- to attend additional reading sessions during registration.
- to have differentiated work set by the teacher within classes.
- to have texts read to them and help with scripting texts.
- to work from pre-printed sheets rather than copy from the board.
- to have small achievable tasks at which to succeed.
- to have alternative ways to demonstrate their knowledge eg. diagrams, role play, verbal input etc.
- to have access to a range of ICT eg. laptop, tape recorders etc. if they are available.
- to have access to specialist support – SpLD Support Centre.

Targets for pupils

To manage their difficulties in the best possible way to minimise its impact upon their learning.
To inform adults of the help they need via LSS.
To work co-operatively with adults to overcome their difficulties.

Target – subject specific (Please include a target for this student appropriate to your subject, this should be reviewed at least twice a year).

Other information/advice
Staff should contact the LSS staff for information on individual students and individual difficulties.

Date of this report: September 2006   Date of next review: February 2007

Figure 4.2 An IEP delineating group support

examination boards, but it has enabled pupils to gain accreditation for knowledge and understanding even though they have an impairment.

Good TAs:

◆ Recognise the need to introduce the children to a collaborative way of working. They make sure pupils are part of the whole class by stopping their activity or speech whenever the teacher speaks to the whole class. As they largely work with small groups of children, they need to be clear within these when the tasks are for individuals to complete and when the task itself is cooperative, for example, in practical science work or a discussion.

◆ Are able to scaffold learning in the classroom and prepare resources to enable differentiated tasks to occur.

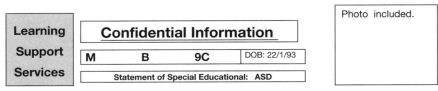

Photo included.

Learning Support Services

Confidential Information

| M | B | 9C | DOB: 22/1/93 |

Statement of Special Educational: ASD

Personal Mentor: Mrs S

General Information

M is a lively, chatty boy who, at his best can be well motivated, caring and kind. He has a wide variety of interests from animals to judo. However his behavioural difficulties, mostly in the area of attention, concentration and social interaction, have caused considerable concern. Frustration can lead to aggressive outbursts, particularly during unstructured times. He can be difficult to calm if he is distressed and benefits from a non-confrontational response.
M lives with his parents and younger sister, but dad works away and is home at weekends.
M has previously been prescribed Ritalin, but is now not taking it. He suffers from asthma for which medication has been prescribed.
NCL: English 3.8 Maths 4.5 Science 4.2 Mar 2006

Nature of Difficulties

M was originally diagnosed with Attention Deficit Hyperactivity Disorder, but in 2003 he received a diagnosis of Aspergers Syndrome in recognition of his difficulties with social interaction.
Assessment by speech and language therapist indicated that M's formal language skills are in the average/high average range. However, difficulties with social communication and understanding are apparent. He has difficulties with humour, conversation turn taking and appropriate termination of conversations. M shows a preference for 'black and white' rules, together with a strong sense of justice, which can lead to problems with peers.
In school M has significant social interaction problems in the playground. His literacy and numeracy skills are developing, but he does find it difficult to transfer his ideas onto paper. M is particularly interested in Science and IT. He finds it difficult to respond to class instructions and changes to routine.

Objectives- as on Statement

- A curriculum delivered at an appropriate pace and depth where teaching tasks, methods and materials are modified according to the level of need
- A structured programme to develop social communication skills
- Support to continue the development of literacy and numeracy skills
- Structured approaches to improve concentration, attention and independent work skills with a high level of positive reinforcement
- Strategies to develop the ability to adapt to the routines and expectations of the classroom and school
- The setting of achievable targets, high levels of encouragement and praise, and the highlighting of personal and curriculum strengths to promote self-confidence and self-esteem

Level of Support

M receives 1.0 TA from Exceptional Arrangements and will be closely monitored by the LSS Department.

Target - subject specific   (Please include a target for this student appropriate to your subject, this should be reviewed at least twice a year.)

-

Review Date: April 2007 (to LA)   ***Date of this report*** – September 2006

Figure 4.3 An IEP delineating individual support

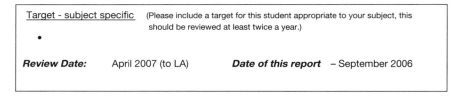

◆ Can support individuals and small groups by being the personal interpreter of the subject matter for the children.

◆ Can both transmit information from the teacher and make sense of it for the groups of children with whom they work.

◆ Can question and challenge.

◆ Come out well when compared with the criteria from texts on teaching skills. Some Ofsted inspectors have observed the quality of teaching of TAs and found it similar, if not better than that of some teachers on occasions. It is the role that was recognised in the HLTA standards. Standard 27 in the draft revised standards (see 3.3.5 in the old standards) states: 'In the absence of the teacher, advance learning in a range of classroom settings that include working with a) individuals, b) small groups c) whole classes' (TDA 2007).

◆ Assist the children to develop skills using demonstration and verbal instruction. Where TAs themselves have skills, for instance in a craft area, they understand the expertise that would be required in the future and are able to present appropriate steps to the pupils.

◆ Provide role models as learners for the children, keen to make the children think about what they are doing and extending their ideas. TAs themselves are learners, often very interested in learning more. They are keen course participants as any adviser who has taken TAs' courses will confirm. They show empathy for the role of the learner and, in cases of school-based course work, present themselves as a role model of lifelong learning. They can be examples of the fact that learning is not just about school or being a child.

◆ Give emotional support, recognising the emotional difficulties of some children that hinder their progress. Attitudes to learning, self-esteem and motivation powerfully affect the learning process.

◆ Give support to pupils with a physical impairment which can mean their participation in mainstream schools, or keeping up with their more physically able peers. Special schools depend on their LSAs enormously.

◆ Use many positive verbal and non-verbal signals to encourage and gave pupils regular attention and praise, boost self-confidence and self-esteem, increase motivation and reinforce success.

School example

One TA said 'I want these children to learn on their own, I'm there to help them learn independently, on their own. The target is to do myself out of a job.' The teacher said: 'They are teaching and guiding. I think they have a different relationship with the children. I think the role has changed though over the years and I think the children do see them far more. It's very hard to describe the relationship. It's hard to put your finger on it. It isn't Mum, it isn't friend, it's beyond that, it's different. It's not that. It shouldn't be that because it's a working situation that perhaps they do see them as there for them more, but that's wrong too. Hopefully, they see as teacher, you're there for them too. But, the responsibility is different. The teaching assistant, to the children, appears to have more time because they're working with a smaller group, therefore for them.' And then later when discussing the possible dependency that such a relationship might engender she added: 'I think that's where you manage as a class teacher and beyond that as well. Having said that, I think the teaching assistants are taking that on more as they are becoming more skilled and learn more about the process. The role of a teaching assistant has changed a lot too, over the years from being a helper to being involved in the children's education. I think, in the past, they were helping and not taking on responsibility for the children's development as they are now.'

(Watkinson 2003a: 19, 20)

These descriptions show clearly how TAs can assist in the government's ideas on personalised learning. If they know the pupils well, better than class teachers, working with them will be imperative to gain a full insight into the needs of individual pupils.

Supporting the teacher

Most teachers acknowledge the support role of the TA and usually say 'I couldn't do what I do without them'. There are still a few dissenting voices who feel that having to plan for the additional adult just gives them more work; 'as bad as or worse than having another pupil in the class' is still being said. Many teachers like the aspect of having the extra pair of hands, eyes and ears in the classroom. Some like the friendship, the sharing, the listening ear to their moans, knowing the TA has also seen the problems encountered that morning. For some, it enables tasks to be achieved that would otherwise be impossible – tasks that need an adult for health and safety reasons or particular guidance. Hopefully, it is this last that is why the TA is deployed, and the rest follows because of the teacher–TA relationship and classroom management strategies. One head said: 'Teachers don't teach in the same way with a TA in the room, there is more relaxation, excitement even with another adult there. It also affects absenteeism of teachers.'

For some teachers, it makes the difference between accepting certain disruptive characters in their classroom or not, or having a person on hand to withdraw the difficult ones and thus preventing their own breakdown through stress. It is sad that TAs have become seen as minders of difficult pupils, enabling the rest of the class to get on properly. If this is happening, it really is time for senior teachers to look carefully at the curriculum presentation and content, and quality of teaching of the teacher that have brought the situation to needing minders. It is recognised that the incidence of behaviour problems, especially low level disturbance in class has increased. It is not only socially acceptable for young people to disturb others, it seems to have become necessary in order to maintain one's 'street cred'. With appropriate deployment, training and support of both TAs and teachers such situations can become productive and not just a holding situation.

The TAs' close and frequent contact with small groups of pupils, allied often with their being able to follow these pupils from class to class as they get older, gives a perception of their competence and a knowledge of what they have already done.

A crucial point that must be remembered is that the teaching activity is always done under the supervision of a teacher (DfES 2003). It is still an area that some teachers find threatening, if not to them personally, to the teaching profession. One of the objections that the unions voiced early on was the possible usurpation of the teachers' role by unqualified staff. You might have to deal with such concerns as you recognise the potential of your TAs. It was clear from responses in the HLTA assessment materials at national moderation that some HLTAs and TAs are taking classes to cover for PPA time like a cover supervisor – following the teacher's plans with no time given for joint planning, preparation or follow-up activities such as marking. Advancing learning is a clear distinction between a cover supervisor and an HLTA appropriately deployed. Conditions of service for such cover must be adequate, as must the remuneration.

School example

An HLTA in a very small village school takes mathematics with years 3 and 4, supported by two other TAs because of the high level of special needs in the class. Next door, on the other side of the partition the class teacher takes years 5 and 6. They plan together and the HLTA feeds back all the necessary information to the teacher.

Supporting the curriculum

The Department for Education (DFE) report examined the different roles of various categories of staff and the boundaries between them (Mortimore *et al.* 1992). The report found it relatively easy to identify the purposes of jobs and benefits, but not so easy to collect information on cost effectiveness and even more difficult in terms of educational value. In the book based on the report it said:

> These assessments of the benefits of the innovation would appear to pass a curriculum 'test', in the sense that the change is having an impact upon the activity in the classroom. As with so many decisions in schools, the assessment of its benefit for learning involves informed judgements and cannot be reduced to an objective calculation.

> (Mortimore *et al.* 1994)

Figure 4.4 The HLTA taking half a class supported by TAs

The study raised questions about the impact that TAs have on learning and curriculum as well as child support and suggested 'greater professional and pedagogical (rather than administrative) commitments' (Mortimore *et al.* 1992: 178). Hopefully, that is now the situation.

In the late 1990s, the introduction of LNS had a further profound effect upon the use of TAs in primary schools. With the insistence of the strategies on group work, it became an essential component of classroom organisation to have additional adults to support the curriculum. Many schools, especially in the primary sector, rearranged their TA provision to cover literacy and numeracy lessons. TAs were much more included in in-house training and government-funded initiatives such as the Additional Literacy Strategy (ALS), resulting in mass training sessions by LEAs for TAs accompanied by a teacher. The partnership of the two was being seen at last as an essential component of the provision for children. The provision of support materials for the use of TAs has increased with most years from year 2 to year 8 having some kind of 'catch-up' or additional work available to reinforce that being delivered by the teacher. I use the word deliver here purposely, for it may be that the increase in curriculum-dominated planning as distinct from needs-led planning has resulted in a greater need for groups to 'catch up' – the schemes of work plough on regardless of whether pupils have grasped the relevant parts.

Learning also has a social context, no one is totally isolated from another human being. Much of what has been described as schooling's hidden curriculum, for instance, consists of what children learn by their social relationships, rather than as a result of what they are formally taught. TAs are often seen in schools contributing in informal times. As well as the social aspect, they can support the English curriculum when talking with children in cloakrooms or the playground, mathematics when assisting changing – matching, pairing, counting. Science in the school grounds, the humanities on school trips, or more generally they can contribute to the pupil's self-esteem through their behaviour management strategies. Ofsted indicated that TAs 'make a significant contribution to the quality and breadth of the curriculum' in the successful primary schools they investigated (Ofsted 2002: 26).

In some schools, the expertise of the TA has been utilised in a particular curriculum area. It is now common to find graduates working as TAs where their family commitments or desired responsibility level has pushed them in a TA direction rather than a full teaching commitment. Some TAs have a particular expertise in, for instance, ICT or French or music. TAs with a knowledge of a local ethnic community language are common to support those pupils with English as an additional language (EAL). Curricular specialisms have been recognised, possibly particularly in primary schools but certainly not exclusively so, by using the TA as the subject coordinator in that area. In ICT, the relative mobility of a TA has led to them being the ICT technician as well.

Supporting the school

Just as diet and housing environment can affect physical growth, the learning environment can affect brain function and learning. Schools with high standards are visibly welcoming and organised places to be. The learning environment includes the physical surroundings or the social, emotional, linguistic and cultural contexts of the learners. Harding and Meldon-Smith (1996) promote the use of a multi-sensory environment, with bright display, plants, well-organised and accessible resources. The TAs' role in helping the school achieve this is an important one, and not to be dismissed just as 'washing paint-pots'. Teachers and TAs can take joint pride in this kind of maintenance.

The WR support staff definitions include a role of Curriculum/resource support (NJC 2003). It defines four levels of support; level 1 being the more simple organisation and maintenance of equipment and supplies, while level 4 sees the role holder as part of the senior management team and responsible for other staff. Cleaning the paint-pots has to be done, but TAs can supervise pupils to do it for themselves even from the foundation stage. TAs encourage pupils to clear up, to work tidily; to manage their resources appropriately. TAs can help with displays and may sometimes have more talent in this direction than the teacher.

TAs support the school in many more ways than just the practical one. Although they are good at making tea, teachers should not turn to them to do it automatically. This was seen in one school but luckily the head was present, who rapidly moved to make it herself, making the point to the teacher that TAs are not just there to be dogsbodies. They can be an advocate for the school within the community, coming from the local community more frequently than the teaching staff. They can also be a listening ear within the community on behalf of the school.

In schools where the extended schools ideas have taken root, it is often the TAs who extend their role to take the Kids' Club or the breakfast club. Brain gym and

Figure 4.5 The TAs put out the display of Easter baskets ready for judging and the Easter assembly

'Take ten', a popular 10-minute exercise routine to music, is often taken by a TA. TAs take break supervision with and without teacher support.

School example

One school in a deprived area of a large town had started a Club 15 at lunchtime. This was run by a group of three TAs for those children who found playing with others difficult, things such as taking turns. Parents had to give their permission for inclusion at the club and the school went to great lengths to make sure it was not a punishment scheme. The MDAs were looking after football activities and the like in the playground. The children had their lunch in the club, so the TA could help with the table meal time social skills, also missing for many children. They had a choice of activities. The TAs took some groups for things such as anger management or emotional strategies mixed in with more ordinary games. They talked about rules and choices.

In all four of the levels of the descriptions of resource support in 'School support staff: the way forward', the support for the school includes:

◆ be aware of and comply with policies and procedures relating to child protection, health, safety and security, reporting all concerns to the appropriate person
◆ be aware of and support difference and ensure all pupils have equal access to opportunities to learn and develop
◆ contribute to the overall ethos/work/aims of the school
◆ work with other professionals at an appropriate level
◆ be involved with, at an appropriate level, out of school learning activities, e.g. clubs, extra curricular activities within guidelines established by the school.

(NJC 2003)

A look at the comprehensive nature of the HLTA standards gives an idea of the range of their role. This is particularly evident in the Professional attribute (new version) or Value and Principles (old version) section.

Those awarded HLTA status:

1 have high expectations of children and young people and a commitment to helping them fulfil their full educational potential
2 establish fair, respectful, trusting, supportive and constructive relationships with children and young people
3 demonstrate the positive values, attitudes and behaviour they expect from children and young people
4 recognise and respect the contribution that colleagues, parents and carers can make to the development, well-being and progress of children and young people

5   have a commitment to collaboration and cooperative working
6   communicate effectively with children, young people, colleagues, parents
    and carers
7   reflect on and improve their knowledge and practice.

(TDA 2007)

Managing behaviour is about having a climate in which teaching and learning can take place; it permeates everything that happens. It is about attitudes and strategies that are consistent throughout the school and classrooms for all pupils, not just those who have problems conforming to whatever is the norm in the school. The new proposals have suggested that dealing with problems of behaviour may be done by people other than TAs, such as learning mentors, who would be specially trained in the role of a 'behaviour and guidance manager', to coordinate or manage a behaviour and guidance team, or coordinate the behaviour policy in a school. Whether people undertake such a specialist role or not, it is imperative that all staff understand the school's behaviour policy and put it into practice. Children very quickly recognise which adults they can take advantage of.

School example

An LSA worked in a middle school in a deprived area of a seaside town with high unemployment. There were the inevitable difficult behaviour problems, but there was behaviour policy in place. The school head was strong and borrowed by the LA on occasions to support other schools. The LSA had left school at 16 and gone to work in a bank. He had become fed up with that so left and went to work voluntarily in his mother's school – she was an administrative assistant in a first school.

He was then 'headhunted' by a friend who was a teacher at the school, to do a paid LSA job and was using this job to fund a distance learning degree. He had recognised, as most LSAs and TAs do, that working in schools can be very satisfying. However, he did not stop there.

He had thought about the behaviour problems, and discussed them with his LSA colleagues. Between them they recognised that one of the problems was the lack of consistency by the teachers, of expectations of what the LSA could or would do about any difficult situation.

So, he talked with his line manager, who asked him to explain the dilemma in a teaching staff meeting. This he did, and offered to run a questionnaire to all the teachers and LSAs about what they thought and would like to happen. They agreed, he did it, collated the replies and fed them back to the teachers. His action had created debate, promoted reflection on the issue for all the staff on the behaviour policy that was already in place and encouraged dialogue between teacher and LSA partnerships.

He also started to develop independently a small whiteboard record of the positive responses of his 'charge' during a lesson. The other LSAs, seeing that this was proving a simple but effective reward strategy started copying it. The Art and Design Department produced an illustrated booklet for LSAs working in their department describing what they wanted LSAs to do and how the teachers would work with them. Being a middle school, the department area contained dangerous tools and equipment which all needed proper handling to ensure health and safety issues were properly covered.

TAs as team leaders

In some schools the growth in numbers of TAs has led to someone either with longer experience in the school or with a more dominant character emerging as a leader of TAs and then their JD being massaged to include that role. At least, when done in this way, the leadership has the consent of the team. It really should be done as a proper appointment, with JDs thought through by the senior management, and the seniority and the increased responsibilities recognised in the pay structure. Senior leadership/management has to decide what that role might achieve. The role of governors in such appointments should be considered. One size does not fit all situations.

The leadership roles of TAs or HLTAs found have included:

◆   a curriculum coordinator role;
◆   induction and mentoring of new TAs;
◆   organising meetings of TAs for information sharing, niggles sharing or CPD;
◆   attending the teaching staff meetings and relaying the information back to the TA team;
◆   becoming a staff governor;
◆   undertaking a small project actually instituting change in schools;
◆   daily organising the TA cover timetable for SEN children;
◆   inclusion in the senior leadership team meetings.

A drawback of having TAs as leaders for them is that there is often a lack of paid time to do the coordinator role on top of their pupil/classroom work. They report that heads can forget that they are hourly paid.

Personalised learning

The principles of personalised learning, one of the current government ideas, are wide, not a crisp menu of plans to be followed as the LNS became. It is based on the ECM agenda, and is a consultative not delivery mode of tackling teaching and learning. It is

a strategy for ensuring that over time:

◆   every pupil experiences success
◆   all pupils are engaged and excited by learning
◆   every pupil will have high aspirations for his/her work
◆   every pupil feels supported in making progress
◆   pupils know that they are valued
◆   parents know that their child is valued.

(Rudduck *et al.* 2006)

There is no way that a teacher of classes of 30 pupils can do this without help. By utilising the warmth that TAs exude, and their skills expertise, knowledge and understanding, it is possible.

The qualities of TAs

TAs cannot just be defined by the job they are employed for or the one they end up doing. Their presence as people, not just a resource must be recognised. There are certain characteristics of TAs that you must take into account when considering their function, appointment and deployment.

Personality

In the early reports, the TA had been described rather as any other piece of equipment in the school. The TA as a person with desires, experiences, capacities or competences which could be tapped or developed was largely ignored. Certain things stand out time and time again when good TAs are watched at work, such as their:

- ◆ Intrapersonal traits and attributes like
  - sensitivity and timing
  - concentration/commitment/perseverance
  - professionalism
  - confidence in action
  - humour, enthusiasm, interest and love of job
  - enjoyment of company of pupils
  - high standards/expectations of self and others
  - using initiative/responsibility within the structure of the class
- ◆ Interpersonal skills
  - relationships with the children and adults
  - showing knowledge and understanding of children's needs,
  - sharing and co-operating with other adults
  - empathy and sympathy with pupils and adults
  - friendliness, bonding, ability to listen
  - respect for other adults and children
  - supporting self confidence and self esteem in pupils
  - being constructively critical of self and others
  - communication with the teacher
  - role modelling learning strategies
- ◆ Physical activity
  - constant mobility and multitasking
  - physical contact – just being alongside the children and appropriate comforting and closeness to children in need of security
  - control or behaviour management through non-verbal gestures.

(Watkinson 2003a: 24)

Comments made in TA course evaluations reflected the enthusiasm that the TAs develop. 'I hadn't been told working with children is addictive . . . seeing the children develop and flourish . . . you can see the excitement in them when they achieve . . . it is something great to witness.' 'It is the best of both worlds: work with children without ultimate responsibility.' Colleague advisers often used to comment on the joys of taking courses for TAs, they would say 'the light is still on in their eyes'. Farrell *et al.* (1999) saw personal qualities as a better criterion for employment than qualifications, a point that you may consider when interviewing for TA posts.

Skills

The skills of teaching assistants are really those one would expect of a good teacher, the HLTA standards are based on those of teachers. They are the skills of teaching and assisting and supporting learning:

◆ planning and preparation, performance assessment, monitoring, recording and feedback;
◆ imagining and creating;
◆ explaining, instructing, questioning, listening, challenging, intervening and not intervening;
◆ organising, reviewing, evaluating and resource management;
◆ caring and empathising, behaviour management;
◆ lifelong learning and reflecting.

Most TAs have these skills by virtue of their role as parents, they have developed the skills as they needed them. Some of the skills are an instinctive reaction of one human being to another who is in a weaker position. In the classroom, TAs watch the teacher they are with and model their behaviour on what they see and assume is the best available. Leaders and managers in schools should be very aware that the skills base of their TAs is unlikely to be better than their teachers in some aspects unless the TA has some basic good experience with children. So, employing parents in the TA capacity is likely to provide a better skill base than employing young school leavers. It is the lack of self-confidence in having a qualification naming their capabilities that tends to mask the teaching skills innate in many TAs.

Knowledge and understanding

The introduction of the LNS has brought about recognition not only of the extra adult in the classroom, but the value of a trained and knowledgeable other adult. The National Numeracy Strategy (NNS), when it was first published, indicated strategies that imply a level of understanding and skill of TAs often previously ignored, while clearly indicating the continuing responsibility of the teacher. One of the standards for HLTA status that has been hotly debated is the requirements for a level 2 qualification in English and mathematics. Yet schools ask assistants to support English (literacy) and mathematics (numeracy) without first ascertaining whether the assistants themselves understand the content of the material they are to teach. This is particularly relevant to assistants working in key stages 3, 4 and 5. You should seriously consider when appointing whether your TAs should have a recognised competence to level 2 – the equivalent of a GCSE at grades A to C. This may be contentious – but worth thinking about.

Knowledge and understanding is also important in curriculum areas that might have specialist vocabulary or methods such as science. It is all too easy for a teacher to ask a TA to support a group in a certain activity, such as measuring capacity without checking that the TA recognises how accuracy in repeated measurements is maintained, or ask children to name items when they are unsure of such items themselves.

I have also seen the reverse occur, as in the following example:

School example

A headteacher used to play for assembly singing in a primary school for two years before they found out that one of the TAs was a grade 6 pianist.

Where previous knowledge and understanding is documented and referred to, changes in the needs of pupils can be addressed internally.

School example

An ex shorthand typist, working with a year 2 child with spinal muscular dystrophy, which prevented the child from holding a pencil, converted parts of the reading scheme to a keyboard skills programme, enabling the child to access word processing more quickly than learning by trial and error.

Competence

With standards for competence being commonplace now in school this is no longer a strange concept. NVQs based on National Occupational Standards (NOS) are now widespread in the community. The idea is that people can show in the workplace what they are capable of (sometimes called 'can dos'), be assessed there, certificated, and recognised for it in terms of career structure and pay.

National recognition and qualifications

From the 'mum's army' of the mid-1990s, through the 1998 Green paper *Teachers meeting the challenge of change* (DfEE 1998), money for recruitment, induction training, NOS and the associated qualifications, and national strategies to WR, TAs are clearly here to stay and nationally recognised as a valuable, if not an essential part of the school workforce. The HLTA status procedure has recognised that many TAs are competent to a high level without formal qualifications, and that experience is a great teacher.

Despite the amount of publicity and funding associated with WR and the increase in numbers of TAs, the issues are still there for schools, of professional boundaries, supervision and management, with the need for more explicit expectations and rationale for employment.

Further reading about the role of TAs

Many surveys have been done on the role and deployment of TAs.

The Blatchford *et al.*/Institute of Education survey (2006) mentioned at the beginning of the chapter will be very comprehensive when completed. The second part (Blatchford *et al.* 2007) is now available.

Two of the most readable, although pre-WR, are: *Teaching assistants in school: the current state of play* (Lee 2002) and *The employment and deployment of teaching assistants* (Smith *et al.* 2004).

A systematic literature review into support staff work is available on the Institute of Education website http://eppi.ioe.ac.uk/.

A quick summary of research and evaluation evidence is in 'The effective management of teaching assistants to improve standards in literacy and mathematics', pages 22 and 23 (DfES 2005b).

Untold stories is a most readable little book of histories written by LSAs themselves (O'Brien and Garner 2001).

Teaching assistants – the complete handbook (Hryniewicz 2004) gives little vignettes.

The first eight sections in *Primary teaching assistants* looks at variations on the role and the significances (Hancock and Collins 2005).

Suffolk LA are compiling a 'Butterflies' publication describing a range of TA activities.

Devon HLTA stories are on the www.devoncc.gov.uk website.

Chapter 5

The whole-school learning environment

The context of teaching assistance

Given leaders with a long-term vision and people with the talents described in the previous chapter, there are still the issues to consider of the context in which you work. The school is an organic whole and consists of people with lives, feelings and agenda of their own. The purpose of schools is to educate young people but research has shown they work most effectively when everyone within the community is a learner, not just the pupils. This means the role of TAs within the school must be seen as to how they fit into an overall pattern of support staff and teacher development. Also, the location and geography of the school building, its community and history all affect what TAs' support is necessary for pupils and what support the TAs themselves might need. The national initiatives and even the global agenda might affect how you consider your workforce appointment and deployment.

The internal context

Relationships underpin how effective a school is. Staff at all levels, managers and TAs, all need support to do their job well. When working with the HLTA group in Devon we were also able to work with a small group of their senior managers on a separate occasion. We asked both groups what their greatest concerns were and gave them some simple questionnaires. It was interesting to compare their lists with each other and with the list of issues that the WAMG had produced. There were some differences of emphasis and some categories not mentioned by some groups, but nearly all the concerns were internal issues:

◆ boundaries and expectations: defining exactly what TAs or HLTAs can and cannot do, should and should not do;
◆ more formal policies and procedures documentation;
◆ communication between staff of all levels and kinds;
◆ use and understanding of language, especially educational jargon, especially in specialist subjects such as science;
◆ whole-school training – especially behaviour management, health and safety and child protection;
◆ induction;

◆ confidentiality;
◆ funding and availability of CPD and training for TAs;
◆ training for teachers to work with TAs;
◆ lack of feedback on performance for TAs;
◆ appropriate contracts, JDs and pay arrangements;
◆ lack of paid time for meetings, planning and performance review;
◆ lack of knowledge and understanding by senior staff of experience and qualifications of TA teams;
◆ governors' involvement in TA and HLTA issues.

TAs interact with many different groups of people in the school community. Collaboration and celebration of good practice within the school contributes to the effective use of TAs and their personal effectiveness. TAs are often very good at their jobs, but self-effacing because of their lack of self-confidence. They are so adept at reading implicit instructions that they are trusted to get on with their job. This may seem a good thing but it could be seen as abandoning control. More than that, TAs need the positive support and encouragement of their class teachers and senior managers to develop their full potential.

The learning environment

Climate and ethos can affect the effectiveness and development of all staff as well as the consistency of experience for pupils.

> School climate is the heart and soul of schools. It is about the essence of a school that leads a child, an administrator, a staff member to look forward to being there each day. School climate is about that quality of a school that helps each individual feel personal worth, dignity and importance, while simultaneously helping to create a sense of belonging to something beyond ourselves.
>
> (Freiberg and Stein 1999)

Hall and George (1999) correlated classroom climate to a school's climate, and both to the impact of the principal.

I have talked with demoralised TAs and watched incompetent ones. Both problems could have been solved by appropriate action from someone in a more senior position – a class teacher, line manager or headteacher. I have rarely come across definitely poor practice in TAs and it has only been in schools with other problems, often an absent or weak head, low morale among the teaching staff and a marked negative ethos. Although these were not necessarily failing or potentially failing schools, the problems were more than poor supervision or lack of management, although these were usually part of the problem. The negative ethos was often most obvious in the staffroom, where pupils' problems were referred to negatively, blame was always on someone or something else, the discussion revolved round anything but the future development of the school or its community. People couldn't wait to leave, if only for an evening by the television. Absence rates among all categories of staff were high.

The headteacher promotes the ethos and climate, has an overview of consistency, and is responsible for setting up systems. The climate and conditions depend upon the ethos and history of the school, and all school staff following the aims and policies of the school. You can feel the atmosphere of a school on entering, it does not depend on architecture or age of the building.

THINKING POINTS

What does a visitor see in your school?

Care of the environment:
Was it easy to find the car park and reception?
Is the entry foyer welcoming?
Are the plants watered?
Are notices up-to-date?
Is there somewhere for a visitor to sit when waiting?
Would you like to sit there if it was the doctors' or a hotel reception area?
Is available documentation reader friendly?
Is there a display showing valuing of pupils' work?
Are rooms labelled, and fire exits clear?

The way people behave:
What is the attitude of the receptionist to telephone calls?
Do receptionists make eye contact with visitors even if they are busy on the telephone?
Do receptionists make sure whether visitors need a drink or the lavatory?
How do receptionists hand over to a member of staff?
Is the visitors' book/fire register properly maintained?
Who shows visitors round the school?
How do adults speak to each other in the corridor
How do pupils talk to visitors?
Who smiles?
What are the noise levels?

(Watkinson 2003a: 57)

One of my research schools in the 1990s used to refer to the 'St So-and-so's way' or of 'one big family' when describing the behaviour of the adults. Ofsted mentions that TAs 'particularly appreciated being recognised as part of the teaching team' (Ofsted 2003b: 9). The paragraph goes on to refer to a small number of schools that still exclude TAs from the staffroom, do not consult with them or use them to their full capacity – it makes TAs 'feel undervalued and resentful'.

An interesting exercise to do with staff is to use an A4 sheet with three columns and headings as in Figure 5.1.

The Devon HLTAs did this in groups using an A2 sheet, trying to come to agreements about what was most desirable. In schools you could similarly get

Values and beliefs	Behaviour seen	School context and support

Figure 5.1 The worksheet for a values exercise

groups to share ideas, particularly using groups of mixed status and job title. Or they could be done individually and anonymously and a composite developed for later discussion.

MacBeath and colleagues (1996) gave the five key features of school climate as:

◆ The school is a happy place to be
◆ There are places for pupils to go and constructive things to do outside class time
◆ Pupils and staff behave in a relaxed and orderly way
◆ Pupils, staff and parents feel that their contribution to the school is valued
◆ The school is welcoming to visitors and newcomers.

(p. 34)

Leaders have to work at developing a culture.

Teaching and learning cultures have to be built and developed through induction, professional development, joint planning, coaching and mentoring, sharing good practice and researching the evidence. The bedrock of this culture are the norms, values and beliefs that bond a community of like minded people into the common commitment of continually improving practice and raising standards of achievement for pupils.

(Brighouse and Woods 1999: 105)

The physical learning environment is not just in the classrooms. Ben-Peretz and colleagues have described how staffrooms (what they refer to as teachers' lounges) in schools are influential in improving the learning environment in schools. 'It is highly probable that lounges, as sites for teachers' interactions, provide the necessary conditions for the development of strong teacher networks and the generation of communal knowledge about teaching. This knowledge might lead to more effective teaching modes' (Ben-Peretz and Kupermitz 1999: 150).

THINKING POINTS

It is worth checking the following:
How do your TAs come to school?
Where do they park their car, bicycle or motorbike?
Is the local public transport school day friendly?
Where do they hang their coat and keep their personal belongings during the day?
Is there room in the staff toilet area for them?
Where do they have their refreshment breaks?
Are they welcome in the staffroom before and after school?
Do they have a sufficient break for lunch?
What do they do for lunch?
What names are your staff known by?
Are they treated with respect by pupils, as well as treating pupils with respect?
What are you doing about any ill feeling about any of the above from teaching staff?

(Watkinson 2003a: 61)

TAs and other stakeholders

In the past, contacting parent or carers and discussing school issues was seen as strictly the domain of the qualified teacher, unless there were exceptional circumstances, such as a profound physical disability where regular contact between the home care and the school care made a lot of sense, or when there is a technical problem with a support aid such as glasses or IT equipment. It is now common for TAs to be involved in IEP reviews and, occasionally even to attend consultation evenings to support a class teacher, usually a primary situation. In some schools, it is now the role of the TA to make the home–school contact in cases of troublesome pupils, where a regular report on behaviour, good or bad is found to be helpful. I have heard of TAs maintaining contact during long school holidays to support autistic spectrum children, making phone calls home when there are unexplained absences and being part of the induction procedure for new children.

I have not ever come across a problem occurring where the TA is a parent at their own child's school. Both sides seem to cope very well, maybe this says something about the parenting skills of many TAs? I have come across a problem where an appointed TA is resident in the locality and has not observed a strict confidentiality code which is necessary in any school. The TA concerned had not been well known to the school when appointed. It is part of your responsibility to ensure that parents and carers are aware of the roles and boundaries of TA responsibilities in your particular school.

Governors are also part of the whole-school team, and responsible, through their delegation to the headteacher, for the employment of all staff and the standards achieved. It would be good to think that owing to the publicity surrounding the increase in numbers of TAs, the existence of TAs in most schools and the WR initiative, governors were well informed about their roles and the potential for increasing standards that they bring, but it is not so. Governors are rarely involved in TA appointments. In all the schools I have visited recently only one had shown any attempt to involve governors beyond the usual references at formal meetings – to agree support staff performance management policy or agree a budget allocation. TAs are rarely the focus of governors' visits. Governors should see TAs at work when they make their classroom visits, and TAs' successes can be mentioned in Governors' minutes and Annual Reports, as well as any policies relating to them. One HLTA in Devon, Susette Barrett, was so concerned about the governors' ignorance of what went on in schools, that she made communication about who the TA staff were, one of the foci of her investigation. She produced the flier shown in Figure 5.2. It was well received and she hopes that it will encourage governors to visit and understand more about their roles. It can be found in full colour as a PDF file on the Devon support staff website.

The good practice guidance (DfES 2000) has a section about creating partnerships with other people involved in education with paragraphs covering:

1 working with outside agencies;
2 regular meetings with SENCOs;
3 a channel of communication with parents;
4 a channel of communication with ethnic minority communities;
5 inviting TAs to participate in school functions.

The need for systems and structures

While ethos, culture, and vision are the essential soul of an organic institution such as a school, they are not enough. Any organisation needs systems and structures to operate. Systems thinking is Senge's Fifth Discipline. 'It enables people to begin to appreciate rather than be confused by the interrelated nature of the world . . . it integrates all the five disciplines and brings about the empowering potential of the learning organisation' (Flood 1999: 67). It is about thinking holistically, putting together the vision, the models, having understanding between people working in teams, releasing them from particular ideologies. Systems in action are very like biological feedback systems. For instance, you can analyse the working of any one of the body's hormones, but until you see how it controls and is controlled by other systems and hormones in the body you cannot see how it works or hope to help when it goes wrong. It is about 'developing an awareness of complexity, interdependencies, change and leverage' (Senge *et al.* 2000: 17).

Inclusion of staff as well as pupils is one of the keys to developing a staff culture that supports TA work. Thankfully the days of separate staff rooms for support staff are largely over. Where the TAs are responsible for the break time cover, meaningful social intercourse is hard. Social mixing at end of term events is also still hard for some schools, and has to be worked at. Different venues, styles of events and timings need to be explored if senior staff really mean what they intend. Ensuring that all the staff are involved in consulting about such simple things and persisting in trying to find a meaningful solution can make one of the biggest differences to the 'them and us' culture possible.

Another simple thing that has changed, albeit slowly, is what TAs are called by the pupils. Where TAs came traditionally from the parent volunteer body and had often previously been involved in the playgroups, they were being called by their first names. Being seen as one of the professionals means being called by their title Mr, Mrs, Ms or Miss and the family name. Calling all women 'Miss' is a pet hate – pupils have names and so do adults; it is a mark of respect to use them, and respect for all is one of the tenets most schools hold high.

School example

The picture in both 1998 study schools of mine was one of constant evolution. There was gradual change, as informalities became accepted ways of working, then incorporated into the systems and then the structures of the schools. The structures of the two schools were apparently different in their way of using TAs, the one for individual children and the other for teachers to support the curriculum, yet the way in which the schools operated showed a great similarity. The senior management constantly referred to developing or evolving systems in both study schools, which may later become structures. Both were:

◆ developing regular meetings for their TAs;
◆ developing planning and feedback systems;
◆ considering policies, job descriptions and appraisal strategies;
◆ committing sizeable portions of the general school budget to TA salaries;
◆ keeping governors informed;
◆ incorporating the TAs in school-based INSET;
◆ committing time to the professional development of TAs;
◆ giving line management to the deputy head;
◆ seeing the appointment of new TAs as important a procedure as appointing teachers;
◆ using advertisements and interview processes;
◆ setting criteria for appointment.

(Watkinson 2003a: 73, 74)

Structures

Managers of TAs at any level – head, classroom or senior TA – need to be part of a whole-school way of doing things. There is a need for some consistency across classes in the use of TAs. Consistency, communication, and a positive climate with the need for whole-school policies and plans, were three of the key factors identified as contributing to what makes effective schools (Mortimore *et al.* 1988; Sammons and Mortimore 1995). Consistency of practice enables pupils to feel secure and provides a learning environment that facilitates curriculum progression. TAs operating the same policies regarding health, safety and security matters, behaviour management strategies and carrying out teachers' instructions in the way that the school has determined, ensure the minimum of confusion.

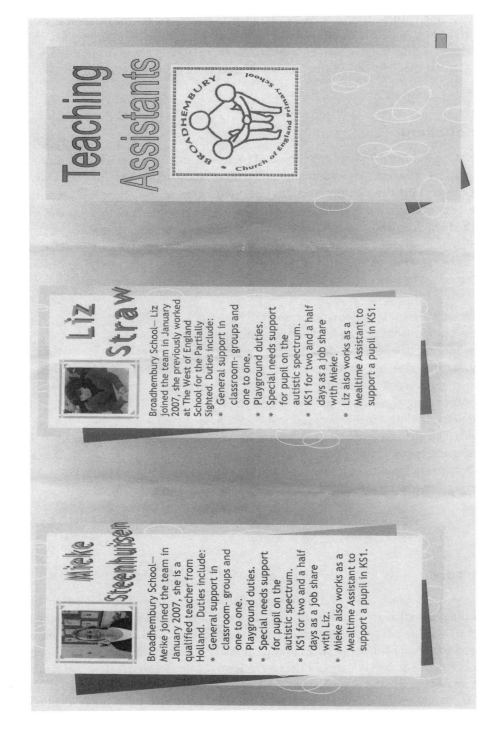

Figure 5.2 The governor information flier

Susette Barrett

Broadhembury School—6 yrs. NVQ3, HLTA undertaking Foundation Degree Level 1. Duties include:

* General support in class.
* Teaching of maths, ICT, PE, art, PSHE.
* Teaching KS2 intervention groups - maths and literacy.
* Subject coordinator for ICT, PE and art.
* PPA cover.
* Responsible for General Curriculum budget.
* Coordinator for TAs.
* Seeks grant funding.
* Playground duties & First Aid.
* In absence of administrator, reception duties.
* KS1 until am break, then KS2.
* Susette also runs the

Jacqui Barrett

Broadhembury School—4 years. NVQ3. Duties include:

* General support in classroom - groups, one to one, whole class.
* Playground duties & First Aid.
* In absence of administrator, reception duties.
* Teaching KS1 intervention group for literacy.
* Special needs support for pupil on the autistic spectrum.
* SENCo admin support.
* Jacqui works fulltime and is deployed in KS2 until morning break, then KS1 for the rest of the day.

Rose Watts

Broadhembury School—2 years. Foundation Degree Level 1. Duties include:

* General support in classroom - groups, one to one, whole class.
* Playground duties & First Aid.
* Special needs support for pupil in KS2.
* Rose works in KS2 on Mondays and Tuesdays.
* Rose also helps run the high fives netball club.

Figure 5.2 Continued

The existence of internal policies as distinct from assumptions of accepted practice, does mean that newcomers to a school world will understand what has to be done when, how and why. Instructions, boundaries of responsibility, levels of action do need to be spelt out explicitly. TAs as well as teachers need to know of organisational or policy changes that are proposed. This will mean attention to meetings and paperwork, sometimes inviting TAs to participate in or receive material originally designed only for teachers and sometimes designing occasions or documents specifically for TAs.

Meetings

Developing regular meetings for and with the TAs has been the turning point for many schools. These can be formal or informal regarding the way they run, who runs them, or when, but fixing a time and place for them and making attendance part of the contractual terms of the job and paying for the time taken shows the importance. It is when 'two or three are gathered together' that issues start to arise. Some leaders or managers see the emergence of issues as the problem, they would rather keep them under wraps. If these issues are small, soluble with discussion, airing them is all that is needed. Apparently insoluble problems once aired at least become shared and, to use another well worn phrase, shared problems are halved. Meetings rapidly move on from being a sharing of issues to sharing practice, and these rapidly move on to be definable professional development opportunities.

Different schools have different kinds of meetings. It will depend on the size and phase of the schools and the deployment of the TAs. If the TAs are organised by the SENCO, then the meetings will be for SEN purposes and led by that person or department. Curriculum TAs will need subject meetings. Senior managers need meetings about procedures and policies. Some schools find it hard to have meeting times after school because of TAs' child care considerations. Other schools make it a condition of service that such meetings take place after school or in the lunch hour or on a specific morning during assembly just so that support staff are included.

Meetings are needed for TAs as a group but also for TAs with teachers. While time for TAs to attend meetings is now much more widespread, time for senior staff to carry out their TA management role and meet with the TAs is less well recognised and needs serious consideration from headteachers when looking at line management and senior management roles.

Communication

This is a main area of unease voiced by TAs when they are asked about problems. Meetings would help, but communication is much more than arranging meetings, which might only take place once every half term. Information on changes in school procedures such as timetables or current behaviour management issues, dates, absences, new appointments, good news and bad is not just needed by the teachers, and this information must be made readily available to TAs.

THINKING POINTS

Check the following:

The staff notice board – do all see it?

The staff day book/diary system – does it reach those it needs to?

The parents' newsletters – do all staff get a copy?

The Annual report to parents – do all staff get a copy?

Are all staff invited to social events?

Can support staff access the policy documentation easily?

Are support staff adequately represented on the governing body?

Do all staff see the governing body minutes?

Are the deliberations of the senior staff meetings minuted? Are the minutes available for perusal by staff?

Are departmental communications as effective as the whole-school ones?

Who knows about: changes in staff responsibilities, changes in staff circumstance which affect their role, changes in the community?

Do all staff reply to consultations and if not why not? (Watkinson 2003a: 84)

Does the support staff handbook need updating?

Are the newest TAs aware of the communication pathways?

What access to any intranet do TAs have?

What mechanisms are there for TAs to feed into communication pathways?

How do you know your communication pathways are working?

Do parents and governors know all they should about TAs and their work?

Developing policies

Schools are required to have formulated certain policies for various aspects of school life determined by law. Some of these policies, SEN for instance, will determine the use and deployment of TAs. It could say pupils will only be withdrawn from classroom activities in exceptional circumstances, then the TAs will have to work with pupils in the classroom, not in a separate small room or the library. If a teaching policy requires all lessons to have a formal whole-class input at the beginning and end, then the TAs should not be working with small groups at that time. Equal opportunities should mean if performance management is in place for teachers it should be there for all staff. Parental liaison strategies may determine the use of TAs as family liaison officers or require their attendance at IEP reviews.

Some schools, although relatively few, even have a special TA or LSA policy. You could use the following list to help get you started.

THINKING POINTS

The policy could contain:

◆ The rationale for employing TAs in the first place
◆ Arrangements for appointment, job descriptions, induction, professional development review or appraisal
◆ Relationship to existing school policies such as teaching and learning, SEN, behaviour management, pay, grievance and discipline, health and safety
◆ Communication systems relevant to the TAs, including consultation, sources of information, line management and help
◆ Any specific things determined by the school such as expectations of attendance at meetings or other out of class provision, personal standards of behaviour
◆ Specific boundaries of responsibility particularly between qualified teachers and TAs
◆ Participation of the TAs in the school processes of long term, medium and short term planning, IEP formulation and delivery, and assessment procedures
◆ Systems for monitoring and evaluation of provision

(Watkinson 2003a: 87)

Circulate a draft copy of the policy to all who might need to see it for their comment: the TAs themselves, the teachers who use TAs, governors, heads of department and other senior managers, especially the SENCO. Meetings can be held, questionnaires used – whatever the current school methods are. A final version may bear little resemblance to the first draft, but that was the point of the consultation. One of the Devon HLTAs, Sarah Webber, has made this part of her investigation. She used a questionnaire to staff to establish what areas they needed to cover. By doing so she was asked to contribute to the teaching and learning policy and was able to say 'I felt TAs were much more at the core of teaching and learning than the policy suggested (resulting in some alterations).'

Line management and supervision

There are as many models of deployment and line management for TAs in schools as there are types of schools and each has something to recommend it. Line managers can be:

◆ SENCO;
◆ curriculum coordinator or head of department;
◆ year group/Key stage leader;
◆ senior TA or HLTA;
◆ another member of the support staff such as the bursar or school secretary.

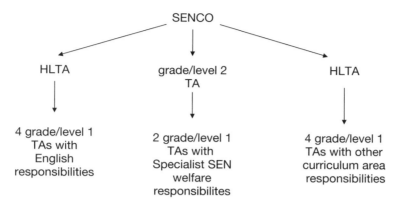

Figure 5.3 A TA team structure

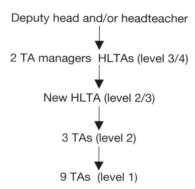

Figure 5.4 Another TA team structure

Whatever is agreed, the new regulations must be taken into account regarding the supervision of the work of TAs.

A person may carry out work specified in regulation 6

[(a) planning and preparing lesson and courses for pupils;
(b) delivering lessons to pupils;
(c) assessing the development, progress and attainment of pupils; and
(d) reporting on the development, progress and attainment of pupils]

Only if the following conditions are satisfied –

(a) he carries out work specified in regulation 6 in order to assist or support the work of a qualified teacher or a nominated teacher in the school;
(b) he is subject to the direction and supervision of such a qualified teacher or a nominated teacher in accordance with the arrangements made by the headteacher of the school; and
(c) The headteacher is satisfied that he has the skills, expertise and experience required to carry out work specified in regulation 6.

(DfES 2003)

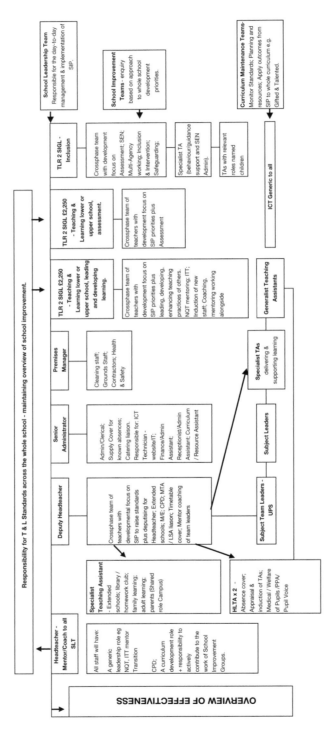

Figure 5.5 A whole-school structure including TAs

This kind of supervision, regulated by law, is generally quite distinct from any arrangement you decide to make for the line management of the TA. The purpose of the supervision is to ensure high standards of teaching and learning.

Recent correspondence from teachers in the TES (2007b) indicated clearly that many of them are unaware of these regulations. All the letters quoted assumed that any learning that takes place while they are not actually taking the class is not their responsibility and they felt affronted to even have to consider it. It is clearly an issue that must be dealt with swiftly in some schools.

Deployment

One of the problems that used to be voiced by TAs is that of following the 'hour here and an hour there' deployment method. With the increase in numbers of TAs and hours of support available this is now rarer; TAs are either spending a longer

Figure 5.6 The TA team of a large secondary school

time with a particular teacher, a particular pupil or in concentrating on a particular subject. This depth of relationship has brought much greater job satisfaction, as it also brings the possibility of greater depth of understanding of the concerns and issues involved in the tasks. The TAs have an opportunity for increased professional development on the job.

Even knowing who is who among a large team is hard and in a very large school teachers are unlikely to be introduced individually to each member of the team if they are being deployed across two or more sites or in varying roles depending on cover for absences. One school displays photographs of all the team just by the entrance to the joint staffroom.

However, the idea of equitable distribution still determines some deployment. Giving every teacher in the primary school three hours support each morning does not necessarily make the best use of the talent or reflect the greatest need. Some teachers get quite upset if their favourite TA is reallocated, and if they are strong characters often get their way for the sake of a quiet life in the staffroom. It takes a strong leader to override some vocal, long-established teachers. This has happened when a TA has been promoted to HLTA status, the school needs the TA to do a different kind of job from classroom support, but the strong teacher might only be able to see their own needs. Careful introduction of the role of HLTA as part of a whole-school reorganisation and review of needs should enable you to show why changes in job deployment as well as title are taking place.

In secondary schools, where the model of individual pupil support is much stronger, it means TAs going to anything up to eight different lessons in a day. Teachers need to be carefully briefed in order that the TA is best used in such circumstances.

THINKING POINTS

So you must decide who has responsibility for:

Supervision as defined in the new regulations
Timetables
Individual pupils' needs
Curriculum outcomes – raising test results
Induction
Appraisal
Ensuring welfare and communication systems are working
Mentoring for course development
Professional development taking place in-house

These can all be the responsibility of one person, or shared, but the TA must not fall into gaps, where one person thinks another person is doing part of the job. JDs of the person responsible, suitable remuneration for the size of task and, especially, time to do what is required, must all be built in to any deployment situation.

Pay and conditions of service – budget implications

Until now, in the view of the DfES, the onus of pay and conditions of service for support staff is quite clearly on the employer. They believed that the national standards, suggested levels of JDs and single status agreements with unions and LAs at a local level would sort the problem. But the iniquities have not gone away. Job evaluation at local level has been fraught and, at the time of writing, has still not been settled in some authorities. It seems that a few Human Resources departments are out of touch with what actually goes on in schools with regards to TAs, and some paperwork problems exacerbated decisions. School decisions on seniority and responsibility have not always fitted the models proposed by the centre.

While pay scales often seem to be generous, very few TAs are paid for non term time working and relatively few are paid for a 37-hour week. So, few people could ever support a family on their take-home pay. It would be interesting if governors and school leaders actually looked at the job done compared to that of a teacher in terms of hours as well as responsibility. Heads say 'but if I paid "properly" I could not afford so many staff'. The TAs themselves will nearly always opt for more TAs to be employed – their colleagues – rather than full remuneration be considered. They are 'their own worst enemies'.

WR did not address this issue. The National Joint Council for Local Government Services has been consulted all along on guidance for employment but this was not about salaries. Qualifications that TAs have should determine the kind of responsibilities for which they are employed not determine their salary scale. Qualified teachers can be employed as TAs, but will not be paid as such, unless their JD determines their responsibilities. Membership of unions has increased but not sufficiently to be a real pressure group. TAs on low salaries are reluctant to pay out money for union fees. The pay may be 'less than a shelf stacker in a supermarket' but there is greater job satisfaction. However, job satisfaction should not mean managers impose on the TAs' goodwill.

Basic rate of pay is not the only thing you need to set, you must also consider the associated conditions of service, such as those shown in the following Thinking Points:

THINKING POINTS

- ◆ all the issues of culture and ethos;
- ◆ the domestic arrangements;
- ◆ ensuring grievance and discipline policies are for all staff;
- ◆ knowing who the union representatives and the health and safety representatives are;
- ◆ where to enquire about employment problems;
- ◆ contracts which reflect their jobs;
- ◆ hours and weeks of work;
- ◆ appropriate names – never non-anything;
- ◆ what kind of job security is available;

♦   whether mentor support will be available for course attendance;
♦   all the policies concerning pay, whether:
    –   paid planning time and meeting time is included;
    –   there is entitlement to superannuation or holiday retainer pay;
    –   contracts and pay rates cover the INSET days or not;
    –   performance pay is for all staff or just teachers;
    –   any cost of courses will be met.

Job or salary reviews

The WR initiative was meant to lead to a full-scale review of staffing for the needs of the school. It would be a good idea if such a review occurred when any major review of the SDP/SIP was being contemplated. It is recognised that just as these WR reviews could lead to possible redundancy and re-appointment procedures so would any subsequent review. Decreasing budgets with falling rolls is very common currently as the birth rate across the country has fallen in recent years. This is causing just such a review of staffing structures.

The key findings of Ofsted by 2005 were that changes had been made; there was an increased awareness of the potential link between remodelling and quality, although few schools were formally evaluating the changes they had made; most schools were at least adequately funded, but 'only in a minority is funding being used to creatively restructure the workforce'; teachers have benefited and ICT was being successfully used to support teachers. Less progress had been made in freeing up headship time, and few governing bodies had helped manage the process (Ofsted 2005). Informal reports from various LA advisers indicate that little further progress has been made by early 2007, and any further developments will be around current initiatives. WR is 'old hat', the funding has finished, many advisers have been absorbed elsewhere.

One of the most difficult issues surrounding the employment of any sort of staff is cost. The response to queries about fair pay for TAs is always 'We cannot afford it'. It is tempting to say as an outsider, 'Well if you saved a bit here and there you could afford something more for the TAs.' Trying to identify how some schools afford more staff than others or employ cover teachers not TAs is almost impossible as heads are very cagey about their budgets and salary allocations. One misunderstanding that exists is that TAs or managers will talk about 'being part time' or 'full time'. By full time they nearly always mean full pupil contact time, i.e. 25 or so hours a week. Where the TAs are working a full 37-hour week, it appears to be only during term time. Few TAs actually work really full time and thus earn the recommended annual salary for their grade, probably only in residential schools. It is not as though TAs, or HLTAs, never do any work outside their contractual hours. They give enormously of their own time. Teachers often work beyond their 32.5 hours a week in term time and this is recognised in a contract that is given in hours per year. The differences in the contractual conditions and pay scales between most TAs and teachers does need consideration when making decisions about whether to employ more people or pay more equitable rates to those currently in post. Particular local problems of falling rolls, parental expectations of year group organisations and small class sizes, and the wishes of the TAs themselves, all serve to complicate the problem. Most TAs, when asked, would rather have more people in the team than higher pay, particularly if it means losing their colleagues.

TAs, in general, are still one of the most exploited groups in the school staff, and of them HLTAs possibly the most exploited of all. They are frequently paid at a higher rate (not that of a supply teacher but of an HLTA rate for their LA) only for the time they are in front of a class, teaching and extending learning. Sometimes they might, themselves, be supported by a TA, but often not. They are not cover supervisors, for they do more than cover. But on reverting to supporting a teacher in class, they are paid at a lower rate. What governing body or headteacher would pay their deputy or assistant head at differential rates according to whether they were taking a class or doing a managerial task? Why should the support staff pay scales be interpreted in this different way? Because it is possible – they are hourly paid, and cheaper. Being hourly paid, they are almost always the first in the firing line when cuts have to be made.

THINKING POINTS

PLEASE: Look at your pay scales and staff structure as a whole.
Does the remuneration really reflect the job descriptions?
Do the paid hours reflect the workload and their responsibility?
Do you know why it is as it is? – history? budget-led necessity?

School example

One school told me that the head and governors had agreed a change in structure and relative remuneration. Their external finance officer had come in and told them it was unsustainable and he had determined what should be the staffing structure in that school. The head, and subsequently the governors felt they had no option but to agree. Guess how the TAs felt.

The school support

The good practice guidance (DfES 2000) makes it clear that TAs can only reach their potential to support teaching and learning where they themselves are supported:

> These four strands of support [pupils, teachers, curriculum and school] are only one part of the story . . . At the same time the school has a responsibility to support the TA in fulfilling the expectations of the role. . . . This obligation

calls for consideration both of the way TAs are managed and of their professional development needs: management support should enable them to perform the job to the best of their abilities, and they should be encouraged to develop their skills and their potential. Clearly this view of two-way support requires the close co-operation of class teachers with whom TAs work as well as of headteachers and other managers.

(DfES 2000: 8, 9)

Lacey (1999) suggested that while the duties of LSAs in managing inclusion in different schools were similar, the greatest differences 'between the schools lay in the area of planning and preparation' (p. 20). She considered the vital ingredients at school level were:

◆ a positive planned, whole-school approach to inclusion
◆ active management support for those who carry out the inclusion
◆ clear and shared aims for included pupils
◆ enthusiastic and knowledgeable teachers
◆ well trained and valued LSAs
◆ sound communication between different sites and units

(Lacey 1999: 33)

Devon HLTAs added some more needs to this list:

◆ paid planning and preparation time;
◆ space of some kind to do the job – whether with pupils or resources;
◆ realistic expectations of workload.

The locality context

The location and geography of the school building, its community and history all affect what TA support is necessary for pupils and what support the TAs themselves might need. The use of a spare classroom for a community pre-school group can change dynamics within the school. The government promise to rebuild many aging secondary schools will affect staffroom accommodation; it could change attitudes towards inclusion when wheelchair access or withdrawal areas become more practical and possible.

Where schools have undertaken national initiatives that are optional, such as the Healthy Schools award, TAs have been vital in developing some of the strategies. An example is The Social and Emotional Attitudes to Learning (SEAL) programme which is about the whole school undertaking strategies to build self-esteem and foster good attitudes and relationships.

LA support varies enormously from authority to authority. A larger authority may have no designated TA adviser, someone might be picking up the responsibility on top of some other job; another small authority, such as Gateshead, has designated advisers able to develop CPD arrangements and give advice as well as manage devolved funds. Hertfordshire has appointed TA consultants to work part time and Devon has a Support Staff Adviser. Most authorities arrange celebrations for their candidates who are successful in certain qualifications and have some kind of

CPD programme. Some LA advisers incorporate TAs into the teacher CPD programmes, especially true of SENCO work.

Where higher education establishments are active in the TA field, running foundation degree courses or similar, they may be the focal point for conferences and courses. There is no common pattern.

The national context

All levels of people in schools talk about initiative overload. One of the most important roles of school leaders and managers is to be able to sort out priorities for their institutions. The deluge started with the NC and local management, the fears and pressure started with Ofsted and league tables, the strategies ratcheted up the outside influences. Much of the description of the impact of national strategies on TA employment has already been aired – the changes were the reason for the book. Parents have become more critical and demanding, so that schools have lost confidence in what works best for them. The weight of initiatives, while aimed at improving matters, appear to be just something more to respond to.

The primary strategy of *Excellence and enjoyment* (DfES 2004b) was an attempt to bring back some of the innovation and exploration enjoyed in the 1960s and 1970s before the national structures. For some, the move to liberate them from the straitjackets of the NC and the LNS is proving hard; they are having to re-engage in strategic thinking about their curriculum planning. If the primary curriculum is to be refocused around topics and themes, it will affect the use and deployment of TAs. Some are making different uses of their TAs as a response, re-engaging them with helping in practical work.

The various current changes being experienced by schools are summed up well in the PwC leadership report. Schools are becoming 'increasingly responsible for the delivery of solutions to issues such as social cohesion, citizenship and childhood obesity' (PricewaterhouseCoopers 2007: 2). They refer to the *New relationship with schools* where a lighter touch inspection means more self-evaluation; the *Learning environment* changes with reorganisation of weaker schools and rebuilding programmes; The ECM agenda with its links to agencies and extended schools; *Personalised learning*, where the system should fit the pupil not the other way around; and *Partnership working for schools and colleges* to work on the new 14–19 agenda.

The report *2020 vision* was the result of a group of senior educationalists attempting to establish what personalised teaching and learning might look like in 2020 (DfES 2006a). Personalised learning is not going to be possible without one-to-one contact between every pupil and an adult in the school at some point. It recognised the need to raise expectations of achievement for all children including the disadvantaged. Among other suggestions for tackling the challenge it includes 'Establishing curriculum teams of staff and pupils to develop plans for improving teaching and learning' and 'Greater use of adults other than teachers to extend the range of skills and support for pupils' (p. 12). They advocate greater use of what they call 'learning guides' in secondary schools to meet with pupils regularly, agree targets, help them learn how to learn, be advocates for them in school and meet with parents or carers to review progress.

For some schools, the initiatives are yet more things to add to the list of those with which they are already struggling. Does that class structure need another rethink to accommodate personalised learning agenda? Should or can the TAs fill the gaps, and enable the teachers to continue in their year-based teaching? Can TAs be the link with agencies? How can parents be convinced of the rightness of whatever decisions the leaders and managers take? What do governors understand of the demands on teachers and the head?

Other outside influences, not just government introduced initiatives have also affected the increase in employment of TAs. That is because of the changing nature of the society in which we all live. Teachers and TAs complain of the increase in difficult, aggressive and disruptive children, whose inclusion is creating an atmosphere less conducive to learning than previously. Whether there is a real increase in numbers of difficult children due to our current cultural decline, or due to increased inclusion in mainstream of children previously in special schools for emotionally and behaviourally disturbed (EBD) pupils, or an increase in expectations by teachers of what can be achieved in an hour, or a decrease on the suitability of the narrowed curriculum to interest them, is unclear, but more TAs are now employed to cope with managing behaviour. It has become a specialism for some, like dealing with speech and language difficulties or visual impairment.

The global context?

Many more schools are making links with schools in other countries and, particularly, developing countries. Exchange visits are more common even for TAs; Devon HLTAs went to Vienna in February 2007. The internet has opened up global communication in an unprecedented and relatively cheap way. TAs travel with groups or have language or ICT skills that support such ventures. Some schools, now Trust schools, are being funded by industrial sponsors or entrepreneurs with global, not just local, connections. It will be interesting to see whether TAs become involved even at this level.

Global migration has created major problems for some schools where a high influx of non English speakers suddenly arrive in their town. Employing TAs who are part of the immigrant population can help at many levels.

Another area where TAs are useful is in the concerted move to consider sustainable or eco-friendly schools because of the raised profile of global warming. Schools are finding it useful for the curriculum, their citizenship agenda or for the return to more practical work to use TAs to take on these additional areas. This concern, along with the healthy schools movement has encouraged schools to look again at their grounds. More schools are growing their own vegetables and resurrecting their wildlife gardens and ponds which have become derelict over the last 10 to 15 years.

Chapter 6

Looking at the needs of the school and of the TAs

The role of the SDP

The chapters so far have been rather theoretical and do not involve any action on your part beyond armchair thinking. Hopefully, that reading and reflection time has persuaded you that, if you are serious, you will need to investigate further. The SDP or SIP is pivotal to managing a school's direction just as a business plan is for any organisation. The effectiveness depends on how it is drawn up and how it is carried out. Completing the Self-evaluation Form (SEF) is probably a first stage as it is based on the Ofsted framework. It also uses the ECM framework. These will probably determine the plan's structure. It should be reviewed annually but monitored continuously in different ways. In order to make appropriate changes in the SDP/SIP regarding TAs, a proper review of the TA provision needs to take place.

If you used the WR materials you might have done this recently, or other school changes might have promoted a special review in this area. It is common practice to undertake a major review, looking at the school's fundamental aims, triennially, or earlier if significant changes have taken place such as a change of head, school amalgamation or change of catchment area, or an Ofsted inspection. In his book evaluating the use of the Strathclyde school self-evaluation framework, Macbeath (1999) describes the stages you go through as follows:

1   create the climate
2   agree a process
3   agree the criteria
4   develop the toolkit
5   focus on teaching and learning.

The National Remodelling Team recommended considering the following when wanting to lead or manage change:

◆   culture
◆   staffing numbers and levels
◆   contractual requirements

- management structures, and
- skills distribution.

In schools where the ethos and culture are good, where there is consultation and communication at all levels of the school community, TAs are already involved at all levels of the plan. They contribute to it, appear in it and help evaluate it. 'School development processes should seek to nurture the conditions that facilitate the tasks of teachers and LSAs working together effectively in classrooms' (Farrell *et al.* 1999: 55). The TA part of the SDP may be a separate part of the plan or, increasingly, their work may appear at different parts. The list below gives the kind of areas that might show up the need for a TA review with a few examples. You might review:

- the SEN needs of the school
    - annual review of wave 1, 2 and 3 demands on an annual basis
    - the arrival of a physically impaired pupil or one with Down's syndrome
    - the diagnosis of autistic spectrum disorder in a child

- the EAL needs
    - the arrival of a new wave of immigrant labour
    - the building of a new university or hospital

- behaviour management
    - need for trained MDAs
    - whole-school training to increase consistency
    - the arrival of a child excluded from other schools whose behaviour raises concerns (restraint issues)

- teacher needs
    - illness/absence of a teacher
    - a weaker teacher
    - challenging children

- the curriculum
    - subject expertise
    - increase in practical work
    - topic-based work
    - strategies implementation

- external changes
    - redrawing of catchment areas or new estates
    - Early Years intake
    - initiatives – internal or external: circle time, counselling arrangements, ECM, extended schools

- WR
    - considering workload
    - taking all the above into account and taking a step back to look at human resource provision
    - independent decision to audit the TA team.

Setting the scene – creating the climate or 'mobilise' and 'discover' (WR)

Schools have developed sensitive ways of investigating their TAs' roles and needs, and also used management tools such as interviews and questionnaires. The WR initiatives reinforced the idea of having a team of people within the school to look at the issues raised rather than relying on one person to do all the donkey work – and possibly take all the flak. Their website is full of ideas, so you might have tried many of these things. Case studies abound on their website and this chapter adds a few examples. All situations are different, so you need to cherry pick the ways forward for yourself from these ideas, audit materials, proforma and real case studies of explorations of TAs: their qualities, qualifications and experience. What you are trying to do is get the best match between the vision and the human resources available.

In order to get those truthful answers, the whole idea of asking them needs to be explored with all the staff whose job is being looked at. The rationale for the exploration needs to be explained. Openness is crucial. If a member of staff sees the exercise as merely an excuse for job shedding they are likely to be cagey. One only has to read accounts of management/union conflict where this happens. It may be that with falling rolls there *will* have to be redundancy but this needs to be up front at the beginning. It can be done, if the budget situation is explained carefully, sensitively, at an early stage and to all concerned, voluntary redundancy might be seen by some as an opportunity not a threat. However, the rationale for remodelling was not to shed jobs but to reorganise more efficiently and effectively. Get people together and talk this through first before starting anything.

No one can take for granted that employing TAs is a good thing, effective, value for money and that there is consistent good practice throughout the school. As there must be very few schools, if any, who are not already employing TAs, the place to start is with what is already happening in your school.

THINKING POINTS

You should know:
◆ how many TAs there are, how long they work for, and where
◆ what they were employed for in the first place
◆ what they are called and why
◆ what they are being used for currently
◆ what hours and weeks they work
◆ what they are paid and why
◆ what kind of contracts they have

But also should find out:
◆ what they are being valued for
◆ what qualifications, experience and skills they have
◆ whether they are the best people for the job to be done
◆ how things could be improved

Although those questions seem obvious, few managers have this information readily available, even in relatively small schools. This basic information in itself is often revealing about the mixed patterns that exist in the school, and immediately prompts questions about effective deployment.

Two schools that I have known over many years both for their general educational quality but also their excellent TA practice, have both recently had outstanding Ofsteds. They coincidentally decided on the same thing – a simple questionnaire to their TA team. They were surprised by the responses, yet they both felt they had known their team and individuals' potential over a long period of time. They got truthful responses because the TAs trusted the heads to deal with any issues appropriately and sensitively.

School example

Market Fields is a special school with children from 5 to 16, staff and TAs. The head's questions, the TAs' responses and his action are summarised in Box 6.1.

Balshaw makes clear that no progress will be made unless the climate within the school is right. She gives what she calls her 'author's health warning'. Questioning practice challenges the status quo and this can be 'an uncomfortable and difficult process and this should be acknowledged at the outset. However, if there is a commitment to collaborative learning, then mutual support on offer to all members of the team should see them through the bad patches' (Balshaw 1999: 22). The schools mentioned above can only go from outstanding to even better, because the relationships in the school are so good. They only needed simple questions because their staff were comfortable to give truthful answers. Trust is so important but only built up over years.

When Ann Melhuish did her HLTA investigation at Whipton Barton in Devon she was clear about her objectives, clear how she would approach staff and promised to monitor change as she went along so that she could make sure she was not making things worse.

Case study: Ann Melhuish's HLTA investigation in Whipton Barton School, Devon

Throughout the study it will be important to monitor the overall effect any changes made to the existing support structure for teaching assistants and new training programmes have on individuals, pupils and the whole-school community. Hopefully, researching each step of the jobs evolution will allow me to monitor my progress and effectiveness and anticipate any pitfalls before they happen.

Preparation
After the initial leadership and management training a discussion was held with the deputy head, who is also the HLTA line manager, and myself. Firstly we brainstormed what was needed in terms of leadership and management of the teaching assistants.

Box 6.1 Market Fields' LSA questionnaire

MARKET FIELD SCHOOL

Support staff review carried out by Gary and Pete - January / February 2007

Summary and Action Points

"What part of the job do you enjoy most?"

An absolutely overwhelming response to this question was – "the children and their achievements". Other frequent mentions were: teamwork; strong sense of personal responsibility; positive environment; happy at work; able to use initiative.

"What can we improve?"

- More time needed to prepare / meet
  Action: Investigating overall budgetary impact.

- Need for career structure
  Action: Implementing HLTA structure (details to follow).

- Sometimes need more medical input
  Action: Discuss ideas with Nik / Dr Coxhead.

- Training
  Action: Organise child protection updates
  Organise input on specific conditions: Downs, Fragile X, PNI etc.

- General need for more space
  Action: Currently working on building proposals.

- Improved staff induction for LSA's.
  Action: Introduce LSA mentoring - possible link to HLTA role or get volunteers for peer mentoring.
  New staff to have "school tour" after first couple of weeks.

- Improve trust and teamwork across "teams"
  Action: Investigate – instigate staff swops.

Gary Smith
26th February 2007

As leadership is such an implicit role a decision was made that this needed to be an important part of the research. Once the brainstorm was completed areas for study were highlighted and an action plan drawn up.

Discussions have been held with the teaching assistants, SENCO, teachers and head so they are all aware of what my plans are. Issues of confidentiality will be dealt with as they arise and all members of staff will be kept informed of any decisions that are made. If information is needed involving any member of staff permission will be asked before the information is obtained.

Research

... As a group of teaching assistants we have been very fortunate that the school has been proactive in involving all support staff in a lot of the vital decision making that has moved the school forward to its present position. However, historically the teaching assistants have often felt that their specific needs have been overlooked. This is particularly true with regard to performance management and communication issues, both of which form a fundamental part of this research. The aim of the study is to improve the effectiveness of teaching assistants by ensuring that they are working in the best way possible without putting too much pressure on other members of staff.

When starting the new HLTA role one of the important objectives was to establish firm lines of communication between myself and the other teaching assistants. It is imperative to listen to what they are saying, whether you agree with it or not.

TAs as part of whole-school reviews

When you start looking for less definable but important information such as effectiveness of communication and consultation or looking at climate, the questions are not so straightforward either.

One whole-school route to consider is that of Investors in People (IiP). This is a nationally recognised framework for improving performance through a planned approach. The framework is based on the simple Plan, Do, Review cycle:

Plan: develop strategies to improve performance
Do: take action to improve performance and
Review: evaluate the impact.

These three processes are broken down into 10 indicators. It is a very structured approach, but recognition for the standard involves registering and being assessed by outside people. During the process, the outside advisers also help the process. While it was originally designed for business and industry, it has had proven success in many thousands of schools. It has evolved into three strands, one following a leadership and management strand, one following a recruitment and selection strand and one following a work–life balance strand. The NFER longitudinal study of 20 schools over five terms showed that:

◆ Overall, support staff gained the most from the whole-school emphasis on the development of staff. They benefited from specifically focused training and development opportunities, as well as from involvement in whole-school activities, and their status and morale had risen as a result.

◆ No direct impact on pupil performance was identified but staff (teaching and support) felt that the improved training and development activities, which they had experienced or were planning, would have an effect in the longer term.

◆ Other identified benefits included, improved channels of communication; clearer job descriptions and systems of line management, a more positive school culture and improved working relationships.

(Easton *et al.* 2003: 1)

'The Standard was perceived as a means of fostering change and developing staff, rather than as an accreditation of their existing good practice' (Easton *et al.* 2003: 1).

School example

Mark Jones, head of Stifford Clays Junior School used IiP when he was a newly appointed head to develop a positive ethos in school. He wanted collegiality and openness, support structures, individuals feeling recognised but working together (Jones 2003). In his paper he describes the processes of performance management and staff development for his support staff that have taken place, their pay reviews and job descriptions, their involvement in policy review. IiP provided an audit of how well the process was going and an opportunity for a wider view on the school. He also documents how the process overcame the sense of 'them and us' that had prevailed and helped him deal with a domineering member of staff, who had to be replaced to enable the other staff to move forward with confidence. Because of undertaking this process, he felt workforce remodelling didn't affect him while the job evaluation scheme did because of the salary schemes suggested for particular job descriptions. Despite the increased cost he will definitely continue with reassessment under the IiP scheme because of its usefulness.

Box 6.2 gives extracts from Mark's Continuing development policy for LSAs and HLTAs showing how he integrated the IiP process into his school processes. (The induction policy mentioned in the CPD policy is reproduced as Box 9.1.)

It is worth looking in detail at the IiP indicators as they relate to schools and seriously considering this process as it has been so successful (IiP 2005). Only you can decide whether the cost is one your school should consider.

Box 6.2 Extracts from Stifford Clays Junior School's CPD policy for LSAs and HLTAs

4. <u>Developing our Staff</u>

◆   See Induction policy for new members of staff and their individual entitlements

◆   Continuous Professional Development Review

    ✓   Continuous Professional Development Review is a process through which employees can plan and review their work objectives and performance, together with their line manager, and possibly their team.
    ✓   Continuous Professional Development Review will need to be continuous to be effective. Once targets, milestones and criteria have been agreed, it is important that these are monitored and discussed regularly.
    ✓   Continuous Professional Development Review looks at past performance and attitudes, but aims to provide a system to underpin the continuous professional and personal development of employees.

◆   What it means to be part of an *'Investors in People'* school (Summer 2002 and then May 2005)

    ✓   Investor in People is a national Standard, which sets a level of good practice for training and development of people to achieve business goals.
    ✓   The Standard provides a national framework for improving business performance, through a planned approach to setting and communicating business objectives and developing people to meet these objectives.
    ✓   The process is cyclical and should engender the culture of continuous improvement.

◆   Training and Development

    ✓   Continuous professional development (CPD) will be actively promoted to ensure our team of Learning Support Assistants are professionally up to date and aware of current best practices.
    ✓   Commitment to training and development for everyone to enable personal development, this will be closely linked with the Performance Review process.
    ✓   Training and development will ensure that employees can directly contribute to improving service delivery and performance.

5.   <u>Investors in People and Performance Review</u>

Investors in People is based on four key principles:
✓   **Commitment** to invest in people to achieve the school's own goals and targets.
✓   **Planning** how skills, individuals and teams are developed to achieve these goals.
✓   **Action** to develop and use necessary skills in a well-defined and continuing programme directly tied to the school's objectives.
✓   **Evaluating** outcomes of training and Performance Reviews for individuals' progress towards goals, the value achieved and future needs.
In 2002 SCJS achieved the Investors in People Standard, demonstrating that through effective management that empowers and has a clear sense of direction, it has exceeded required standards in:

✓   The quality and planning for service development.
✓   The quality of communication and interaction with staff on those plans.
✓   The quality of training and development provided to staff to enable service targets to be delivered.
✓   The value for money of the training investment.

Policy for Performance Management Procedures for
Learning Support Assistants (including HLTAs)

INVESTOR IN PEOPLE

Simple audits

You may be able to jot down a list of roles and needs that you already know about. After an initial list has been compiled, get each TA to complete something like this:

THINKING POINTS

Name; Job title; Location.

Detail tasks in brief.

Does the job description cover the tasks undertaken?

Who is the main line manager and how regularly is there contact?

Do other staff regularly share functions with or do work for the postholder, if so which posts?

Do you consider any tasks which are currently undertaken are no longer necessary?

Qualifications held by postholder and any training undertaken

Skills of postholder which are not currently being used

Are there any training needs for the current job?

Location of current job, is access to equipment, co-workers and line manager adequate?

Any suggestions for improvements to current work?

(FAS 1998)

Other questions could be:

THINKING POINTS

How much does your school rely on the goodwill of the TAs to enable the communication to take place between them and the teachers? Is this right?

Do all the teachers know what the TAs do in classrooms other than their own?

Do the TAs meet together? with each other? with teachers with special responsibilities in whose area they might be working? with senior staff?

Do your TAs have a job description? . . .

Have you a shared ethos?

Are all staff consulted when formulating the schools development plan? Are all views valued even if the decisions are opposing?

Do all staff know all the relevant policies. Is there a staff handbook for all staff?

Does your staff development strategy include support staff?

Who attends which meetings? Why? . . .

Do you utilise the training budget in your school for the best development of all the adults in your school?

Have you thought of a mentoring system for all your staff?

How do you know what the adults in your school feel about themselves in relation to your school?

Is your whole school a learning environment?

Do you know the professional development needs of all the staff?

Does the school employment and pay policy reflect the needs of the school and the qualities of all the staff?

What determines the number and hours worked by the TAs in the school? . . .

Do you know what training opportunities, resources and accreditation routes are available in your area?

Do you know what other schools in your area are doing?

Do you know what funding may be available for adult learners?

(Watkinson 1998a: 3; 1998b: 4)

Despite the date on the preceding list, it is surprising how few managers know the answers to some of these questions. Maybe it is a reflection on the increase in numbers in each school that managers have lost track of the answers; maybe it is a reflection on the demands on the managers from all the other sources that have decreased the opportunities to carry out such information gathering exercises; maybe it just smacks of yet more bureaucracy. I hope you can see the value of knowing the answers to many of the questions.

The DfES *Good Practice Guide* has what is still possibly the best collection of audit materials despite its 2000 publication date. The content was not only suggested by a major research project (Farrell *et al.* 1999) but was also evaluated by the authors of the original report (Balshaw and Farrell 2002). For the TA project leaders, the most comprehensive and trialled materials can be found in Part 3 of the guidance. It is specifically directed to the work of TAs to help you to query your existing practice, in order to identify the next moves.

There are eight lists of questions covering six indicators of good practice in the guide. Each page is set out with a four-point scale for each question asked. There is space on the page for comments. These pages can be photocopied and used as a questionnaire, retrieved and collated. The audit contents are as follows:

1   Schools should have clear policies outlining the roles and responsibilities of TAs.

2.1 Managers' and teachers' management strategies provide clear guidance as to how TAs should work in their classrooms.

2.2 The expertise, skills and knowledge of TAs is used flexibly to foster the learning of pupils.

3.1 TAs work cooperatively with teachers to support the learning and participation of pupils.

3.2 Teachers and TAs learn together to improve the quality of their work.

4   TAs develop effective working partnerships with people involved in education.

5   TAs meet with others for the purposes of planning, problem solving and staff development.

6   TAs are supported in relation to their induction, mentoring and development needs.

I suggest you choose only a limited number of indicators in the first instance, rather than trying to look at the whole field of TA practice.

THINKING POINTS

You need first to decide:

◆ Which member of staff should lead this audit review?

◆ Which staff members could constitute a task group to take it forward? (ensuring that TAs themselves and at least one senior manager are part of the group)

◆ When should the governors be informed and could/should one be involved in the process?

◆ Is there anyone else who should be informed of our intentions: pupils, other staff, parents, advisers?

◆ What budget can we commit to the review?

◆ What time in the year would it be best to proceed?

◆ Is this to be part of a larger review of school practice?

◆ Does this fit in with any other project coming up in the next year?

◆ What kind of audit would fit our perception of the current circumstances?

◆ What are the priorities of the school? Where should the school focus?

◆ What will happen to any report or recommended action produced by the task group?

The task group then needs to:

◆ Prepare a costed action plan and submit it to any relevant school authority for approval

◆ Inform all staff of the existence of such a plan.

Then consider:

◆ Who needs to be involved?

◆ Which bits of which audit framework are to be used, in what order?

- ◆ What paperwork needs to be prepared?
- ◆ What meetings need to be convened?
- ◆ Where will they be and what records should be kept?
- ◆ What will be done with any data obtained? Who can have access to it?
- ◆ What data can be trawled from existing data banks?
- ◆ Will interviews or observations be undertaken?
- ◆ What protocols will need to be set up?
- ◆ How will any report be made?
- ◆ How will any action be taken as a result of any conclusions reached?
- ◆ Who is to do what by when?
- ◆ Are there any required outcomes which must be addressed as a priority?

It is then up to the individuals named to prepare materials, inform, collect data, collate information and report back as agreed.

(Watkinson 2003a: 39, 40)

In their book evaluating the guide, Balshaw and Farrell (2002) highlight some key issues:

For the assistants:

- ◆ effective examination of role through a focus on job descriptions, flexible deployment and management practices in respect to these;
- ◆ staff development opportunities and induction processes.

The key issues for management were:

- ◆ senior teaching staff and school leaders developing awareness of the issues identified within the indicators of effective practice;
- ◆ an appreciation of the need to change management practices;
- ◆ resulting developments in both policy and practice.

In addition important factors within the action research were:

- ◆ a senior member of staff strategically fulfilling a leadership and advocacy role;
- ◆ this role kept the 'voice' of the action researchers on agendas for staff meetings and in discussions with key groups of people such as senior managers or governors;
- ◆ self-advocacy generated by both the lead researcher assistants and the whole teams of assistants.

(Balshaw and Farrell 2002: 98)

There is a detailed school self-evaluation grid in the DfES materials on *The effective management of teaching assistants to improve standards in literacy and mathematics*.

It takes their suggested six 'levers' for efficacy in using TAs and plots them against the four strands of improvement: focusing, developing, establishing and enhancing, on two A4 pages (DfES 2005b: 4, 5). This would give a useful discussion document for opening the debate in a staffroom by asking those present to ring where they thought the school was in each respect. This document goes on to describe a provision map for an anonymous primary school, looking at the various waves of provision, and what interventions will be needed for each year.

School example

In Carlton Colville Primary School the teachers annually undertake a provision mapping for the children as they see them at the end of the summer term ready for the September class changes. They undertake this for each year group following their SEN audit for the LA. They consider all the children whose progress is causing any concern according to their needs as determined in the four SEN areas: behavioural and emotional, communication and interaction, cognition and learning, and sensory and physical. They put them in concentric circles on a sheet of paper, those with the least need being in the outer circle. These will receive Wave 1 teaching, the innermost circle of greatest need requiring Wave 3 or individual support. When they see how the numbers pan out the headteacher and SENCO provisionally allocate their TA team for the following year to classes not to individual children. This transitional document is then discussed at a staff meeting where a more detailed needs analysis is undertaken and TAs matched to teachers. Within their TA team they have one TA with a speech and language specialisation, one who does a gym trail, one with counselling skills who can work with nurture groups, anther skilled in anger management, one who is good with children who need a boost in self-esteem, one with understanding of autism who is good at working with social stories and one with expertise in the Early Years. They have no HLTA.

Balshaw and Farrell considered that TAs can be placed

firmly at the forefront of staff and practice development and school improvement. The lead that assistants took at the national dissemination conferences was impressive, their appreciative audiences applauding them and their presentations, their confidence and their work. Listeners were impressed with the accounts of the development of confidence and self-esteem that came from their involvement in action research. The assistants are rightly proud of these achievements.

(Balshaw and Farrell 2002: 98)

Clearly, while this could be seen as a very time-consuming process in an already overloaded timetable, the very act of delegating the TA review to the TAs themselves, with the manager taking the lead role, is valuing the role. It seems an ideal tool for a newly appointed HLTA or senior TA.

Using questionnaires or meetings

You can use paper questionnaires. A facilitator might help by introducing teachers and TAs to the questionnaires which ask slightly different questions of each group. They take away the results, compose a composite answer from them, which is then fed back to the two groups assembled together. In this way, answers are anonymous and all hear what has been said. The outcomes can be discussed much more openly and positively.

School example

Lakenheath Primary School decided on questionnaires to their senior leadership, the teachers and the TAs. Each set was about a page and a half of questions, but because they had all agreed to do them, they were completed. The TAs read through all the information given so that the process was very open. Box 6.3 is their summary.

Holding meetings of TAs is another way schools use to ask questions about how the job is perceived. It still surprises me how few schools encourage their TAs to meet, or provide time and a place for them to do so, let alone recognise this as paid time. The results are astounding. If you have not done this before, then please try it. TAs unused to such meetings or the thought of observations or individual interviews do feel more secure when surrounded by their colleagues. I have seen it used as a way of introducing performance reviews, the meeting becomes a sort of joint review before introducing the individual approach. What happens though, even in the best schools, is that the initial outcome is likely to reveal some negative issues, but these are often small and easily dealt with. It is exactly the dealing with these issues that is going to improve the situation of the TAs, their confidence in your management and open the opportunities for further work with them. If the issues are large, then you will realise that you might have some serious work to do to get a motivated workforce.

A simple SWOT analysis with TAs

This tool is often underrated because it is so simple and comes with the 'fly swatting' connotation of the acronym. Just looking at strengths, weaknesses, opportunities and threats can give a lot of information for development. You don't have to call the sections by the SWOT names. Ann Melhuish undertook hers as part of a meeting (Figure 6.1).

Looking at TAs at work in the classroom

You might decide to do this as part of a review of TAs or support staff as described above or it may be part of a performance review. Procedures for this process are described in the next chapter. It is a very sensitive procedure which can be misinterpreted, so it is important that things are well discussed beforehand to prevent later problems. Most TAs welcome someone watching them at work and

Box 6.3 The Lakenheath questionnaire

The questions.

TA questions asked about:
Did they feel they were being given responsibilities?
Space to work?
Were their skill and contributions valued?
Were they and would they like to be involved in planning?

Questions for teachers asked about the relationship between the class teacher and the TA.
Their job descriptions i.e. did the CT know what the TA's was?
Did they want/have time for planning?

Questions for SLT
Asked about TAs' qualifications and achievements.
Were these taken into account?

Results

Generally felt that time was needed in TA contract for planning and admin.

It was felt that these meetings would improve partnerships and good practice.

Also felt that parents needed to be informed of TA role i.e. not all parents are aware of their qualifications and experiences. A few thought of them as "paid helpers".

What have we done?

Each TA had 1 hour added to contract to plan with Class Teacher.
The exact timing of this is decided within each pair.
The TAs feel this is beneficial.
Teachers equally value the time spent with the TA instead of "snatching" odd moments or feeing guilty at TAs staying after school for no extra pay.

Letters to parents explained that some TAs may be working as Cover Supervisors. They are planning with the Class Teacher and may be delivering some of the curriculum.

Strengths	Areas for Development
a) A good strong team b) A large team c) Approachable and friendly d) Wide range of strengths and knowledge e) A sense of community f) Loyalty and honesty g) Good relationships with the children h) Good role models i) Mutual respect j) Good team work k) Good school ethos l) Good support from colleagues m) Wide range of lunchtime, after and before school clubs n) The backing to get more training o) Feeling valued p) Clear guide lines for behaviour q) Comprehensive planning r) Talented teachers s) Good communication t) Empathy u) Developmental opportunities v) Views recognised	1) Being honest during meetings 2) To know what courses are available 3) Group training in key areas e.g. ELS and Springboard 4) TAs are often linked to named children and therefore do not always have the opportunity to work with other groups 5) Group working spaces – where do you take children to do small group work, particularly where it is quiet 6) Numeracy and literacy training 7) Interactive and utilisation of whiteboard and basic ICT 8) Them and us attitude with the Infant School 9) A chance for airing grievances 10) Passing on of knowledge and training 11) Wasting money 12) Follow up on performance management 13) ICT and development for SEN children 14) Very limited access to computers with TA/SEN children 15) Resources 16) Training 17) Assessment 18) Active support throughout lesson 19) More time for TA/teacher to meet every week
Opportunities	**Barriers**
➤ Gardening – to develop Kevin's garden ➤ TAs weekly meeting is good for sharing but maybe focus could be a bit clearer ➤ Some of the agendas for the TA meetings needs to come from them ➤ Further training opportunities ➤ Make training opportunities more accessible e.g. print off from the Internet	➤ Quality time at meeting rather than being rushed because of other demands ➤ Money to pay for courses ➤ Dictation of timetables ➤ Budget ➤ Time constraints ➤ No place (specific) that is quiet ➤ TAs are asked to carry out some tasks without the relevant input ➤ Sometimes there are too many other children in need – especially when working with a named child

Figure 6.1 A TA SWOT analysis

feel valued by the process. If there is not any school guidance on the procedure, then start the process to get some, consulting all involved for best results.

Interview procedures

Any formal observation of any member of staff should be followed up with a one-to-one interview in order to share perceptions, ensure understanding and avoid misunderstandings and to maintain the openness of the procedure. The meeting should take place in a quiet place in quality time (i.e. paid time). The content of any such talk should be confidential, and any recorded outcomes agreed by both before they part. In order to really find out what is going on during the time the TA is observed, it is necessary to talk to them, the teacher and, if possible, the pupils – first separately and later the teacher and TA together, so that it is all open. It is in-depth work, but you will see how the school context is affecting the way the classroom dynamics operate, and understand the issues for the partners better. Again, there is more on this in the next chapter.

Monitoring and evaluation

The major concerns of schools appear to be, either 'What will Ofsted say' or 'How will our place in the league table be affected'. The short inspections under the current framework depend on hard data of test results, just like the league tables, but the school's self-evaluation does allow for the school to look at soft outcomes. The main criticism on many research reports about TA work is that schools do not evaluate the provision of this human resource. Monitoring impact is discussed in the DfES material on managing TAs for literacy and mathematics (DfES 2005: 4, 5).

Probably the most difficult question to answer is whether the TAs are directly affecting teaching and learning in a measurable way. It seems likely that the value of TAs is in the facilitation of school systems, their contribution to the team of staff, and their support of the learning process in class rather than in measurable learning outcomes at the end of the year. Only the school can decide where they wish to attribute value.

TAs can:	*Possible monitoring action*
Support inclusive policies enabling pupils otherwise excluded from mainstream school, to attend the school	These pupils can be identified
Enable more of time of pupils with SEN to be spent with their peers	This can be counted in hours Examples would be the presence of a TA enabling pupils to be in a science or PE lesson they would otherwise miss, or to take part in a class plenary session
Enable teachers to function in a less stressful way	Ask them Count the teacher absences Monitor time spent by teachers and TAs on various tasks
Enhance the systems of the school	List the tasks the TAs are actually performing
Raise the self-esteem of learners	Watch the pupils in class and at informal times Look at truancy rates, staying-on rates, and participation of pupils in school functions

Provide counselling sessions	Monitor pupil stress
Provide liaison with parents or outside agencies	Monitor time spent by teachers and TAs on various tasks
Manage resources	Monitor time spent by teachers and TAs on various tasks
Assist learners to understand about their own learning	Monitor pupils' activities when they have left – how many go on to further education immediately or later?
Bring additional skills and dimensions of challenge and support to the school	Audit them

(Watkinson 2003: 81)

You could collect hard data. For example:

◆ the names of pupils who regularly get certain kinds of support with the times and dates of such support;
◆ track the groups of pupils not on the SEN register, needing 'a bit extra' over several years;
◆ quantify the time that TAs are involved in such initiatives as Catch-up or ALS;
◆ IEP data might be collated where TAs have been directly involved in attaining targets;
◆ 'P' levels of assessment data is included for those with SEN;
◆ the rate at which support can be decreased where there is effective TA support.

ICT software in use in schools should make it possible to make these connections. The rate and number of pupils who come off the SEN register would be an indication of the success of the school's provision. Too often, once a pupil is 'labelled' and the school's funding is earmarked to their support, the support is not reviewed with a view to decreasing it.

Blatchford et al. (2002) looked at school entry booklets and submitted termly questionnaires. From that, they calculated measures of class size, pupil–teacher ratios, pupil–staff ratios, pupil–adult ratios both registered and experienced. However, they found practice was so diverse they could not come to any firm conclusions.

Some of the so-called 'soft' data can be converted to numbers as there are rating scales for things such as behaviour, self-esteem and teacher stress. You will need to consult people who are trained in such techniques to have access to these and, again, such collation will be time consuming. However, the Ofsted framework being now in terms of the ECM agenda is a hopeful move towards recognising that the affective domain of learning is important.

Ofsted (2002) reported that:

◆ Teachers value the support.
◆ The quality of teaching in lessons with TAs is better.
◆ Training has improved TAs' knowledge of subjects.
◆ The DfES training helped TAs' competence, confidence and management.

◆ Career progression for TAs is increasing.
◆ TAs contribute to the wider life of schools.

They also noted the need for management to recognise competing demands on TAs' time, and for them to enter into monitoring and evaluation procedures. Teachers, while valuing the support that TAs can give, also found this took time to organise.

Blatchford and colleagues (2006) have only the baseline results so far from their questionnaires where they have collated feelings and opinions. Their second phase in evaluating the WR (Blatchford *et al.* 2007) monitors some of the changes taking place. They reported:

◆ 'Support staff who work closely with teachers are most likely to have a large positive effect on teachers' job satisfaction' although some negative cases were recorded.
◆ 'TA equivalent staff and technicians were . . . most likely to reduce stress.' Only 46 per cent felt support staff had helped workloads and they were usually administrative staff.
◆ 'most teachers felt support staff had a beneficial effect on pupil learning and behaviour. The main ways that support staff affected learning and behaviour were in terms of:

1 bringing specialist help to the teacher and into the classroom, e.g. in terms of skills in technology, counselling, careers advice, equipment and resources;
2 affecting pupils' attitudes, e.g. in terms of confidence, motivation, pride in their work and improved social skills;
3 helping pupils' understanding and misconceptions;
4 having a positive impact on pupils' discipline, social skills or behaviour.

Teachers felt support staff had benefited their teaching in a number of ways: enabling teachers to concentrate more on their teaching, bringing expertise to teachers and pupils, improving the quality of teachers' teaching, facilitating planning and preparing for lessons, and freeing teachers from routine tasks; and allowing teachers to differentiate the work for more pupils.'

(pp. 92, 93)

The second report (Blatchford *et al.* 2007) identified a significant increase in numbers of TAs employed, but less change in management practices. A third of the staff were working unsupervised and paid time for extra work had even decreased. WR had decreased teachers' workload but not always by using TAs. Lack of paid planning and feeddback time in over two-thirds of the workforce was still undermining good practice.

One outcome that is rarely measured is that of the effect of valuing and developing the TAs themselves. Their personal growth as people and educators is an indicator of their usefulness. Such a measure is likely to be very rewarding for them, and impressive for their colleagues and the teaching staff.

They are certainly value for money as much of the provision is of a high level, some definitely equivalent if not better than teachers. They are being employed in preference to supply teachers because of their better effectiveness but they are not being paid as supply teachers. Many schools justify TA cover of the PPA time on budgetary grounds, while others are still paying teachers for this cover. School leaders must decide a proper rationale for PPA cover and pay appropriately, even if it means cuts elsewhere. Anything else is exploitative and taking advantage of TAs' goodwill. If the school has determined its rationale for the employment of TAs, then evaluation must be against that rationale. If they are teaching then they should be monitored in the same ways as teachers; if taking a class, they should be observed and evaluated as teachers would be.

One measure, which is growing in visibility when reviewing TA teams, is the ability of the school to 'grow' their own people, enabling and encouraging them to grow professionally and personally. This can mean greater turnover of teaching staff as they leave for promotion, but with TAs often the loyalty to the school and the domestic need to stay in the area means an increasingly highly experienced and qualified staff, 'grown' in the ways of the school. There is a significant number of teachers in schools now who have come through the TA route, becoming graduates and training on the job.

Even in 1992, Mortimore *et al.* recognised that looking at a proper cost evaluation of staff might end in the

> reduction in the absolute numbers of teaching posts in a school . . . (but which) . . . would be likely to lead to an enhancement of the teachers' role. This enhanced role will be more challenging and have greater professional and pedagogical (rather than administrative) commitments. It may not be to everybody's liking, but it may lead to more effective schooling and more efficient use of resources.
>
> (p. 206)

Poor practice and possible negative outcomes

It is rare to record poor practice in TAs, but it does happen.

> I found in schools with poor practice:
>
> ◆ it is difficult to disassociate the TA from the class teacher, as the directions given by the teacher delineate the task for the TA
> ◆ schools with serious weaknesses which included weaknesses in the quality of teaching, also had poor TAs
> ◆ some schools had given no directions to the TA
> ◆ relationships were sometimes strained
> ◆ communication was lacking
> ◆ TAs were underused.
>
> (Watkinson 2003a: 52)

Blatchford and colleagues (2002) suggested that 'more support does not necessarily mean more effective support, even when the staff involved are individually effective' (p. 47). Their case study evidence picked up a class where individual observation of TAs' skills were described as excellent but there were so many adults supporting (this included volunteer help) that the teacher could not brief them all properly and planning was difficult. Lack of TA preparation, missed opportunities for learning, complexity of arrangements and the possibility of 'dead' time were also described. The list below highlights some of the features that seemed to apply when helpers were not effective:

- inflexible and didactic
- see role as dealing with correctness of work and behaviour
- limited warmth and praise
- little probing or questioning or efforts to help children understand why they might be mistaken
- little knowledge of the task undertaken by the children
- little effort to ensure equal opportunities for all.

(Blatchford *et al.* 2002: 43)

Clearly, poor practice concerning TAs can rest with the TAs themselves or the teachers or the management. You have to decide whether it is appropriate that your least well-trained, least experienced and lowest paid staff should be working with your most challenging pupils. This is why it is important to ensure you know what is going on, and how the TAs are actually working in practice.

Dealing with poor practice

If you do discover practice that could be less than effective for the learning and teaching of the school, you must do something. One of the main difficulties managers seem to face is that of actually telling the ineffective person of the problem. It really does make a difference just being frank but supportive. Remember, the people involved should be told of the problem away from the classroom and other people. You must make suggestions as to how it could be improved and offer to help with support. The aim is always to improve practice not condemn it. Hopefully, this situation will be rare. If poor practice needs to be dealt with it should be done immediately and not left until performance review.

Don't mix the good with the bad, keep it simple and direct but supportive. If your advice is not heeded or the situation deteriorates, always take advice as to proper procedures. There will be policies to take note of and legalities to follow. If they are not followed the process can be long drawn out, demanding on your time, degrading for the member of staff and demoralising for other staff.

After monitoring and investigating

Hard decisions may need to be made. But, by carrying out any of these processes you will raise the profile of the TAs in your school and hopefully have found out how much they do and could do. The next step is to identify what changes you want to make.

One of the biggest challenges facing school leaders has been to win the support of their workforce in order to challenge established patterns of working and effect a change in the school culture. The management of change is more successful in those schools where all the staff develop the capacity to question existing practice and consider what they might achieve by first recognising barriers to progress and planning action.

(Ofsted 2005: 11)

The Ofsted report goes on to describe situations where staff have not been fully consulted, or induction or performance management procedures are weak and communication breaks down. Governing body support and challenge can help but is not often forthcoming. LA support is on offer but not always used well.

Chapter 7

Performance review

All staff deserve the process that is a legal requirement for teachers. Anything other is actually discriminatory as well as possibly ignoring some hidden gems. Not only is performance review important for all staff, the outcomes should also be important for the leaders and managers in the school. There should be objectives set relating to the overall school plan, and the professional development and training needs of all staff should be included in the budgeting and planning for the next year. This is not only true for TAs but for all support staff – caretakers, cleaners and kitchen staff where employed by the school, MDAs, clerical and administrative staff. All support staff should have some sort of formal review process at the end of a probationary period, after about six months and certainly before the end of the first year. Some schools or people may refer to reviews as appraisal, so long as you and the appraisee are clear as to what the process entails, the name is immaterial.

Performance review has proved contentious from its first introduction into the teaching profession as peer appraisal in 1991. Where it is well done, it has proved its value for teachers and TAs. Crane's research involved looking at review systems in the RAF, the Derbyshire Building Society and Toyota UK.

> The mechanistic approach of the current performance management process led the teachers interviewed in this research to conclude that the system failed to connect with their authentic learning, and instead was about 'performing for the management' . . . In schools where performance management continues to be a bolt-on activity, it has little impact upon the progress of students, the performance of staff or the overall achievement of schools.
>
> (Crane 2002: 3)

TAs respond well to the process as they see it as being valued for what they do and what they could do, given support or training. The links with performance-related pay have not been helpful and it is interesting that as the teachers move towards this, next September, many industries move away from it. It proves either divisive or useless because everyone gets a pay rise. Some industries do have a rather prescriptive performance review system whereby items are scored, that has not come into schools. What is happening for support staff in many cases is that they only get a 5- or 10-minute annual interview or a collective opportunity for a gripe meeting. Despite recommended observation and interview procedures taking time and organisation, where it takes place it is productive and valued. As with teaching staff, it must be introduced carefully to get the best out of it.

The indicators of IiP include:

> '3. Strategies for managing people are designed to promote equality of opportunity in the development of the organisation's people
> 6. People's contribution to the organisation is recognised and valued'

This latter one means 'Systems need to be in place through which headteachers and principals can give recognition to what people have achieved and contributed. This can be achieved through performance reviews or staff meetings, for example. Individuals should be able to describe how they have contributed to the school or college and give clear examples of how it has been recognised and valued by their management.'

Indicator 8 looks at all people learning and developing effectively while Indicator 9 looks at evaluating performance, and says this means 'other individuals should be able to explain how training and development has improved their personal performance while managers and their teams should be able to explain how it has impacted on them' (IiP 2005: 4, 5).

School Support Staff – the way forward states:

> 4.2 For training and development to be effective, every member of staff must receive a rigorous, constructive annual appraisal leading to the development of an individual plan for development. Following the four-stage appraisal cycle for teachers of planning, development, monitoring and review, the process should take account of the employee's personal objectives and the school's goals. It should be conducted as part of a cycle complementing that for teacher, so that shared objectives can be established.

> 4.3 Support staff appraisal should take place during normal working hours but when this is not possible, the time should be paid for.

> 4.4 Whilst all school-based employees should be encouraged to take responsibility for their own learning, ultimately head teachers, governors and managers all have a role to play in helping individuals to achieve their full potential and fit new and emerging roles in schools.
>
> (NJC 2003: 41)

The Essex guidance gives the purposes of the performance management review scheme which it recommends to schools as:

> communicate the schools strategic plans and objectives;
> give clarity to individual roles within those plans;
> set standards of performance;
> evaluate individual past performance and development;

evaluate learning and development received;
set service-related and personal objectives;
plan individual learning and development;
provide a mechanism for the assessment of pay progression (where appropriate).

(ECC 2002: 1)

Indicator 6 in the *Good practice guide* has questions to ask concerning development and support for TAs. For instance:

Are job descriptions reviewed with TAs on a regular basis? . . .
Are TAs appraised as a means of developing their contributions and account-
abilities in the school?
Are TAs given staff development opportunities in relation to career progression?
. . .
Does the school structure responsibilities for TAs reflect their qualifications,
experience and training? . . .
Are there clear means of identifying appropriate and relevant external training
courses to support TAs' further development?

(DfES 2000: 49)

How development supports the individual

Senge's First Discipline is about personal mastery for all members of the organisation. This entails people taking responsibility for their own learning and professional development, finding out what their potential is and what the opportunities are. While this responsibility can and should be written into a JD, you as the leader or manager must enable this to happen. Each of us needs a second opinion on our ways of working, an opportunity to discuss options, some pointers to our role or potential role in the organisation and support in developing that potential – that is what performance management is about. Senge himself says:

As individuals practice the discipline of personal mastery, several changes take place within them. Many of these are quite subtle and often go unnoticed. In addition to clarifying the 'structure' that characterises personal mastery as a discipline (such as creative tension, emotional tension and structural conflict) the systems perspective also illuminates subtler aspects of personal mastery – especially integrating reason and intuition; continually seeing more of our connectedness to the world; compassion; and commitment to the whole.

(Senge 1990: 167)

The original NOS values and principles state:

Continuing Professional Development
Teaching/classroom assistants will take advantage of planned and incidental self-development opportunities in order to maintain and improve the contribution that they can make to raising pupil achievement. Asking for advice and support to help resolve problems should be seen as a form of strength and professionalism.

(LGNTO 2001: 5, 6)

The old HLTA standard 6 ensured that 'They are able to improve their own practice, including through observation, evaluation and discussion with colleagues' (DfES and TTA 2003). The draft new HLTA standard 6 is much simpler and merely states 'Those awarded HLTA status: reflect on and improve their knowledge' (TDA 2007: 2). It will be interesting to see what the guidance for candidates on these standards will request of TAs in order to fulfil this standard in future.

One of the biggest things which holds TAs back is lack of confidence. This may seem surprising given the feisty nature of a few TAs, but their very historical invisibility has hampered their self-confidence in putting themselves forward and challenging the more senior staff. Attendance on external training and getting qualifications has been a significant boost to morale.

> It was clear from informal feedback that many students saw a growth in confidence in the classroom as a critical effect of the course. Part of this may have derived from greater knowledge and understanding; informally students also hinted that the course had enabled them to share a technical vocabulary and set of concepts with the teachers that made it easier for them to take part in educational discourse.
>
> (Swann and Loxley 1998)

They have been seen as enthusiastic amateurs by many qualified teaching staff and have regarded themselves as such in many cases despite sometimes being more highly qualified in their own field than the teachers. Valuing, encouraging and celebrating success has helped enormously where it has taken place.

The very emergence of the HLTA status, as distinct from a qualification, was recognition of the high level of experience and expertise many TAs have without nationally recognised qualifications and training routes.

TAs are gluttons for development and usually seize every opportunity even if they sometimes seem indifferent to qualifications. The DfES recent research (Blatchford et al. 2006) showed only one third needed specific qualifications for their jobs and only 44 per cent required experience. The report indicates that 40 per cent of TAs only have qualifications below GCSE level. This is even higher in their 'pupils' welfare' category but lower in the 'other pupil support' category. The second report (Blatchford et al. 2007) indicates some increase in the requirements for qualifications by schools. They want to do their job better. They are eager to attend school-based INSET even if it is unpaid time, and despite domestic difficulties with child care and transport make considerable effort to attend off-site training if available.

Farrell et al. (1999) found that TAs 'valued the opportunity to receive training, both accredited and non-accredited, particularly if it related to their daily work' (p. 3), but stated such training had no impact on salary or career progression, both of which concerned the TAs. They wanted to be 'better LSAs and to be valued for doing just that' (p. 64).

The following is an example that I noted some years ago now:

School example

Advisers and trainers like tutoring TAs, often commenting that they were much more responsive than teachers coming out of school, 'they listen, work with their schools, produce materials of high calibre off their own bat'. TAs will buy themselves computers to undertake study, stay up when the rest of the family has gone to bed to watch videos, and complete work under strained domestic situations. It is rare for them to give up and even rarer for them to fail. Once they have a flavour of personal success, they want more (Watkinson 2003a: 150).

The DfES report says that 'HMI and Smith *et al.* [Smith, Whitby and Sharp 2004] both suggest that TAs who had taken part in training – particularly for those for intervention programmes such as ALS and Springboard – had proved to be more effective in supporting literacy and numeracy' (Blatchford *et al.* 2006). We also know that more TAs watch the *Teachers' TV* channel than teachers (Anon. 2007b).

Sensitivities

Performance review can be threatening to teachers let alone TAs, yet anyone who has been in business or industry finds it odd that educational staff still have a fear of the process. One way round this is to start with discussing things generally in a TA meeting, but this should only be a preliminary to individual reviews. Teachers or HLTAs unused to the process must have training as this process deals with sensitive personal issues and can elicit information that is confidential or critical of other members of staff. Schools that have taken this process slowly over years have quelled fears and overcome problems. Unfortunately in some areas this is new and job evaluation procedures have come in apparently heavy handedly. TAs have been presented with model JDs which do not fit what they do and lack of time for negotiation and compromise has created an atmosphere of resentment.

School example

One large secondary school used PowerPoint slides to introduce performance review to the support staff. These restated the school vision of service, the expectation that staff should meet the school's aims and objectives and the need for all to access appropriate development. They outlined the purposes, the cycle and how it is to be implemented for support staff. The school uses 'Accelerate Achievement' software to support the county recommended paperwork. The IT system has replaced the portfolios which took too much time for such a large staff. The individual sheets are printed out before the end of the review interview, signed and dated. One copy goes in the school file and one is for the member of staff. The pay decisions are all made by the headteacher who has access through the IT system to all the reviews. The organisation of the information is based on Ofsted criteria and can also be used to inform the SEF. The HLTAs had training before undertaking any reviews.

Doing the review

Who does the review? Taken that this should be repeated annually and should not just be the 10-minute interview by the head, this is a commitment to a lot of time by the appraiser(s). The 's' is on the last word advisedly because no one should be undertaking a review of more than four to six people. If senior managers are already undertaking the review of this number of teachers then who should do the TA reviews and when? For some schools the appointment of the HLTA has been the answer to this question. Maybe you should appoint another senior TA or HLTA if your team is larger than six. The other route is to get various teachers to undertake this, a class teacher who has a partner TA would seem ideal. You will need to provide professional development for the teacher as well as TA, but it is good CPD for the teacher too. Heads of department, key stage or year group leaders might be another route but you must consider their workload. If the TA is taking whole classes then a qualified teacher should be the person to comment on their performance.

School example

One school has an annual performance management review for each TA following termly observations by teachers and team leaders. The reviews are undertaken by the HLTAs.

Ann Melhuish's case study describes the process.

Extract from Ann Melhuish's case study

Teaching assistants along with the teachers complete a performance management interview where they too have the opportunity to express their opinion as to the targets they would like to work towards over the coming year. The problem is they frequently feel that the forms are filed in a drawer and there is not enough support to help them complete their targets especially if they involve training. This is by no means detrimental to the school it is merely a reflection of work load, priorities and who takes responsibility for organising and adequately supporting the teaching assistants. . . .

For the teaching assistants having a line manager in place specifically for them was quite a novelty. Some saw it as an opportunity to express concerns and ideas for improvement, for others it was a challenge in the fact that they had always managed in the past without this additional support so why did they need it now.

Her school's performance management process looks like the following.

School example

In a full appraisal system the stages should comprise:

◆ a self-review
◆ an observation of the TA by a more senior colleague

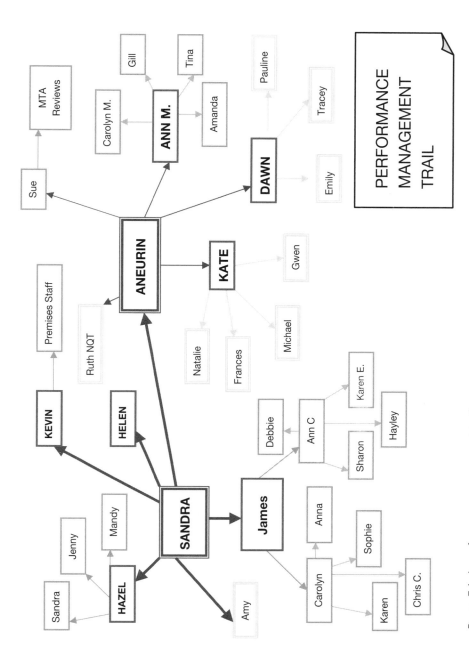

Figure 7.1 A performance management trail

◆ an appraisal meeting with feedback (sometimes called dialogue), review of JDs and previous targets, and any training needs
◆ agreement about future targets and additional training
◆ agreement about interim review procedures
◆ regular repetition of the cycle.

A self-review

If your TAs have attended the TDA induction training run by the LA, they will have a TA file and will have been through an introduction to the process. The materials in the DfES file are excellent. There is a very helpful and simple self-review form for them as well as explanations as to the value of the process and what they should be able to expect from the school. The training materials and the file materials can be downloaded from their website if you wish to use them for all your TA staff to introduce the process.

A self review should be an honest appraisal of:

◆ Your strengths and development needs in respect of working in support of the school, the curriculum, pupils and teachers
◆ Any extra contributions you have made to school life, in particular in relation to your key responsibilities
◆ Any appreciative or critical comments you have received from others
◆ Your future professional development needs.

(TDA 2006a, 2006b: 2.39)

A self-review is useful for anyone about to have an appraisal. If there is a school policy giving formal forms for self-review then use them. Most TAs will appreciate some kind of prompt list if not a formal form. The TA should keep ownership of any self-review form and decide whether it is shown to the reviewer.

Anyone going into an appraisal or performance review needs to think about:

◆ Their JD
◆ Completion of any targets set at a previous interview or reasons why targets have not been completed
◆ Quality of support received since the last appraisal
◆ Any formal observations that have been made and the outcomes
◆ Any comments that have been made, appreciative or critical
◆ Good and less welcome things that have occurred since the last review

◆ Using and availability of resources for the job
◆ Working with pupils in care, support and learning activities
◆ Teaching activities of planning delivery, assessment, feedback
◆ Completing records and other data handling
◆ Working with colleagues
◆ Contributions to school life other than in the classroom
◆ Time management

◆ Quality and usefulness of any training received
◆ Successes and concerns
◆ Ideas for change: other areas to work in, improving anything
◆ Future progression or career – aspirations
◆ What works well
◆ What gives them satisfaction
◆ What helps and what hinders in their job.

School example

Whipton Barton has a prompt sheet for people:

PREPARATION FOR PERFORMANCE MANAGEMENT

How relevant is your job description?
What aspects of your work are you especially pleased with?*
What aspects of your work have not gone as well as you would have liked?*
What aspects of your work have enriched, supported and stimulated the school?*
What would you like to focus on in the coming year?*
In what ways would you like to develop your experience and strengthen your expertise in the coming year and the long term?
Are there any other issues about your work you wish to raise in the meeting?
* see professional activities chart for guidance

School example

Oaklands Infant School has a simple self-evaluation form, quick to fill in and yet you can see what a lot it tells you about the work of the TA. This one was not only shown to the reviewer but filed in her personal file. See Figure 7.3.

Looking at TAs at work in the classroom

TAs teach, whether with individuals, groups or whole classes so they should be observed at work by someone who understands teaching. Provided the ground rules are adhered to, relationships are in place, and full discussion takes place between both parties before any observations are made, then there should not be problems. It shows an interest in a person's job to shadow them or watch them at work.

Observation procedures

Any observation procedure needs protocols to ensure there are no misunderstandings as to purpose, that the methods are open and clear, the results are confidential

Whipton Barton Junior School

Performance Management for Support Staff

Self-assessment and Skills Audit

Name: ....

The main focus of my work in school:[Is my job Description relevant]
The following aspects of my work have been particularly successful and / or rewarding during the past year:
The following aspects of my work have been particularly difficult and / or challenging during the past year:
I consider these to be my main professional skills and areas of interest:

Figure 7.2 Whipton Barton Junior self-review form

between observer and observed and that there is proper feedback. For TAs, the needs of the pupils must come first, to reduce intrusion. Extra adults observing are now a common occurrence in schools, and are usually largely ignored by pupils, but they have to be considered. It is not possible to see a situation as it would be without an observer, because an additional adult of any kind changes the dynamics. In some cases, it appears that formal observation of teachers has become excessive, so much that recently some teaching unions have been demanding a restriction on the occasions on which it should be done. Maybe, the purposes and methods of

Courses / training / meetings I have attended / undertaken during the past year:
Continuing Professional Development (CPD) or additional training I would like considered for next year:
The following personal skills and interests / hobbies could be used more fully in school:
Any other comments:

Signed: ....

Date: ....

Figure 7.2 continued

observation have not been properly discussed in some schools. No manager can say a person is working well unless they have seen them do it or had a proper report from an observation done by someone else. There is also, or should be, a difference between a formal recorded observation for review purposes and either visiting a classroom for another purpose or working alongside another member of staff. Just assuming all is well because no one has complained or been disruptive is not good enough.

All staff need to:

◆ know that all the people involved, the observer, the observed and any other adult in the room, e.g. the class teacher if a third person is observing a TA, are quite clear as to the purpose, timing and nature of the observation;

Performance Management meeting 2006

Name........ S............................

- **What I think has gone well in school this year:** – *enjoyed wi*
  Yr2 IEP Work
  enjoyed working yr2 s / whole class /
  enjoyed working with Guy watching the

- **What I have particularly enjoyed:**

  Yr2 Work – "learning to learn"
  Circle time/

- **Where I feel I have developed my knowledge, skills or understanding:**

  S+L course
  OU Maths degree work –

- **What could have gone better:**

- **The support I would like to help me develop knowledge, skills or understanding:**

  More S+L / continued support.

- **Any other comments:**

Figure 7.3 Oaklands Primary School self-review form

- ◆ feel they have a way of dealing with concerns;
- ◆ know that the observer would stop if circumstances within the classroom were not settled;
- ◆ recognise that anything seen that contravenes school policy would have to be dealt with.

So, it is important to have written protocols such as the following.

THINKING POINTS

Purpose: e.g. to try to find out how TAs A, B, etc., actually work with children

Intended outcome: e.g. a synopsis of the variety of roles seen for general circulation among TAs and teachers

Plus individual feedback session for each TA

Protocols to be observed could be:

◆ Either side should make comment at any time in the process if there is any discomfort or suggestion about what is taking place or being said.
◆ Openness, honesty and integrity will help, as sometimes what is left unsaid can indicate issues.
◆ The main audience of any summary written material will be the relevant TAs and teaching staff.
◆ It might be that this process will show up matters within the school which need wider dissemination (say to governors), then all participants should agree on the format to be circulated.
◆ Anything written for this purpose will be shared first with the staff involved so that comments can be made and points of accuracy checked.
◆ All names are to be changed in the final report to preserve confidentiality.
◆ Photocopies of all that is written down about any member of staff in observing or talking to them – scribbled notes or observation sheets shall be given to the member of staff concerned. The originals will be kept by the observer securely until the end of the process and then destroyed.
◆ Individual comments should be anonymised, or amalgamated with others to preserve confidentiality.
◆ The observation material will be fed back to individuals, who will not be able to change what is seen but could add comments.
◆ If others are involved, then they will be covered by the same sort of protocols.
◆ Permission of the parents of any children known to be closely involved will be sought by the school.
◆ The taking of video and photographs needs separate negotiation.

(Watkinson 2003a: 42, 43)

Similar protocols need to be established with the teacher and pupils so that everyone knows what is going on. This cannot be a hidden process. Recording changes or differences in behaviour, to find the range of what is taking place, is more productive than working to a strict time observation schedule, although some people like doing that. People working in classrooms react to circumstances – or should, you cannot teach properly to a script. You need to catch interactions as

```
Narrative:
Date and time:

Context

Teacher's name

TA's name

Room

In classroom or not

Lesson focus

What went on before

Introduction of me to class

Other adults

Children's activities and learning objectives if known
```

Figure 7.4
Cover sheet used
for observation schedule

they occur. The observation sheets in figures 7.4 and 7.5 can be used for observing. They are similar to those in the TA files of the induction materials (TDA 2006a, 2006b). Watch the TAs for about half an hour while they are carrying out their normal activities, particularly when working with children. Figure 7.6 shows the detailed observation sheet used in King Edward VI Community College.

Criteria

It is possibly difficult for any of you new to this system of management to judge what is good performance for a TA. A useful idea for professional development before such a review is to enter into discussions on just this subject. You could even list the criteria to guide both reviewer and reviewed. As an exercise it would certainly help with the problem some HLTAs identified, that of understanding educational vocabulary, or at least bring a shared understanding of what is to be valued in teaching and learning in your school.

School example

Feniston Primary School have developed a whole set of criteria for successful teaching assistants to support their performance management system.

Their headings developed to date are:

Reviewing and developing:
- Health and safety
- First aid

Time	TA's activity	Children	Teacher	Comment

Figure 7.5 Observation schedule for watching TAs in the classroom

LESSON OBSERVATION FOR TEACHING ASSISTANTS

TEACHING ASSISTANT _____ OBSERVER _____

DATE _____

LESSON
SUBJECT	SESSION	YEAR GROUP

NUMBER AND NATURE OF ANY SEN STUDENTS

MODELLING   Satisfactory   Further development

Is the Teaching Assistant -

Punctual

Modelling good behaviour based
On 'Starting the Lesson Well'

Calm

Professional

Good-humoured

Patient

Other comment

RELATIONSHIPS   Satisfactory   Further development

*Does the Teaching Assistant have a good, working
relationship with -*

Named student

Other students

Teacher

Other comment

Figure 7.6 The TA observation sheet from King Edward VI Community College

STUDENT LEARNING   Satisfactory   Further development

Does the Teaching Assistant show evidence of -

Annotating work to show what support
has been given

Encouraging independent learning

Differentiating work where appropriate

Other comment

Strengths

Areas for Development

Signatures: Teaching Assistant: _____

                   Observer: _____

Figure 7.6 continued

- Registration
- Reading to pupils (story, poem, other text)
- Work with an individual pupil or groups
- ICT in school
- Your own professional development

TO FOLLOW:
- Cash collections
- Lunch money collections
- Questioning pupils
- Planning
- SEN
- Resource management
- Extra curricula
- Guided reading

Feedback

In order to really find out what is going on during the time you observe the TA, you must talk to them, the teacher and, if possible, the pupils, first separately and later the teacher and TA together if you can, so that it is all open. A class teacher will have much more understanding of why the situation was as you saw it, as they should have directed the proceedings originally. Getting two perspectives on the same question can be illuminating. Pupils can say what they thought the TAs were doing, supposed to be doing and what the TA was there for. You could just ask before you leave the room:

THINKING POINTS

Have they always been there?
Are they there all the time?
Do they make any difference? If so, what?
Will you still have a TA helping you as you get older?

(Watkinson 2003a: 46)

This is not the appraisal/review interview so the feedback is about reassurance and clarification. For some TAs this will be the first time anyone has ever watched them like this and it can be daunting. Teachers have all been through college and had many such observations. Any notes are about clarification and copies should be available to both the watched and the watcher. This is in-depth, time-consuming work, but you will see how the school context is affecting the way the classroom dynamics operate, and understand the issues for all those working in those conditions or with that group of pupils. The feedback must be in a quiet place and notes, if any, shared.

The sorts of questions are really simple, they might be:

THINKING POINTS

- What did you think was going on?
- 'Was this different because I was coming in?
- What was the objective for the session for you?
  for the teacher?
  for the child/ren?
- How do you know what to do?
- Did you plan together?
- What assessment and/or recording do you do?
...
- Can you describe your relationship with the teacher?
- What helps this relationship? What hinders?
- What is your relationship to the child/ren?
- What changes would you like to make?'

(Watkinson 2003a: 45)

The appraisal/review meeting

This should take place as soon after the observations as possible.

Confidentiality

There is a valuing of individuals when someone senior gives them their undivided and private time for at least half an hour. This is surely the minimum needed to explore personal and professional issues that both sides will wish to discuss and allow time for the usual preliminary courtesies, such as a cup of tea or coffee or similar. The time should be uninterruptible, comfortable and in a private place. Do make sure the appraisee knows what the process you embark on will entail, why you do it, who owns which bit of paper and what happens to any outcomes. This should be a confidential process, where both sides feel free to explore issues without redress, and agree on any written outcomes before they leave the room. Again, a school policy may have formal outcome forms to be completed and kept on record, but the dialogue is confidential. The ground rules for the process should be clear, and part of the school handbook of which everyone should have a copy.

The meeting should cover:

- Consideration of how well targets established in the last appraisal have been met
- A self assessment by the person being appraised
- Observations on the performance of the person being appraised by the line manager

◆ Dialogue, including any problems raised by the person being appraised
◆ Setting targets to be achieved by the next appraisal
◆ Agreeing the actions required to meet those targets including any training needed
◆ Consideration of the JD and agreeing any changes, if necessary
◆ Setting a date for the next review
◆ Agreement as to what is going to go on the recorded note for the headteacher/ staff development manager/governors.

(TDA 2006a: 2.40, 2006b: 2.40)

SMART targets

The word 'targets' has become derided because of its overuse in political domination of public services. You may well want to use another word – 'objectives', 'aims', or whatever – to make the process seem less bureaucratic. When explaining the process to anyone new to it, just explain what you mean by them.

The

Specific
Measurable
Attainable
Relevant
Time bound

acronym is usually used in association with performance review targets. This can also seem a bit officious, but if these points are clear in the final agreement that is written down, these actual words need not appear. Look at the examples of forms given in Figure 7.7 and you will see how the spirit of SMART targets can be incorporated but in softer language.

For instance, there is no point writing out targets for a TA that do not relate to them and their work. You must write them in terms by which, by the next review, you can see whether they have taken place. The TA must be capable of doing what is suggested, either intellectually or physically, and it must be sustainable within budgets or timeframes. The school must be able to support the suggestions. The targets must be within the areas wanted by the school, that is, can be related to the school development or improvement plan. They must be 'doable' within the year that will elapse before they can be reviewed.

Recognising value – celebrating good practice

There are little things that can be very meaningful to staff, just as with children. The word in the ear when you have seen a good lesson or heard a positive comment is very effective. Continual praise devalues its effect. Sometimes what might seem childish ways to show appreciation can be appreciated – you will know your staff and what might embarrass, or what might be liked. I have known a TA who, on returning to school after completing a course, had her course certificate presented to her by the head in assembly when the children received theirs for various things. She was clapped, and at playtime children came up to her and asked her what she

Whipton Barton Junior School

Performance Management Individual Plan

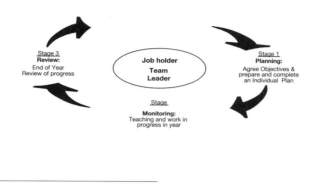

Name:_____

Job Title: _____Date started current job: __/__/____

Main responsibilities

_____

Initial Review carried out by: _____

Date of initial review: __/__/___

Period covered by review: __/__/___ to __/__/___

Figure 7.7 Whipton Barton Junior recording forms

had had to do to get her certificate. This same head used to put smiley face stickers in children's books from time to time and had special adult versions for the portfolios that the TAs maintained for their courses.

By doing the performance review you not only show the whole staff that each person is as valuable as the next, but you might well discover some hidden talents that can be used more publicly and recognised. Photographs of all staff can appear in the foyer in a small school or in relevant places in a larger school. Any kind of celebration needs to include everybody.

Whipton Barton Junior Performance Management

Name: _____　　**Job Title:** _____

Review Statement

Overall assessment of performance, including achievement of individual objectives
(summarising relevant information)

Statement agreed by: (signature and date)

Post holder: _____date: __/__/____

Post holder Comments:

Team leader: _____ date: __/__/___

Figure 7.7 continued

Carrying out the targets

The process does not stop with the TA. You should have agreed any training or
resources that might be necessary for them to be completed. This information
along with that from all the other school staff reviews needs to be collated, costed
and programmed. If on doing this a staff development manager or finance officer
indicates some things are not possible, then you might have to renegotiate targets
and rethink the training programme possibilities. Maybe an in-house session can
replace an off-site course. It is important that this whole review process for TAs
is linked with that of other staff, not just for budgetary reasons but in order to
plan properly. The following few pages give you some ideas of what kind of
developments are reasonable for TAs to expect, and possible for schools to support.

Development and training to support achievement of objectives   Postholder ……………

Development and Training (including target knowledge and skills, and target dates)	How to be achieved, support required	Notes from in-year discussions	Notes from end-year discussions	Date completed
Objective 1				
Objective 2				
Objective 3				

Post Holder's Comments

We agree this is a true record of our meeting and objectives agreed

Post holder: _____   date: __/__/__   Team leader _____   date: __/__/__

Figure 7.8 Whipton Barton Junior targets grid with CPD included

They are not entitlements but will value and enhance your human resource and support the concept of the learning school.

The process should not be just a yearly exercise or it becomes a bureaucratic chore. There must be opportunities between each full review to see how things are going. Dates are formally written in for these in the headteacher review system. You might want to do this to ensure they occur, or set up a system akin to that in the Essex Wildlife Trust. There they have what they call 'one-to-ones' every six to eight weeks. These might be only 10 minutes or a telephone conversation. They are merely logged as having taken place but just enable line managers to check all is going according to plan and that things in general are 'OK'.

Chapter 8

Professional development for and of TAs

In-house provision for development

Informal training and development

Anyone in teaching these days will be aware of some of the learning theory which describes how pupils learn. We are but grown-up children so our learning styles and processes are merely extensions. If you are leading a CPD session in-house, rather than just sending people off on courses, remember the sorts of things you would consider with children. For example:

> **THINKING POINTS**
>
> ◆ We don't learn well at the end of the day – so should training be after school? Can you have TAs' training sessions in the morning?
> ◆ You need a balance of activities for different learning styles – interaction and dialogue is required – participatory and active things help.
> ◆ We stop listening well after five minutes.
> ◆ Watch out for 'death by overheads' – and so on.
> ◆ It is very useful to think about learning styles both for yourself and with your group of TAs. Consider their learning styles when planning in house training.

Hodgson and Kambouri (1999) discuss some of the underlying principles for teaching adults, pointing out that there is no one best way, and that it might take time to find out how each learns best. They give six principles, emphasising facilitation rather than formal courses:

◆ participation in learning is voluntary;
◆ effective practice is characterised by a respect among participants for each other's self worth;

◆ facilitation is collaborative;
◆ action and reflection are placed at the heart of effective facilitation (action in the sense of exploring a whole new way of interpreting one's own work, personal relationships or political allegiances);
◆ facilitation aims to foster in adults a spirit of critical reflection;
◆ the aim of facilitation is the nurturing of self-directed, empowered adults.

(p. 185)

One of the ways in which TAs have learnt best over the years is by role modelling. Few TAs in the past went on courses, and few teachers ever directed their activities, so they watched and copied. Therefore, one useful in-house training method can be for a TA to watch a different teacher at work. In some schools this already happens because of the timetabling. If it doesn't then you can set it up. The old style 'open plan' schools used to offer lots of opportunities for getting ideas.

What turns such observation into a learning situation is not just setting it up but encouraging TAs to reflect on their observations. If you can create a climate of professional discussion about teaching methods or use of resources or behaviour management styles, without it being criticism, this can be invaluable.

School example

Three TAs from one school went on an OU STAC course where they had to be paired with TAs from other schools. They therefore went to three different schools in similar catchment areas and relatively close to their own school for five days, all different from their own. On returning to their own school they compared notes. The ways in which the schools were organised differed as well as the buildings, the systems of management and the resource usage, including the ways TAs were used. Such were their findings and their interest in how different schools went about teaching differently they discussed it with the head. At her request they attended a teaching staff meeting to share their observations. This resulted in some very interesting discussions for the school.

If it is not possible to observe and discuss practice with your own teachers then there is good video and DVD material available. Usually an LA adviser will have access to such material in a particular subject area, or a local training college might have a library of such material.

Having all staff become reflective practitioners is part of developing a learning school. Talking with each other, sharing ideas, commenting without being derogatory is so valuable and should be encouraged at every point. All staff should try to read something about their professional role regularly, if only skimming a magazine or a couple of websites. I have put a list of references for journals, websites and the subject associations at the end of the chapter. Regular meetings of TAs are essential for professional development to encourage just such discussion.

Figure 8.1 SENCO and HLTA

Meetings and opportunities for in-house professional development

You can use the *Good practice guide* (DfES 2000) Indicator 5 to find out whether TAs meet with other TAs for purposes of planning, problem solving and staff development, and Indicator 6 (p. 49) to find whether TAs are supported in relation to their induction, mentoring and development needs.

The *Good practice guide* also has paragraphs on holding meetings and sharing in its section called 'Creating partnership among teaching assistants' (DfES 2000: 31–3). Informal opportunities are not sufficient. More formal arrangements must be made particularly to encourage professional dialogue, for sharing information about pupils, the school and support groups; planning, problem solving and staff development.

Once the meetings become regular and the opportunities for gripes have been got out of the way, these meetings soon become opportunities for in-house professional development which can be led by different members of staff. HLTAs may do this or a different curriculum leader for a different subject of the SENCO or line manager. The opportunity for minor negative things to be said is important. As one head said 'if nobody says – you don't know!'.

Some useful topics for meetings that have been used by managers have been:

◆ any area of interest or concern raised by the TAs themselves;
◆ questioning – using video material of teachers in action;

Figure 8.2 The informal meeting over coffee between HLTA and TAs

◆ supporting IEPs and implementing other strategies to support those pupils with SEN;
◆ the value of play, hearing reading – using video material;
◆ using the materials from the LNS;
◆ using a visiting teacher, educational psychologist (EP), literacy or numeracy consultant, school adviser or therapist to explain parts of their work.

Your LA might have an adviser for TAs who could visit. Your School Development Adviser or School Improvement Partner might be available to give a session to TAs. The LA SEN advisers should help if your TAs are used for that purpose.

These advisers might have to charge for taking an in-house session for you. It is worth asking what advice is available in your local area, although usually this will now come at a price.

Tracey Brighton's HLTA project gives many reasons why such meetings can be valuable.

Case study

My investigation's key focus is communication, after my colleague and I had observed that many of our TAs work part-time and communication can sometimes prove difficult. Consequently some TAs are beginning to report a negative attitude towards their working environment with undue feelings of

- Exclusion
- Being undervalued
- Stress on both the TAs and teachers when messages have not been received

This research project gave me the opportunity to investigate and as a result I decided to set up a support group for TAs to provide regular opportunity for communication and training. I asked all TAs if they would be interested in supporting a group especially designed for themselves.

I discussed my idea of a support group with the Head Teacher, Deputy Head and the Senior Management Team.

I worked closely with Tina Casson (HLTA) to develop this idea in conjunction with the intranet facility for TAs that she is creating. I gave the TAs the opportunity to make comment through an evaluation. Time was allocated on two occasions to discuss and evaluate the case study with the Deputy Head. I have kept a record of the agendas prepared for the meetings together with TA evaluations in my HLTA portfolio.

With the Head Teacher I planned a suitable agenda for our first meeting on the September INSET morning and printed copies for the TAs. I sorted a date, time and place to carry out meetings.

I prepared letters informing TAs about the new 'TAgs' (Teaching Assistants' support group) group and informed the teaching staff at a staff meeting. I started my research by questioning the TAs about how they felt they were supported in our school and what could be done to improve it. The following feedback resulted.

- Lack of communication and often felt isolated
- Would like more training tailored to their needs
- No opportunity or time to share TA concerns

I put the same question to the teaching staff who also felt that communicating to all the TAs was often difficult.

I realised that there was a need in our school for the opportunity for all TA staff to meet on a regular basis and decided to set up a support group to meet this need. I discussed this with the Head Teacher and Deputy Head who both supported the idea and felt that it could also provide an opportunity for TA training sessions. The support group would be run in conjunction with the intranet facility for TAs set up by Tina, so we worked closely to develop ideas.

The remainder of my research involved organising a meeting time and place, planning an agenda for the first meeting and notifying TAs. Although still in the early stages, a regular support group (TAgs) has been set up.

There have been two meetings where the agenda has covered topics such as 'How a TA Can Support Their Teacher', 'First Aid and Medical Duties' and 'Instruction on the New Codes for Completing the Class Registers'.

Through the TAgs group TAs have also been instructed in how to find the new TAgs site on the school network, set up in conjunction with this research project by Tina Casson (HLTA).

Regular meetings are now to take place every half term – the next two already booked!

The Head Teacher asked me to share the TAgs initiative with the Senior Management Team and Tina reported successes at the staff meeting. Inset training commitments for TAs has begun to cause difficulty in finding an alternative date to hold TAgs meetings; however, negotiation with the Head Teacher to incorporate training within the TAgs meeting has solved the problem.

Sharing information during meetings has successfully resulted in guaranteeing all TAs are well informed and TAs have supported this success through their evaluations of the new TAgs group. Good ideas have been provided for future meetings by the TAs through their evaluations of the new support group. The TAgs group has provided an opportunity for regular training for TAs and at present this is the main focus of the group.

TAs have said they enjoy the new group, and I have already observed closer teamwork:

◆ TAs and teachers are working together outside their key stage to provide training on guided reading
◆ TAs are sharing problems – 'Can you help me log on to the computer?'
◆ TAs are helping each other sign up for courses

At present the TAgs meetings are providing opportunity to train TAs, however, to enable TAs to share concerns and feedback from staff meetings, I need to prepare a standard format for TAgs sessions to incorporate both training and any other issues. Many TAs have said they would prefer meetings to be in school hours and as a consequence one meeting per term will take place on inset days and the others during lunchtime. I need to discuss TA ideas for training with subject coordinators and the Head Teacher and prepare relevant training programmes.

Planned INSET

The training programme for the National Literacy Strategy (NLS) required attendance of the TAs at the in-house training and was undertaken willingly by the TAs, despite, in some instances, lack of payment for the time they attended. In the

Figure 8.3 The Feniton TA staff meeting held by the HLTAs

NNS, guidance was given in the training materials and the framework itself. TAs received their own copies of the guidance. 'Make sure that they know not only what the children are to do but what they are to learn', recognised that adults other than teachers could understand 'why' as well as 'what' they were doing (DfEE 1999). The additional booklets that appeared from time to time such as vocabulary lists are also useful for TAs.

Now the strategies are becoming history, but hopefully the tradition of including TAs in teachers' in-house training will not. How else will you get the consistency you want, the understanding of the subject matter, the professional dialogue about concerns over resources, which pupils might benefit and what the initiative means for the school? Hopefully, you have a climate in your school where a TA in a joint teacher/TA staff meeting can ask about what they don't understand without feeling stupid. Also, hopefully, there will be opportunities for TAs to ask for further help in areas the teachers find easy or obvious.

Other joint training areas

Behaviour management

There are some other areas where it is essential that staff are trained together. One of these is the principles and practice of behaviour management. When the DfEE/DfES Induction training included modules in this area in 2000, the teachers

Box 8.1 An example of a planned INSET programme in Whipton Barton Junior School

Teaching Assistants Training Timetable

Friday December 1st	9.00 – 4.00 First Aid Training – Infants School Chris Conibere Sophie Mynors Hayley Ford Carolyne Malpass
Tuesday December 5th	10.10 – 11.10 Clicker Training – Computer Room With Pauline Gulliver All TAs
Wednesday December 6th	10.10 – 11.10 Assessment Training – In Staff Room with Dawn Hallett All TAs
Tuesday December 12th	10.45 – 11.10 Speech Therapy With Kelly Redding All TAs
Tuesday January 30th	10.10 – 11.10 Mental Health Support Training with Pauline Simpson All TAs
Tuesday February 13th	10.10 – 11.10 SEAL/Behaviour Management Training with Graham Fisher and Judith Dunn All TAs
Tuesday February 27th	10.10 – 11.10 SEAL/Behaviour Management Training with Graham Fisher and Judith Dunn All TAs
Tuesday March 13th	10.10 – 11.10 SEAL/Behaviour Management Training with Graham Fisher and Judith Dunn All TAs
Tuesday March 27th	10.10 – 11.10 SEAL/Behaviour Management Training with Graham Fisher and Judith Dunn All TAs

in many schools had not had similar training. Now, thankfully, this is an area most schools cover with all the relevant staff – the TAs and the MDAs.

School examples

At a meeting with the TAs and MDAs of a school to provide some behaviour management training, they shared a problem which is possibly not uncommon, 'How can we stop a child sliding down the banisters, when the deputy head does not stop them?'. When I shared this concern with the head, it turned out he was having a general problem with that member of staff.

Another school had not only sent all their staff together to cluster training days given by Bill Rogers, but had had him as a regular visitor to the school. He showed by example how children can be treated positively yet firmly, as well as taking whole-school INSET sessions. After several years, all the staff had developed this way of talking to children with some remarkable results. The school was in a deprived area, where social skills were often lacking at home, and any consistent discipline also lacking. Five-year-olds could be found on the street alone at night in that area of the town. The head reckoned the attitudes were beginning to rub off on the parents as well. This school not only achieved high levels of behaviour but the children did well academically, and were keen learners.

Safeguarding children

It is vital that Child Protection training should take place for all staff. This should be done in the context of the ECM agenda so that keeping children safe is discussed as well as the negative and emotive areas of child protection issues. The school must have clear child protection policies which are agreed by the governors and known to the parents. There are two aspect to this: (1) how to deal with a child or pupils who reveals information; and (2) protection of staff against false allegations. TAs are particularly likely to be the ones to whom pupils reveal, along with other support staff such as MDAs, as they work so often with individuals or small groups. These are the staff with whom individual children can make close relationships, often talking about home or leisure situations. The TAs often help small or physically impaired pupils change their clothes and may see body marks, or recognise emotional distress. All staff must know about not questioning such pupils but providing a listening ear. They need to know what is important and what not, which member of staff is the Designated Officer to deal with incidents, and the whereabouts of the LA guidance. All staff need guidance on when to touch or comfort is appropriate for younger or vulnerable pupils and how to help in intimate situations, such as changing wet or soiled clothing. If restraint is to be allowed, training in proper procedures is essential.

Other joint areas of concern

First aid training is another very useful whole-staff training session. It does a lot for team work, developing a sense of humour and morale when the elegant female school secretary has to settle the 'hunky' male physical education (PE) teacher in the recovery position, or the deputy head has to bandage the site manager.

Any school briefings given in the areas of equal opportunities, celebrating multiculturalism and/or developing strategies to support pupils with EAL and their families, should also be for all staff, not just the teachers.

Cascading

One of the problems in any school is the cascade model of in-service, where only limited numbers of staff go off site to 'receive the message' and then have to come back to inform or train other staff. You need a system whereby all staff attending courses feed back in some way. The TAs, particularly, need to feed back about the ways in which they are being trained, otherwise the teaching staff do not know what their TA is capable of. Where the TAs have been asked to take part in a staff meeting and tell the teachers what they were studying, it boosts their own confidence as well as exchanging information. Now teams of TAs are often represented at teaching staff meetings by a senior TA or HLTA, the cascading is done within the TA team. This method does sometimes mean that the messenger inadvertently changes the message because they have not understood, or they leave out bits, so it is worth keeping an eye on the system.

Use of ICT

Many schools now have internal networking with computers in every room, ICT suites, staffroom computers for support staff, teacher laptops and interactive whiteboards. With the network set up with a password system, the system becomes an intranet. The potential of such systems for professional development for TAs is enormous, their only problem is access to a computer. Few TAs have laptops although some HLTAs do. Communication systems using a staffroom computer are more reliant on proactive logging in than a personal system because of the physical effort involved. Nevertheless, available on the school intranet will be plans, schemes of work, pupils' assessment details and SEN, subject plans, resources and communication notices of many kinds. This area is probably in its infancy for TAs.

This is a description from Tina Casson's HLTA project

Case study

In conjunction with Tracey Brighton (see her case study, p. 133) I decided to look at ways to improve communication within the school for the TAs. My focus was the setting up of an area on the school computer network specifically for the TAs. My intention was that it would include relevant information that had been brought up at staff meetings, important dates for their diaries, training opportunities and a forum where they could raise questions or issues that others might find interesting or be able to offer help and guidance on. I hoped by doing this it would give the TAs a central point which they could access easily that provided both information and help. I also hoped that it would bring the TA team closer and give them an opportunity to share their knowledge with others.

Together with Tracey we took our ideas to the Headteacher to find out whether he felt it would be useful. I also discussed the idea with members of the teaching staff. I discussed the outline of the project and asked for their permission to share e-mail addresses. I decided to allocate an area on the network that is easily accessible and could be viewed by all TAs and teaching staff. I confirmed this would be acceptable with the ICT co-ordinator.

I prepared written instructions on how to find the site. I set up the TAGS area on the school network in time for the beginning of the new school year. Tracey and I then had a meeting with all the TAs during the INSET day where we told them our plans and showed them where to find the site. We decided to give it a name and chose TAGS.

I gave a set of clear written step-by-step instructions on how to find the site to each TA. I hoped this would help those less confident with IT. I told all the teaching staff about the site at a staff meeting and invited them to add any information they felt would be of use to the TAs. Each week I updated the site with the latest information, I felt this was vital to keep the TAs aware of current issues and to stop the site becoming 'stagnant'.

Off-site training

Visiting other schools

Local cluster groups have started up in some places, where the heads have supported meetings in their schools. The TAs visit each school in the cluster in turn, say once a term, talk to each other and about their schools, and may have visiting speakers. Some schools' cluster INSET days have special sessions for their TAs, as well as MDAs, caretakers and so on. TAs who work with children with SEN can visit special schools to watch TAs and teachers who work with children with more profound conditions than those they work with. If there are specialist schools, say for autism, it would be worth not only visiting these but setting up ways of keeping in regular contact to discuss problems and share ideas. Hospital schools might help TAs who deal with physical problems, hearing impaired units help with the problems of deafness.

Courses

Most authorities run short or one-day courses in special areas for TAs. These may be about curricular areas or SEN or EAL concerns. Courses to promote the strategy support materials have been common and useful. All courses provide an opportunity for TAs to meet, share, discuss and extend their learning.

Long courses are usually accredited in some way and certainly will have a cost implication – for cover for the TA when absent if nothing else. But, as one head said to me when describing how he justified funding various courses for his support staff, 'Give a little – get a lot'. He felt identifying training needs and enabling the TAs to develop had unlocked potential. One of his LSAs was doing a foundation degree for which the school paid, and two others were being assessed for the HLTA status.

Funding

Funding has been an issue for the TAs, being so poorly paid, and realising no amount of training or qualifications would change their rate of pay. There is a difficulty here. Teachers might choose to undertake an OU degree or further study not required by the school. They would fund this but they do earn more than TAs. Sometimes a TA will fund their own course, some can be funded by the school professional development budget and others are sometimes free, being funded through the LA from designated funds. But, of course, funding for TAs does not stop at fees. TAs are often required to attend in their own time, not paid time. They might not have access to a car, or access to the family car means expenditure or inconvenience to other members of the family. Public transport is not an option in rural areas as it rarely provides something in the right direction at the right time. Some schools do recognise all the above and make efforts to provide additional support to enable the TAs to go to off-site training, knowing the school and pupils will benefit as well as the TA. If you feel this is not possible you do need to explain this to the TA and a welcome gesture would be for you to provide paper, files, set books or other materials suggested by the courses, none of which cost a great deal, but show an interest and support of the TAs' training.

Courses put on by local Further Education (FE) and Higher Education (HE) colleges and universities will attract funding through the LSC or equivalent. Thus, the real cost of such courses as they appear in the handbooks is already subsidised. It is possibly worth considering local sources of funding: charities, industries or businesses who might see bursaries as a way of supporting local communities. Such activity can be time consuming for you, but can build up useful local contacts. TAs should be paid for their time if they would normally be working, and you could consider helping with travelling expenses. Where schools are 'growing their own', governors are usually only too supportive of providing such finance.

You could consider releasing a teacher to accompany the TA but of course the cost would be high. If joint TA and teacher courses are available, despite the initial cost, they are very cost effective because immediately each member of the partnership knows what the other has heard or done and the subsequent debate about which bits are relevant to the school and their situation is not only helpful but also builds the relationship. Sometimes such a joint course may need mentor release time and paid time for the TA to complete tasks for the course back at the school. All the TA courses will demand some TA participation, observation and recording of school activities. TAs need access and time to do these. Often the cost of back-up activities comes to the school in the guise of a small grant that can be used for coursework on site.

Qualifications and experience

Whatever award or course your TAs undertake, you as manager should try to make contact with the college, provider or course tutor. All courses will have an element of school-based work in them, carrying out activities or observations. Not all colleges are good at liaising with host schools and providing them with details, largely because of the time/cost implications for them. Some are not very good at backing up the student's work or taking into account the local circumstances. If you and the TA are to make the most of any training, it should be a joint effort.

A lot of the following information is taken directly from the TDA website, which is the best source of further information. The website has links to the various organisations mentioned.

I assume that all your TAs whom you have reviewed will have undergone some kind of induction process and many of them completed the DfES Induction course. If you have an apprentice TA, they will already be into the NVQ route of development. You then have to consider with them at what level they might be ready for further external qualifications if that is what they are looking for. The NOS are based on the National Qualification Framework (NQF) proposed by the Qualifications and Curriculum Authority (QCA) – see Table 8.1. For a full list of all accredited qualifications in the NQF, please visit the National Database of Accredited Qualifications at www.accredited qualifications.org.uk.

A Career Development Framework for school support staff is available from the TDA which gives a lot of detail about the various possible routes, standards, qualifications programmes and links (TDA 2005). It is a document that will date, so needs to be checked for changes.

NOS are drawn up by the National Training Organisation (NTO) to reflect the expertise and interest in the particular occupation under scrutiny. The NOS are then used by the QCA to regulate any awards in the occupational area including NVQs, and can be used in personnel discussions with employers and unions. For TAs, the original NTO was the Local Government NTO (LGNTO), it is now the TDA. The NOS and, subsequently, any approved NVQs, are organised in levels to correspond with traditional levels of qualifications to fit in with the NQF.

The LSC or equivalent funds courses and testing procedures for any adult wishing to avail themselves, generally operating through Further and Adult Education Colleges.

Table 8.1 The National Qualifications Framework

National Qualifications Framework(NQF)		Framework for Higher Education Qualifications (FHEQ)
Previous levels	*Current levels*	*Levels and Examples*
Level 5	Level 8	D (doctoral) Doctorates
	Level 7	M (masters) Master's degrees, postgraduate certificates and diplomas
Level 4	Level 6	H (honours) Bachelor degrees, graduate certificates and diplomas
	Level 5	I (intermediate) Diplomas of HE and FE, foundation degrees and higher national diplomas
	Level 4	C (certificate) Certificates of HE
Level 3 A levels		
Level 2 GCSEs Grades A*–C		
Level 1 GCSEs Grades D–G		
Entry level		

The current NOS for TAs only cover levels 2 and 3 and use 42 and 111 pages respectively to describe them. The updated version (TDA 2007c) uses 102 and 292 pages respectively. Coming into effect from September 2008, they can be found on the www.uk.standards.org website. The units list performance indicators and knowledge base of all aspects of a role. The scope of the indicators is also determined. If a TA undertakes assessment against these standards, each and every indicator has to be assessed in some way, by observation, assignments, witness statements or some other means.

It is not possible to use a tick sheet of these competences, even in a tabular form, for observation purposes, as TAs do not show all that they are capable of in half an hour. This is also true for the HLTA assessment and is the reason direct observation of the HLTA by an assessor is not part of the process. As level 2 shows a comprehensive coverage of what a competent TA can do, it is obvious beginner TAs will not have achieved this level. Job evaluation and the support staff guidance notes also use the levels of the NQF.

Levels 2 and 3

NVQs at levels 2 and 3 for TAs are now widespread and much better understood. These qualifications are specifically for TAs, and are designed to assess how skills and knowledge are applied to real work practices, using evidence from work situations. The TA needs to be in a TA post that includes the required range of responsibilities or can be adapted to do so. Level 2 is suitable for people new to the role or whose responsibilities are limited in scope; level 3 is suitable for experienced TAs whose working role calls for competence across a varied range of responsibilities. The beauty of NVQs is that TAs can work at them at their own pace, working on just one unit at a time if they choose. They will need a mentor within school and will use previous learning and experience in school as evidence. They might also need some external training to cover the knowledge requirements. Some colleges offer these qualifications through a taught route, getting the evidence from assignments and witness statements. This is not the intention. TAs should be assessed by as much direct observation and interview as possible by qualified assessors. More and more schools now recognise this internal assessment process, and line managers are much happier in undertaking the task and getting the assessor qualification, and the school recognises the value of developing staff in-house. The assessor qualification is also based on a competence model, with observation and interviewing as they do the job. To undertake this you have to have occupational competence and be registered with an assessment centre. Some LAs operate as assessment centres for this purpose. This totally in-house assessment process does away with any need for peripatetic assessors and, thus, a lot of the cost. Secondary schools have been aware of this type of assessment for years, in connection with the GNVQ (General NVQ) courses they offer.

NVQs are based on NOS, which are the nationally agreed set of competences for specific roles at specific levels. There are some awarding bodies that offer qualifications which are not called NVQs but are also matched to the standards and so are levelled and nationally recognised awards. The awarding bodies are CACHE, Edexcel, OCR, and City and Guilds. Links to their sites are available on the TDA website and their websites are listed at the end of the chapter.

Level 2

These awards are intended for people who are looking for recognition of a basic level of competence. Intellectually and on the NQF they are equivalent in level to GCSEs. Currently, you have to achieve seven units of competence from the NOS. There are four mandatory units and you can choose three more from the optional list.

Mandatory units
2–1 Help with classroom resources and records
2–2 Help with the care and support of pupils
2–3 Provide support for learning activities
2–4 Provide effective support for your colleagues

Optional units
2–5 Support literacy and numeracy activities in the classroom
3–1 Contribute to the management of pupil behaviour
3–10 Support the maintenance of pupil safety and security
3–11 Contribute to the health and well-being of pupils
3–17 Support the use of ICT in the classroom

Level 3

A level 3 qualification equates to 'A' levels and so is intended for experienced assistants. For a level 3 qualification, currently you have to achieve 10 units of competence from the national occupational standards. There are four mandatory units, and you will also pick six from the optional list, spread across the range of categories.

Mandatory units
3–1 Contribute to the management of pupil behaviour
3–2 Establish and maintain relationships with individual pupils and groups
3–3 Support pupils during learning activities
3–4 Review and develop your own professional practice

Optional units
Select six units from the following options: one unit from each of sets A, B, C and D, plus any two others.

Set A
3–5 Assist in preparing and maintaining the learning environment
3–6 Contribute to maintaining pupil records
3–7 Observe and report on pupil performance
3–8 Contribute to the planning and evaluation of learning activities

Set B
3–9 Promote pupils' social and emotional development
3–10 Support the maintenance of pupil safety and security
3–11 Contribute to the health and well-being of pupils
3–12 Provide support for bilingual/multilingual pupils
3–13 Support pupils with communication and interaction difficulties

3–14 Support pupils with cognition and learning difficulties
3–15 Support pupils with behavioural, emotional and social development needs
3–16 Provide support for pupils with sensory and/or physical impairment

Set C
3–17 Support the use of ICT in the classroom
3–18 Help pupils to develop their literacy skills
3–19 Help pupils to develop their numeracy skills
3–20 Help pupils to access the curriculum

Set D
3–21 Support the development and effectiveness of work teams
3–22 Develop and maintain working relationships with other professionals

A list of the new units of the NOS for use from September 2008 can be found in Appendix 1.

There are a few Specialist Teaching Assistant courses accredited by the universities which might attract credit points towards their foundation degrees. You or the TAs will have to investigate local possibilities regarding these courses.

HLTA status

This is a process of recognition intended to accredit those TAs who have a lot of experience. The original standards were drawn up with the intention of recognising people working at the equivalent of a second year degree level, (Level 5 on the NQF) who had never had the opportunity of achieving conventional qualifications, and who, by virtue of their more mature years would probably refuse to undertake such a course and all the preliminary qualifications that might prove essential. Some say it was a devious route to teachers on the cheap, but it has served to recognise the large group of people working at a higher level in schools who were without any previous recognition. The difficulty for some TAs has been the completion of the paperwork, for it was not designed to rubber stamp years of service but to be a rigorous and worthwhile status to achieve. So, the three-day assessment training was introduced.

For some, there is a wish to attain the standards but there are bits of experience missing, so various training routes, usually modular in nature are on offer. There is still funding available for the process through the LA. The training needs of a potential candidate will be assessed by the LA in consultation with your school. Some of the providers have on-line needs analysis tools which are worth exploring. The so-called National Association for Professional Teaching Assistants (NAPTA) is not a national association but an outlet for Pearson Educational to market a needs analysis tool to ascertain at which level the TAs need training. It is available through some LAs or their website.

There are potentially four steps to achieving HLTA status, which are: applying for funding, training, preparation for assessment and assessment. It is a status not a qualification. People interested in it have to be assessed against the standards. These standards can be downloaded from the TDA website with notes on terminology or a simple list can be found in Appendix 2. Before applying for funding, it is worth reading through the 'Literacy and numeracy requirements' section where the details of the level 2 qualifications required are detailed. There has been some difficulty in verifying old qualifications because of the changes in examination boards over the years. The word 'training' is misleading as the basic three-day course available is training for assessment not for becoming an HLTA. The demand for the 'assessment only' route is likely to decrease as the need for training to actually do the job becomes more obvious, the most experienced TAs having been assessed in the first years of the initiative.

Your regional provider of assessment (RPA) or LA will have details of training in your area. Contact details are available in the 'LA and RPA contacts' section of the TDA website.

Preparation for assessment involves:

◆ making sure of understanding of the professional standards and how they relate to work in school;
◆ preparing for the four assessment tasks, which are used to record achievement against the standards;
◆ receiving formative feedback on the assessment tasks; and
◆ preparing for the visit to the school by an assessor.

Assessment involves a half-day visit to your school by an assessor approved by your RPA, during which evidence on how the TA meets the standards will be assessed.

The school visit enables the TA to:

◆ explain in more detail the activities they have used as evidence in the assessment tasks;
◆ make available the documentary and oral evidence that supports these assessment tasks;
◆ have the evidence verified by the headteacher (or representative) and class teacher(s).

At the end of the visit the assessor will reach a conclusion as to whether the standards have been met, which will be verified by your RPA who will normally notify the outcome within eight weeks of the school visit. It is very important that you as a manager understand this process in order to support your TA, and can give informed evidence at the school visit time. This is also true for the teacher(s) involved.

Foundation degrees

Foundation degrees are HE qualifications at level 5 of the NQF. They are available in a wide range of subjects, but there are some specifically designed for support staff including degrees in classroom support, learning support and Early Years. A foundation degree can act as a stepping stone to a full honours degree or other professional qualification. Colleges and universities decide their own entry requirements and you might find that experience is as relevant as previous educational qualifications. The pattern of study and time taken to complete the qualification vary from one course to another. For a full list of providers and their foundation degree subjects, see the UCAS website. Alternatively, go to the DfES foundation degrees site.

The school workforce development board

The school workforce development board (SWDB) is the sector-wide body concerned with training and developing the wider workforce. Chaired by the TDA, the SWDB was established in the autumn of 2004 to guide the TDA's work on training and development for support staff. The SWDB consists of representatives from the national bodies most closely involved in funding, promoting learning and skills, and providing training for school support staff.

The SWDB consists of:

◆ the Department for Education and Skills (now DCFS);
◆ the Employers' Organisation for local government;
◆ the LSC;
◆ the National College for School Leadership;
◆ the National Strategies;
◆ the national support staff Centre of Vocational Excellence;
◆ Ofsted;
◆ the QCA; and
◆ the Workforce Agreement Monitoring Group (WAMG, which includes workforce unions).

They identified three early priorities for school support staff:

◆ remove barriers, for example by providing better access to training and development information and by helping schools to access funding;
◆ improve supply, for example by ensuring support staff have the training they need, when and where they need it; and
◆ strengthen quality, for example by developing a framework of skills and competences for each school occupation and by finding ways to increase the impact of training and development on day-to-day practice.

Routes to teaching

Again this is best investigated by going into the TDA website and following routes to 'Get into teaching'.

The range of different initial teacher training (ITT) courses and programmes available is designed to provide something for everyone, whatever your circumstances, qualifications, experience or preferences.

All programmes lead to QTS which is a requirement to teaching in state-maintained schools.

Programme type	Course type	Abbreviation
Undergraduate	Bachelor of education	BEd
	Bachelor of arts/science with qualified teacher status	BA/BSc with QTS
Postgraduate	Postgraduate Certificate of Education	PGCE
	Teach First	Teach First
	School centred initial teacher training	SCITT

| Employment based | Graduate Teacher Programme | GTP |
| | Registered Teacher Programme | RTP |

Self-study for TAs and their line managers

TAs may find it hard to read much outside school because of the family commitment that so many have, but will appreciate ideas.

Handouts from courses are usually helpful and stimulating. Some TAs try out the TES in the staffroom, and there is a relatively new magazine just for TAs in primary schools called *Learning Support*. The magazines in the Scholastic series (*Junior Education*, *Child Education*) are also designed for those working in primary schools. Secondary TAs would find the journals from the subject associations interesting.

Magazine subscription details can be found at www.learningsupport.co.uk and www.scholastic.co.uk, and www.subjectassociation.org.uk will give you the website addresses of the individual subject associations.

Books for and about TA practice are much more numerous than they were. Again the David Fulton Publishers (Routledge) list carries maybe a dozen or so depending on the area of interest and level of the TA. Fox (1998) and Watkinson (2002a) are useful for TAs at the beginning of their career. Watkinson (2003b and 2003c) are for level 2 and level 3 respectively, and Watkinson (2005 and 2006) are for HLTAs. Bold (2004), Alfrey (2004), Cable and Eyres (2005), Hancock and Collins (2005) and Tyrer *et al.* (2004) are designed for use by those studying a foundation degree. Hryniewicz (2004) claims to be the complete TA handbook.

Selected sections from Pollard's reflective teaching books (Pollard 2002a, 2002b), a few straightforward teaching text books: Kyriacou (1997, 1998), Wragg (1994), Wragg and Brown (1993), E. Dunne and Bennett (1994), R. Dunne and Wragg (1994), Brown and Wragg (1993) and any teacher's handbooks to a set book series would all give further study reading for TAs. Any of the David Fulton Publishers (Routledge) titles on dealing with particular SEN problems could be very helpful.

Leaders and managers might like to dip into:

◆ *Effective in-class support* (Lorenz 1998)
◆ *Help in the classroom* (Balshaw 1991)
◆ *Teaching assistants – practical strategies for effective classroom support* (Balshaw and Farrell 2002)
◆ *Working with support staff* (Kerry 2001)
◆ *Teachers and assistants working together* (Vincett *et al.* 2005)
◆ *Working with support in the classroom* (Campbell and Fairbairn 2005)
◆ *How to support and manage teaching assistants* (Birkett 2004)
◆ *Appointing and managing learning support assistants* (George and Hunt 2003)

Useful websites for TAs could be:

◆ www.TDA.gov.uk
◆ www.DCFS.gov.uk/standards or /strategies
◆ www.teachernet.gov.uk

Examination boards:

◆ www.cache.org.uk
◆ www.cityandguilds.com
◆ www.edexcel.org.uk
◆ www.ocr.org.uk

The National Database of Accredited Qualifications can be found at www.accreditedqualifications.org.uk, and information about the location of foundation degrees at www.ucas.com.

Chapter 9

Good practice in appointing and developing TAs

Assuming you are in a financial position to appoint new staff, either through an increase in budget provision, or a decision taken as the result of some audits of needs or to replace someone who has resigned, you have several options.

Apprenticeships

These are designed for young people under 25 years old who want to make their way through a workplace-based route. You would probably need to be able to guarantee them a job for a certain number of years but places are funded through the LSC. Apprenticeships offer a programme of work-related training and education that covers key skills, plus NVQs at level 2 or 3. They provide a mixture of work-based and off-site learning at two levels: apprentice and advanced apprentice. At the end of an apprenticeship, a person would have:

◆ an NVQ at level 2 for the apprenticeship or level 3 for the advanced apprenticeship;
◆ key skills qualifications in communication, application of number and, usually, information technology; and
◆ a technical certificate at level 2 for the apprenticeship and level 3 for the advanced apprenticeship.

An apprentice can gain the NVQ through on-the-job training and assessment, whereas the programme leading to the technical certificate is taught off-site and provides knowledge and understanding that supports the NVQ. Whether they start at level 2 or level 3 depends on their level of ability and current job. If they start at level 2 they can still progress from an apprenticeship to an advanced apprenticeship. From there, a foundation degree could be the logical next step.

The LSC apprenticeships site does not offer much more information than I have given so I advise you to contact the TDA or your local LSC office direct if you are interested in this kind of employment. I have not come across a school with such an apprentice. I am assured they exist, but I cannot comment on the efficacy of this route.

Pre-employment access courses

These are a relatively recent phenomenon. They can be run by the school – usually a larger secondary school – or the LA. They offer sessions about the job and, usually, an opportunity to listen to experienced TAs describe the jobs – the joys and pitfalls. When they can be run in the school, they usually link with an opportunity to 'be a TA for a day' as a volunteer, provided they do not work directly with the pupils but merely shadow an existing TA in the school. They will not be checked by the Criminal Records Bureau (CRB) to work with children (includes all pupils up to 18 years old). This process means that those who then go on to apply for jobs do so with their eyes open and an understanding of the kinds of things they are letting themselves in for. Devon has developed an access course for TAs enabling them to familiarise themselves with the TA role before applying to a school.

Just having a pre-advertisement 'open house' time to allow potential TAs to see what goes on in school can help both them and you see whether they would fit into your way of working. Outsiders, even parents, do not always understand the demands of working in schools. This is particularly true if you work in secondary schools. Parents do still volunteer to work in primary schools, if in fewer numbers, but this is rare in secondary schools.

Outward-going characteristics must be considered by those appointing. One teacher can appreciate a TA's initiative, but another can feel threatened or resentful. Boundaries need to be established both by the school and individual teachers.

School examples

One secondary school runs a pre-induction access course over five mornings. They have various inputs about:

◆   the way the school supports SEN;
◆   the SEN Code of Practice and the four areas of need;
◆   how needs are identified and tracked;
◆   outside agencies involved;
◆   levels and methods of support;
◆   the roles of TAs and their support in the school;
◆   the team structure within the school.

The potential TAs then have an hour shadowing. They find the difference when interviewing later between those who attended and those who did not is very clear. They also will say 'this isn't for me' or 'I think I'll go to primary'.

One primary school invites potential TAs to the school for four days. They give them lots of little jobs in different parts of the school. There is no interview attached. They find the process does show up some inadequacies and limitations on both sides so that when formal advertisements go out, people applying know what is involved.

One head suggested that the TAs and the schools now recognise that TAs need to be trained before they start the job. Her local FE College was running a Level 2 course and had many people applying. Part of their course may include some kind of placement or visits to local schools.

The recruitment process

'The recruitment of staff is one of the most important management activities and it is therefore worth investing more care and time to select the best' (Brighouse and Woods 1999: 116). The appointment of support staff is no less important than that of teaching staff, although in the past it has followed a rather informal and ad hoc route. There is a need for properly instituted procedures to make things open, equitable and fair, and to provide the best possible staff for the education of the children. Whatever recruitment procedures the school has in place for teachers should apply to all staff. Even if you think there is a person within the existing staff who might like the job you have on offer, and be suitable, it is best practice to go through open procedures. You can ring fence appointments internally to start with if you wish. You would then only advertise in the staff circular or on the staff notice board.

THINKING POINTS

Things to consider

What is it you want from this recruit: purpose, length of time, level of competence, experience, etc.?
Where this appointment sits in the school development plan.
What do relevant staff consider important?: senior staff and the teacher(s) who will be working with the potential candidate; the rest of the TA team; the personnel/people-related governor committee or members of the governing body delegated to deal with staffing matters.

You could discuss the role with advisers outside the school: SEN, Early Years, curriculum, behaviour management, general school, Personnel/Human Resources departments.

Decide what will be the line management of this recruit.
Consider what the future opportunities are for this person within the school.
Think about the implications for other staff in the school, your training programme and domestic facilities.

Then, decide on a job description and a person specification, including qualifications, experience, type of contract and pay scale to be offered.
Advertise appropriately – consider parents' magazines or newsletters, community newsletters or local papers, the local LA staffing circular.
Decide on the wording of the advert to reflect your needs and the ethos of the school.
Decide the time, place and nature of the selection process.
Will it just be a simple interview? What questions do you need to ask?
Prepare a simple pack for the administrative staff to send to applicants, with some details of the school, the job description and person specification.

Shortlist with a senior member of staff or a relevant teacher, and an appropriate governor. The support staff governor should not be involved in case the appointment would affect their status. Send for references, considering them at an agreed point within the process.

Meet them informally beforehand if possible to answer their questions and enable them to be shown round the school if they have not been before.

Interview as for any other member of staff, remembering all the equal opportunities issues and answering their questions.

Discuss and agree a successful candidate with panel. Notify successful and unsuccessful candidates.

Prepare an induction programme.

School example

A special school head described his procedures. He puts an advertisement in the local paper with a telephone number that people can ring to come and visit. They then have to submit a letter of application, a CV and make the visit. He shortlists from these and sends out the job specification and application forms. The headteacher, deputy and a governor interview.

They are looking for passion, drive, determination and commitment; personal qualities not qualifications.

The person specification

With personality and competence so important in the work of a TA, the appointment process for them is crucial. You will know what kind of personality will fit into your existing teams, both whole-school and TA teams, and can define the qualifications and experience. While you should not just appoint a good volunteer informally, you could put 'volunteer experience desired' in your advertisement. The person specification is a set of criteria against which each candidate can be matched and, if desired, scored. Each characteristic can be marked E or D – essential or desirable, and can cover the experience, knowledge, skills, qualifications and personal qualities which would ideally fit the needs of the school.

Entry level

As induction levels are not defined in the NOS, there is no national guidance about the basic levels expected of a person who can be employed in a school. All potential employees are subject to checks of: identity, academic qualifications, references, employment history, CRB and health checks. Information on employing and recruiting staff are in DfES guidance *Safeguarding children and safer recruitment in education* which came into force on 1 January 2007 (DfES 2006c). They were developed because of the distressing cases involving child protection cases and school support staff. The ECM developments are also instrumental in bringing about concerns. These guidelines should be followed in all cases.

You might find the following list of qualities useful. It was part of the proposal put forward for an orientation programme during the consultation for the qualification framework for those working in the Early Years sector (QCA 1998). It is still a useful list to use when considering basic level entry to being a TA.

Essential criteria for suitable personal characteristics of candidates

◆ ability to relate to children; warmth
◆ potential to change attitudes and question own values; respect for differences amongst people
◆ willingness to learn and evaluate own practice
◆ commitment to complete training and assessment and to sustain work/ training programme including assignments and other set course work
◆ personal maturity appropriate to the age of the applicant; not seeking to work with children in order to meet own emotional needs
◆ ability to assess situations and know own limitations; willingness to seek advice/support
◆ ability to remain calm under pressure or in crisis/emergency
◆ understands the physical requirements of working with young children (or pupils of age of institution)
◆ enthusiastic
◆ good timekeeping
◆ potential to develop the ability to prioritise and judge relative significance of conflicting demands
◆ anti-discriminatory attitudes, awareness of prejudice.

(p. 33)

'School support staff: the way forward' (NJC 2003) suggests the following for a level 1, but whether these are qualities to look for or items to be included in a JD is not entirely clear.

Experience:
◆ working or caring for children of the relevant age

Qualifications:
◆ good numeracy/literacy skills
◆ completion of the DfES Teacher Assistant Induction Programme
◆ participate in development and training opportunities

Knowledge/skills:
◆ appropriate knowledge of first aid
◆ use basic technology – computer/video/photocopier
◆ ability to relate well to children and adults
◆ work constructively as part of a team, understand classroom roles and responsibilities and your own position within these.

For higher levels you could refer to this document or even the NOS, but these latter are rather detailed. You must also decide whether any particular qualifications are required. These could be in the SEN area, for instance – a qualification in signing or dealing with a particular disability.

HLTA standards include the necessity of having a level 2 qualification in English and mathematics. It is arguable that this kind of level of competence, basic literacy and numeracy, should be required of anyone working with pupils in class. It would be really good if all aspiring TAs would consider this. If you are involved with access courses of the kind just described, then do recommend aspiring TAs to think about this. There is plenty of support available to help people get up to level 2 in literacy and numeracy. Local colleges and training centres offer funded level 2 training and qualifications in mathematics and English. The *Move on* website (www.move-on.org.uk) offers a free skills check, a free brush-up course for the literacy and numeracy skills needed to pass the national level 2 tests, and a list of local centres.

The job description

It is not easy to give an exemplar JD given the diversity of role of the TA, and each member of staff may need a different one. It is usual for TAs' JDs to follow the practice of having general, generic and specific sections. Use 'School support staff – the way forward' (NJC 2003) for more detailed suggestions. Consider each of the four strands – pupils, teacher, curriculum and school – when formulating job descriptions and be sure to add in what support the school intends to provide and the supervision arrangements for whole-class cover time. While some exemplars are given in the list below, they cover a range of levels of expectations. The JD should clearly reflect the level at which the TA is expected to work, which is also reflected in the appropriate pay scale for the job being described. The following headings would not suit any one TA. The items in quotes would need to be replaced by names.

THINKING POINTS

Some examples of descriptions for each area:
Main purpose of the job:
Duties and responsibilities:

Support for pupils:
◆ Develop an understanding of the range of learning support needs for 'a named pupil'
◆ To meet the child's physical needs as required by the IEP
◆ To reinforce the pupil's self-esteem and promote independence
◆ To implement a 'named programme'

Support for teachers:
◆ To provide practical support to 'named class teachers'
◆ To participate in specified planning time and provide feedback about the pupils to the teacher(s)

- ◆ To contribute to the maintenance of pupils progress records
- ◆ To liaise with 'named agencies'
- ◆ To support 'named teacher(s)' while they take PPA time
- ◆ To provide emergency cover for 'specific classes' when requested
- ◆ To manage particular resources
- ◆ To support a 'named teacher' (e.g. SENCO) in their work

Support for the curriculum:
- ◆ To deliver a 'particular booster programme'
- ◆ To select and prepare resources for pupils for whom English is an additional language
- ◆ To attend relevant in-service training
- ◆ To understand and adhere to relevant school policies and procedures
- ◆ To be included in the staff development programme

Support for the school:
- ◆ To work with parents
- ◆ To maintain particular databases
- ◆ To understand school policies in relation to 'named subjects'
- ◆ To observe pupils' learning in 'named subjects'
- ◆ To take responsibility for the maintenance of 'named resources' (e.g. library)

Management responsibilities for a team of TAs

Support to be provided by the school:
- ◆ Annual review of job description through performance review
- ◆ Opportunities for career development
- ◆ Access to all relevant documentation
- ◆ Provision of mentor and line manager support.

Supervision arrangements:
- ◆ Line management including performance review by 'named teacher'
- ◆ Any class teaching will be done under the supervision of the responsible class teacher
- ◆ Meeting arrangements
- ◆ Class teacher planning and feedback times

(adapted from Watkinson 2003a: 101, 102)

The JD changes with time – hence the need for constant review along with performance review. Specific tasks could include anything from making the tea/coffee, carrying out photocopying, maintaining the CD/DVD library, timetabling the TA team, to particular support for a particular pupil which might entail specific training. Whether or not the TA is to undertake whole-class supervision, act as supply cover, or undertake other specific tasks traditionally carried out by teachers must be specifically spelt out and the supervision arrangements to match indicated. All JDs should be drawn up with the agreement of the person who is going to carry out the job or they can be meaningless, and in the case of TAs it surely makes sense that the teachers or agencies named both be consulted and given a copy of the JD. They then know what their responsibilities are as well as what they can expect the TA to do.

School example

Many schools were kind enough to let me have copies of their job descriptions. They are not reproduced in this book because they were rightly so idiosyncratic to the needs of the schools and the particular job. The diversity reflected the thought that had gone into trying to define what the job was and hence the need of each school to draft their own for their own circumstances.

Advertising and interviewing

After making the decisions regarding a potential new employee, the procedures are identical to those for any other member of staff.

Do remember in interviewing, appointing successful people for the job, or debriefing unsuccessful candidates for a TA's post, that the TA might never have been through the procedure before, and might be unaware of the use of criteria for selection purposes or how the school proceeds from that point. TAs who are mothers retuning to work after having their family or young people new to the job scene are probably very nervous about the whole procedure and would appreciate some briefing at the beginning to explain what they might expect. You might even like to tell them the sort of questions they will be asked so that they can prepare. If you do this you must do it for all candidates for that particular job.

Some schools ask teachers to teach a class at interview, you might consider asking the potential TAs to work with a group, say read them a short story or describe to them an incident or event relevant to the subject they are being asked to support. If you do this do give them time to prepare and ensure that you do it for all candidates, that the pupils concerned are happy with the process and that the unCRB-checked person is not left alone with the children.

For teachers and HLTAs new to interviewing, do take advice from your line managers or the headteacher. All candidates have to be asked the same questions – not in the same words or same order, but cover the same topics or areas of interest. Team interviewing is recommended practice, do not interview alone as you leave yourself open to allegations of unfair treatment. You start with introductions, then a general question, then move on to specifics and end on something general again. Always close by asking the candidate if they have questions for you and describing what will happen after the interview – how they will be notified if successful and what feedback they could expect. Questions must not be asked about domestic circumstances, especially child care arrangements or future family plans. The questions must abide by the school's equal opportunities and anti racial policies. Questions about outside interests or hobbies, where they might be relevant, are permissible. Do ask advice about your chosen questions if you have any concerns.

If teachers or pupils are asked to comment on the candidates, their views can be used in discussion to inform the interviewers especially if they have been involved in the group observation exercise. General comments about demeanour when waiting or being shown round the school should not be the defining criteria for success or otherwise.

Induction programme

The DfES programme

The DfES teaching assistant induction programme is designed to inform TAs of the context in which they will be working and how they will support teachers. LAs run the programmes, which are funded centrally. The primary TA induction programme includes modules in literacy, mathematics, promoting positive behaviour, role and context, and inclusion. Optional modules are also available in understanding how children learn and ICT. The secondary TA induction programme includes modules in role and context, literacy, mathematics and promoting positive behaviour. Optional modules are also available in inclusion and science. Separate programmes for the foundation stage in literacy and mathematics are also available. The materials are downloadable from the TDA website.

Part of these courses is the requirement to do some investigative and observational work back in schools. While these courses only attempt to provide the off-site input for a more lengthy induction process undertaken by the school, its content has been matched with the NOS so that if the TA wants to progress to level 2 or 3 NVQs or their equivalent they can use the evidence they glean to start with for their assessment portfolio. TAs successfully completing all the off-site days and the tasks required of them back at school, will have covered many of the competences, knowledge and understanding components of a level 2 TA and some of a level 3 TA.

> To perform well you need to know what it is you are supposed to be doing . . . Because the role of the TA has been evolving, and as it varies according to the school and the experience and qualifications of the TA, the task may well require more thought than it does for other members of staff whose role is better established. It may require more monitoring and follow-up.
>
> (DfES 2000)

It could be easy to forget the induction of a member of staff who may only be working for a few hours a week, but given the closeness with which most TAs work with pupils, it is essential. Because TAs have in the past often come to the post via the volunteer route there is sometimes the assumption that they know all they need to know about the school processes. Although, being people who have been appointed for their initiative and sensitivity, they are also likely to be able to find out what they need to know, it is still helpful to induct them properly; it is another way of supporting and valuing the new member of staff. The same person does not carry out all the induction procedures but the newly appointed line manager needs to make sure the various bits are completed. Box 9.1 is an example of an induction policy from Stifford Clays Junior School.

Box 9.1 The induction policy from Stifford Clays Junior School

STIFFORD CLAYS JUNIOR SCHOOL
POLICY FOR – Induction

Lead Co-ordinator: Mark Jones
Governor Responsible: Dave Harper

Rationale

'Induction is the effective introduction of an employee to a new role within an organisation. The employee may be a new recruit or maybe an existing employee whose job has changed due to promotion or other reasons'.

The following is evidence of an effective induction package in operation

- People *can explain how they contribute* to achieving the organisation's aims and objectives
- People who are new to the organisation, and those new to a job, *can confirm* that they have *received an effective Induction*
- The organisation can show that people *learn and develop effectively*
- People *understand why they have undertaken development activities* and what they are expected to do as a result
- People *can give examples of what they have learnt* (knowledge, skills and attitude) from development activities
- Development is *linked to external qualifications or standards* (or both), where appropriate

> *"A newcomer can take in only a limited amount of information at a time. Too intense an induction programme is likely to be ineffective."*

Aims

To ensure any new member of staff is –

- Provided with information on the school's policies and procedures.
- Provided with Child protection training and is aware of who the designated person is.
- Aware of the part they will play in contributing to the improvement and development of the overall effectiveness of the school, helping to raise pupil achievement, and meeting the needs of pupils, parents and the wider community.
- Familiar with the school's Code of Conduct to ensure that they understand what is expected of them at the school.
- Provided with training which is specific to their needs.

In addition our induction process will -

- Identify the role we expect our new member of staff to play within our organisation and to explain how we will help the new member of staff to make an effective contribution.
- Clarify how we intend to support new members of staff. To make them aware of the support structures in place to enable them to be able to carry out their role effectively.
- Explain other regulations relevant to the workplace such as health and safety legislation, emergency evacuation procedures etc..

Who is included in our Induction Programme?

- Lunchtime supervisors
- Learning Support Assistants
- Caretakers / Site Managers
- School Administrators / Bursars
- Members of the Governing Body

- Members of the Senior Management Team
- Teachers taking up a post of responsibility within the School
- NQTs
- Student teachers
- Supply teachers

- Parent helpers

What is included in our induction programme for <u>all</u> new members of staff.

Prior to start date -

Half Day Induction for Educational Support Staff and new teachers (other than NQTs) - The purpose of this half day is to provide the new member of staff with some useful information in advance of their start date which will help to prepare them for their first day.

Early start for Newly Qualified teachers starting in July – NQT's will have opportunity of starting in July to get to know the school's structures and routines in order to prepare them for the new academic year.

Induction Pack – All new members of staff will receive an induction pack which will contain important and useful information about the school.

From start date -

Welcome session by Headteacher to include the following;
1. Our <u>vision for the future</u> and <u>ethos</u> and the part which they will play in contributing to this
2. The <u>Key aims and objectives</u> of the school
3. <u>Key targets</u> in the School Development plan. (As appropriate).
4. What the school can offer in terms of <u>training, development and support</u> including the Performance Management and how they will fit into this Process.

Induction Partner / Mentor Support – All members of staff will be partnered up with a mentor who will provide the following in the first few days of starting;
- Guidance and support in getting to know the structures and routines of our school along with day-to-day information (including timetable).
- To give them a guided tour of the school and introduce them to all members of our community and the role they play in it.
- Someone the new members of staff can shadow when they first start.
- An opportunity to go through the general and specific duties in relation to their particular role.
- Someone who will familiarise them with the relevant information / documentation as listed on the 'Induction Checklist' sheet.
- To make them aware of regulations relevant to the workplace such as health and safety legislation, Child Protection Procedures, emergency evacuation procedures etc

In addition to the above the mentor will also provide the following -
- Ensure that the new member of staff is provided with Child Protection training within the first half term and has read through the school's CP policy.
- Help to identify and address any specific training needs.
- A listening ear and someone they can turn to for help and advice.

Monitoring our induction programme

All new members of staff will be asked to complete the induction questionnaire at the end of their first term, to help identify how positive an experience they have had particularly in terms of the level of help and support on offer.

The responses to the questionnaire will then be used as a guide for discussion between the mentor or Headteacher and new member of staff. Any outcomes from this will then be used to help improve our induction programme for future new members of staff.

Induction Checklist

All new members of staff will receive the following in their induction pack: -

1. Induction Programme (NQTs will in addition receive additional material from the LEA)

2. The School's Mission Statement / Aims and objectives

3. Map of the School

4. School Timetable

5. A list of the different members of staff and Governors along with their areas of responsibility

6. The 'Useful information guide'

7. Health and Safety Information

8. Child Protection Information

9. Term and Holiday dates

In addition new members will also receive the following: -

'Plan on a Page' which is an overview of targets on the School Development Plan

Job description / Terms and conditions

Emergency Evacuation procedures

Induction checklist (which the mentor will work through with the new member of staff)

Staff Handbook

The DfES induction process begins by asking TAs to find out certain information about their schools before they attend the first day of the course. (TDA 2006a, 2006b). Do look at the list, it would be a very useful one to use to prepare materials to give to all new staff. If you have not got a TA actually going on the course the materials can be downloaded from the TDA website. The headings are as follows:

1 *Do you know the key facts about your school setting?* This includes items about numbers of pupils, teachers and support staff and key stages, any specialisms or defining characteristics of the school.
2 *Do you know about the local community?* This includes items about the locality itself and who makes up the community, employment patterns and community activities.
3 *Do you know what the governing body does and who the governors are?*
4 *What regular visitors from the local authority, other services, agencies or teams come to the school?* This includes what contact the TA may have with such people.
5 *How is the school organised?* This includes class groupings, guidance on systems and procedures, policies, resources, internet access, etc.

THINKING POINTS

The following list might be useful to check against, some of the items will be dealt with in greater detail elsewhere.

Before the TA starts:

The TA needs:
- a copy of a map of the school, with a detailed timetable for his/her first day – and beyond if it is available;
- a copy of their job description;
- the expectations of the school in terms of dress code, titles and names used;
- car parking, time of arrival and where to go in the school when they arrive.

The school needs to:
- be aware of a new arrival to be ready to welcome them – children and all other staff;
- have a welcome pack of appropriate documentation, or a list of where it can be found;
- appoint a mentor for their first year, whether or not they are undertaking any outside course;
- ensure somebody greets them, settles them in for the first day,
    - introduces them to the teachers and pupils with whom they will be working closely
    - briefs them on the contents of the documentation.

On the first day, if possible, the new TA should:
- be shown round the school and introduced where possible and appropriate including:
    - where to keep their personal belongings;
    - staff facilities for toilet, refreshment and rest/sickness;
- be introduced to the mentor if that is a different person;
- meet the people with whom they will be working closely;
- shadow an experienced TA;
- be given the document file/school support staff handbook and the contents briefly explained.

During the first week the following policies and procedures should be made clear to the new TA:
- health, safety and security strategies, particularly in dealing with emergencies
- confidentiality
- child protection.

(Watkinson 2003a: 103, 105)

6 *Are you familiar with school procedures?* This refers to a school handbook and procedure on health and safety, confidentiality and child protection, security, expectations of behaviour management.

7 *How does the school provide for pupils' differing needs?* This is about access to the Code of Practice for SEN, and resources and people who can support SEN or pupils with EAL.

8 *What do you know about the curriculum?* This asks about familiarity with key stage demands of the NC, the strategies, assessment procedures and inclusion implications; SDP/SIP and accountability strategies including inspection.

9 *What is your school/LA doing in relation to the ECM agenda?* This asks questions about each of the five areas.

10 What training and development opportunities are available in your school/setting or local area?

The secondary induction includes a separate section asking 'What do you know about qualifications?' This is referring to the qualifications the school offers pupils, not what is available to the TAs.

You can also see that the detail of information proposed really does need explanation, hence the vital value of appointing a mentor for the induction process. Boxes 9.2 and 9.3 show a three-term induction plan and a checklist for each new TA to tick off as they go through the process from Whipton Barton Junior School. This school has now indicated that they feel some version of the process is needed for all staff at the beginning of each year to ensure that everyone is up to date with changes made over the year and any concerns thrown up by end of year reviews.

Appointing a mentor

Anyone new to a post in the school should be allocated a mentor – a guide, a friend, usually someone other than the line manager. When a mentor is appointed, do remember to include a commitment of resources of time to a teacher or the senior TA who is to carry out the major tasks and to the TA themselves. Just because they are new and need mentoring, or on a course with a particular cost, does not mean that the mentoring process has to be in voluntary time. Just making the appointment without recognising the implications is not enough.

The mentor does not have to be a superior in the school hierarchy, but someone who has more experience of the ways of the school. A senior TA is ideal for the job, they will have sufficient knowledge and expertise, particularly regarding the more domestic support strategies, and it will be good management experience for them. The nature of the mentoring should be explained to both parties, and routes to particular expertise explained and facilitated, for example, to the SENCO or subject leader.

You can recognise the importance of such a role by making it public to the rest of the staff, even allocating temporary responsibility salary recognition to the person concerned, or providing extra pupil contact release time. The school and teachers quickly recognise the benefits of having well-informed, welcomed TAs

Box 9.2 The three-term induction plan for Whipton Barton Junior School

The line manager is responsible for the induction and support of the Teaching Assistant in conjunction with the CPD Leader.

Phase 1 :- After appointment

Information	• Overview of induction. • School prospectus • Planning. Termly / Yearly overview. • Copy of Job description. • Allocation of 'buddy.' • Data on named child (if applicable). • Pre-visit (if possible) see pre visit/day 1 checklist. • Discussions with Head and/or Deputy/Line Manager/Senco/classteacher.	• Deputy • Line Manager • Classteacher. • Head/Deputy • Line manager • Senco/c.teacher

Phase 2 Joining – 1 st Term

Information	• As above if not already allocated. • Weekly /unit planning. Termly overview • PSP/IEP info	• Class teacher • Line manager
Support/ training	• Day 1 entitlement see checklist • Meeting with Senco, 1 every half term on a 1 to1 basis. • Meeting with TA group every week. Discuss Support issues. • How to help to fill out annual review sheets if applicable • Week 1 entitlement see checklist • 1st month see checklist • Observation and feedback • Performance management info and discussion (if applicable)	• Line manager • TA • Senco/classteacher HLTA/line manager Line manager

Phase 3 Developing Relationships – 2nd term

Information	• Weekly /unit planning. Overview of terms planning.	• Class teacher
Support/Training	• Meeting with Senco, 1 every half term on a 1 to1 basis[if needed] • Meeting with TA group every week. Discuss support issues. How to help teacher carry out statement reviews (if applicable). In year performance Management discussion	• Senco • TA • Senco/Classteacher

Phase 4 Consolidation – 3rd term

Staff Develop. Support	• Performance management feedback, prep for next one. • Meeting with Senco, 1 every half term on a 1 to1 basis. • Meeting with TA group every week. Discuss Support issues. • Evaluation of induction policy.	• Line manager • Senco • TA
Self Reflection	• Preparation for and participation in performance management interviews.	• Line manager
Information	• Unit/weekly planning. Overview of term	• Class teacher

Box 9.3 The TA induction checklist for Whipton Barton Junior School

Induction Pack Checklist

New TA's should be provided with or have information on the following

Have you got:
Before Starting

☐ An appropriate and clear job description which sets out what you will be doing and to whom you will be responsible, holiday etc

☐ A copy of the school prospectus

☐ Staffing structure

☐ A plan of the school

A copy of the following policies:

☐ Performance Management

☐ Behaviour – including rewards and sanctions

☐ Health and safety – including emergency procedures

☐ Child protection

☐ Intimate care and handling (if appropriate)

☐ Confidentiality

☐ Dress Code

☐ School expectations – time of arrival, departure, school timetable etc.

☐ Term dates

☐ Attendance at staff meetings

☐ Arrangements for tea, coffee and lunch

☐ Golden rules (school rules)

☐ General information on key stages in school

☐ Where to go on the first day.

Before Starting / Day 1

☐ A tour of the school including where to find resources

☐ How to use the photocopier, riso, laminator etc

☐ Codes for storage cupboards and rooms

☐ Passwords and access codes to computers and email

☐ Sickness procedures – who to phone if unwell and phone numbers

☐ Where to find information on grievance procedures, sickness and absence (with particular reference to page 13) and handling and abuse by staff (Red books)

Meetings and child related information

Have you had:

☐ Data on named child / children you will be working with

☐ A meeting with parents (if appropriate)

☐ A meeting with the SENCO (if appropriate)

☐ Approx. 30 minutes meeting with the class teacher to discuss clarification of your role, responsibilities and expectations

☐ Introduction to a TA buddy and time to spend with them

☐ Access to relevant IEP's and PSP's

☐ Introduction and meeting with line management HLTA

Week 1

☐ Child protection training / input

☐ Had copies of the termly planning / yearly overviews and weekly lesson planning

☐ End of week meeting with line management / class teacher / head / deputy for feedback on how the week has gone and discussion on issues that may have arisen

☐ Look at finer details of your role

☐ Opportunity to observe / work alongside buddy

☐ Knowledge of clubs during and after school

☐ Knowledge of how to deal with children in an emergency

First Month

☐ Weekly meeting with TA's – ongoing throughout the year

☐ Regular discussions with line manager / SENCO / HLTA

☐ Identified your individual training needs

☐ Discussions with class teacher on planning and assessment procedures e.g. maths and literacy groups

☐ Knowledge of termly literacy and numeracy targets – ISP + RAP

☐ Daily discussions with class teacher re planning and observations

First Half Term / term

☐ Access to appropriate training

☐ Regular meetings with TA's – sharing of expertise

☐ Attended INSET training sessions

☐ Further observations of TA's

☐ Line manager / HLTA – observation and feedback of your progress in the classroom – continue half termly

☐ Training on how to write IEP's and PSP's and statement reviews (if applicable)

Yearly

☐ Performance management meetings / Reviews

☐ CPD – continuing professional development – relevant to yours and school needs

Signed .... Date ....

HLTA .... Date ....

Please sign and date the checklist after each meeting

and teachers who understand what the TA is capable of, and both being part of a whole-school team. In the early days there was a lot of resentment from teachers in being appointed mentors for courses such as the STA one and even the DfES induction courses, or refusal from heads to bother with troubling other members of staff, but where it happens it is always repeated because the value to the school becomes evident.

When mentoring off-site courses it is important that the mentor should be aware of the content of the course, and hopefully, not just the mentor. If the school is to be able to make full use of the TA once trained, all need to know what the training was about. TAs can, encouraged by their mentors, take part of a teaching staff meeting to explain briefly what they are studying and why. Teaching staff have been known to borrow TA course material such as videos and use it for their own discussions.

Devon runs a TA mentoring course which goes through the course content along with the role and scope expected of the mentor, the programme that should take place in the school post-induction and some of the management issues that can occur for mentors and TAs. They also give details of the local CPD opportunities open for TAs.

Figure 9.1 The Whipton Barton Junior HLTA with her mentor, the deputy head

Mentoring

Mentoring is not just used in schools but also throughout business and industry and not just for courses or induction. It is unrealistic to expect one mentor to be all things to another member of staff. A mentoring or 'joint working' policy would help those people given a mentoring role. It spells out the sort of expectations the school has of such a role and what school support the mentor, as well as the person being mentored, can expect. All the outside courses, from induction to HE level include some kind of in-house activity or observation, and all recommend mentor support, to enable these processes to take place. It needs the mentor to interpret the course contents in the light of the in-house practice and policies.

The mentoring concept can permeate a school philosophy; 'mentoring schools' have been recognised by colleagues. Kerry and Mayes have a useful model showing stages in mentoring (Kerry and Mayes 1995). In the first stage, the apprentice emulates the experienced practitioner, by practising under their guidance. This is particularly necessary for a new TA, who needs information and a role model in order to develop appropriate skills and understanding. The TA needs to be able to ask questions. This can lead onto systematic training by the mentor of the TA where there is a realisation of the competences needed and the underpinning knowledge required. The mentor can observe the TA and provide constructive feedback. The TA is allowed to experiment, with supervision. This, in turn, can lead to the teacher or mentor and TA working as a partnership, focusing together on the needs of the pupils, looking at their learning, and talking about how best the partnership can develop. This needs both to have open minds as it might confront the beliefs or values of either, and might necessitate changes in practice.

You need to monitor the process and to review it as it goes on. It is rare for poor relationships to sour things if you have set it up carefully, but there needs to be a watching brief to make sure other staff are helping, supporting and encouraging appropriately. There could be personality clashes or clashes of values, beliefs or educational philosophy, e.g. multiculturalism, attitudes to discipline. Pupils like to know that adults are still learning, and can help. Governors need to know of the process and what it means for the school in terms of resource allocation, care and professional development of their staff. Parents of individual children might need to be included if the appointment was for individual support of a particular need. They are often interested and provide extra information about the child if the TA is undertaking a child study or particular investigations as part of their course. This may well feed back to increasing the value of the support for the child.

Do bear in mind though, that the professional relationship of a TA to a teacher if the teacher is the mentor is not that of a peer, certainly in the career, pay and status realms. Prior experience and training can be very different and not necessarily one way. The TA could be a graduate, with specific understanding and skills in a subject area, and the teacher be a very experienced teacher but without a specialism in that subject. The assistants might have children of their own, and other life experiences which the teacher has not. TAs, keen to develop, can overtake their teacher in enthusiasm, and may become more informed as to current issues in education than the teacher. TAs might have more time for reflection with less paperwork. Vocabulary sharing is important as the educational jargon which is second nature to the teacher is not so well understood by the TA.

School example

One secondary HLTA commented that she solved the problem about ensuring that the new TAs had some kind of mentor by using the more experienced teaching assistants. They were paired up with a buddy from their year group wherever possible so that they could call upon them easily if they needed help.

Professional development portfolios

The rationale of a portfolio

These seem to be less used currently and I am not sure why. Since working with TAs and advisers using the idea, I have kept my own and found it invaluable when asked for information about myself, or to be able to find particular documents. Maybe it is seen as too much trouble or even cost, but I still think it is worth

considering their potential value. Newly qualified teachers in some LAs are still given ring files with particular content for the induction year. If it is a good idea for them, then why not TAs? They are helpful for professional development management and very helpful for the individual whose file it is. It is really just a ring binder with sections, contents can be photocopied where relevant for the assessment and verification process of an NVQ if necessary. Completing the personal section at the beginning of a file just for them immediately gives the TA a feeling of self-worth and belonging to an establishment that cares about who they are and what they are going to do within that establishment.

The portfolio construction

A portfolio is really just a loose-leaf collection of information and evidence about the person with sections and prompt sheets. They can become quite bulky if too eclectic, a separate staff file for relevant school documentation and information and separate files for out-of-school courses are needed. Provide a sturdy ring binder, if you use ring files that have a plastic pocket front cover, you can personalise the ring binder to your school with a crest or logo and appropriate titling. Dividers separate the sections, which can be defined by the school or left to the owner. Provide a sprinkling of plastic pockets to take certificates; and section dividers, the wider ones which will overlap the plastic pockets for areas something like the list on p. 170. Each section can have prompt sheets for the new member of staff to complete if you wish or some of the information ready printed in them as listed above. Some schools have introduced electronic versions of portfolios for their staff to cut down the paper use or clutter.

The first action of the mentor can be to explain the purpose of the file, suggest the completion of a few personal pages and set a meeting time to discuss the school pages.

School example

I have watched a SENCO introducing a professional portfolio to a new TA in a school, and watched the TA grow as she turned the pages, anticipating completing the personal pages, listing courses and undertaking a self-review. She recognised that how she progressed in her new job mattered to others as well as herself.

The new TA can insert their own JD, school map or other papers sent to them before their first day. Appraisals or review material will be agreed on separate sheets as per the school policy and procedures then kept by the owner in the file. It is reference collection for the owner, a positive record of things they have done and can do. They should take it with them if they leave. The ownership of the file once given remains with the TA. This is not something to be handed to a manager for perusal but a reference document carrier by the owner. The contents are specific to the TA, and whatever system is used, should be confidential and private for them. The school/staff handbook is much more formal, containing relevant school documentation, which should be kept up to date by the school and returned to you when the member of staff leaves.

THINKING POINTS

The sections and prompt sheets of a personal professional portfolio could be:

◆ Personal section
  – name, address, telephone number etc.,
  – other important numbers – car, national insurance, hospital, telephone number of next of kin, etc.,
  – educational history (places and dates)
  – examinations taken with results
  – qualifications, grades and dates (certificates and diplomas can be kept here)
  – any other courses undertaken (dates)
  – life experiences (clubs etc.)
  – employment experiences (dates)
  – records of anything produced (a booklet, a craft object, a child (photos?))
  – major life events (travel, disasters coped with, celebrations)

◆ The job and place of work
  – job description
  – induction material
  – school description
  – school staff responsibilities
  – some key policies or a list of policies contained in a separate school file
  – useful contacts

◆ Progress and reflections on the job
  – record of meetings attended
  – record of courses attended
  – jottings about personal progress
  – self-review

◆ Appraisal or Professional Development Review process
  – whatever the school policy and documentation is for appraisal or review

◆ Notes on courses attended (not course handouts, there will not be room) or evaluation sheets

◆ A section for personal jottings or diary

(Adapted from Watkinson 2003a: 111)

From Ann Melhuish's case study

What has already become obvious in my research is that simple strategies that make life easier for teaching assistants can be as effective as more complex ones. One thing that I realised was that teaching assistants were constantly being presented with pieces of paper in the form of policies, timetables and planning sheets etc. The problem was they had nowhere to store it all. The solution was to provide them all with files and file dividers.

School documentation

Copies of school documents

TAs need copies of certain school documentation, including relevant curriculum policies. Behaviour management, Health, Safety, Security and Safeguarding Children are essential. It may be that the school has a special TA policy, SEN, EAL, assessment (including marking), teaching and learning policies, and others. It would not be helpful just to present these to the TA on their first day without explanations; a list of their locations in the above portfolio and timetable for their introduction by the mentor would be much better.

THINKING POINTS

The school documentation relevant to TAs:
- ◆ Its aims, philosophy and ethos.
- ◆ The staff structure with roles and responsibilities of the class teacher, roles of senior staff, duties of ancillary staff including the role of the governing body, and the support staff governor's name.
- ◆ Basic school routines and procedures, e.g. registers, duties, marking, record keeping, reports, parents' evenings, sanctions, legal obligations (*loco parentis*) and health, safety and security.
- ◆ The school policy for child protection, including the identity of the named person; the policy for confidentiality, and behaviour management.
- ◆ Copies of relevant documentation for literacy and numeracy, and any other curriculum areas.
- ◆ The school's SEN policy and arrangements for working with IEPs, reviews and statemented children where appropriate.
- ◆ Arrangements for staff meetings, working parties and consultations as relate to the TA.
- ◆ Arrangements for line management, the whereabouts of pay, discipline and grievance documentation, union membership if desired.
- ◆ Resources available in the school and how the TA should access them: stock and curricular equipment including SEN resources; the school library and

ICT facilities including audiovisual aids, e.g. television, radio, tapes, films, video etc.; reprographic equipment.

◆ Resources available locally: curriculum development/teachers' centres, libraries, museums, field study centres etc.

Some suggestions for a school handbook relevant to TAs

While a handbook of some kind should be available for every member of staff, there will be differences depending on the category of staff for whom the handbook is intended. This should be a separate file to the personal portfolio and, as explained above, the property of the school.

THINKING POINTS

The TA handbook could contain:
◆ General staff guidance: confidentiality, expectations of dress, punctuality, code of courtesy etc.
   – job descriptions, pay policy, discipline and grievance procedures, role of governing body
   – line management systems; staff structure; staff support systems
   – professional development procedures
◆ Fire and first aid practices; health and safety procedures, security, and off-site responsibilities
◆ Behaviour policy: expectations, roles of all staff, responsibilities and strategies
◆ Safeguarding children including child protection issues and procedures
◆ Communication systems, including emergencies, bad weather etc., rotas and timings, dates including meetings and agenda/minutes, newsletters from school
◆ Systems for recording incidents or assessments where appropriate
◆ Siting of relevant school policies and support materials
◆ Equipment and resources: roles and responsibilities, access
◆ Wet playtime procedures

School example

Oaklands Infant School handbook given to new TAs contains:
A welcome and the school mission statement
Lists of: school staff
            children who have regular medication and/or emergency medication
            'special children'
Breaks and emergency procedures

Job descriptions
Class timetable
Fire drill procedures
Things they should be told, shown and do
Notes on behaviour management
Health and safety policy and reporting form
Equal opportunities policy
Child protection policy and diagram for completion if anything untoward is noticed
Anti bullying policy
Behaviour policy
A gender checklist
A playground management plan
Some photocopies of articles: Catch them being good
                                 Talking to children
                                 A guide for teachers on child abuse from the NSPCC
                                 Some basic first aid
A list of who to talk to in school about various things
A list of local organisations and school contacts
A list of Health and Safety codes of practice

Learning support assistants (Teaching assistant)

You should be given -
Job description and contract.
Class timetable

You should -
arrange your hours with your class teacher.
be shown where various kinds of stock are kept.

In the class-room
Teachers work in different ways, but you will be told what kind of support you are to give on that day, and if something specific is needed, the day before.
You will be expected to -
support and encourage children in their work.
encourage children to become independent and try for themselves [you are not there to 'do it for them' - the work should be the child's].

Kinds of activities -
working on daily task set by Mrs Langley for certain children
supporting a specific child who needs a little extra help
supporting a group of children with an activity
talking with the children and encouraging them to talk
listening to children read [do check how the teacher wants it done]
science activities [ensure you know from teacher what she expects]
craft activities
Practical tasks to lighten the teacher's load, e.g. making books, mounting work, mixing paint etc.
Supporting during numeracy or literacy activities.

If you are asked to use any equipment you have not used before, e.g. strimmer, photocopier, laminator, etc. do ask to be shown the first time.

Figure 9.2 An early page from the Oaklands Infant School handbook

School example

Feniton Primary School TA handbook also includes their absence procedure, a class conduct code, a conduct code and the arrangements for performance review.

Further induction process

Giving it time

Induction is a lengthy process, and is not one sided. TA, mentor and school all need to participate, with any off-site course merely adding extra dimensions to it. The DfES induction course is designed to be a four-day course taken off site after about a half a term working in a school, with induction probably taking a full year to complete. This should enable regular dialogue between the mentor and the TA to ensure further understanding. It means the TA will experience the range of activities the school undertakes, from performances to examinations, parents evenings, social events and sports days. The development of relationships and partnerships essential to the work of TAs takes time.

For new TAs, there will be a probationary period of six months as with all support staff under single status agreements. Personnel/human resource advisers will always give recommendations about such things. In this way you can see how the TAs perform, give appropriate support and feedback, and can give people previously unknown to the school as fair an opportunity as the in-house volunteer who is better known. You should never refuse to confirm a probationary period at the end of six months if you cannot show your processes of supervision and support during that time.

Chapter 10

Empowering TAs to support the learning process

Teachers and TAs in the classroom

While good practice is much more than regulations, it was clear from the replies reported in the TES (2007b) that not all teachers understand the significance of the regulations even if the headteachers do. It is important that all teachers working with TAs in their class be aware of the statutory conditions. Legislation does not promise that the TA and teacher will work well together, or that the teaching and learning in the classroom is enhanced by the TA presence, or enable the teacher to support the TA rather than 'supervise' them, but the teachers do need to be aware that they are responsible for the TAs' work while in their classroom. The heads in the TES cases may have told the TAs this – but not the teachers.

There are clear regulations that whatever happens in the classroom in terms of delegation of teaching strategies: the person carrying out any work in the classroom, 'is subject to the direction and supervision of such a qualified teacher or nominated teacher in accordance with arrangements made by the headteacher of the school' (DfES 2003: 10). The guidance associated with the regulations puts it like this: 'Accountability for the overall learning outcomes of a particular pupil rest with that pupil's qualified classroom/subject teacher and . . . that each class or group . . . must be assigned a qualified teacher to teach them' (DfES 2003). The guidance goes on to describe the ways of establishing a system of supervision: 'An inexperienced assistant would require direct supervision and should not be left alone with a class, while an experienced teaching assistant . . .would not require the qualified teacher assigned to that class to be present at all times.' It describes the kind of qualities a headteacher should have regard to when looking for a TA to undertake work at a higher level (DfES 2003). All the copies of the professional standards for HLTA status carry the sentence 'teaching and learning activities should take place under the direction and supervision of a qualified teacher in accordance with the arrangements made by the headteacher of the school' (p. 17).

Two distinct types of supervision are defined:

1   supervision of activities relating to teaching and learning; and
2   line management.

Much of this book to date has been about line management. This chapter is particularly concerned with the management of teaching and learning. The guidance refers to the possibilities of one TA being directed by several teachers, and the needs of less or more qualified TAs for more or less direct supervision. It does emphasise the 'Supervision arrangements for all support staff undertaking activities to support teaching and learning should include time for teachers and support staff to discuss planning and pupil progress within the contracted hours of the support staff' (p. 17).

Teachers are paid two to three times as much as a TA for taking responsibility. They are answerable to parents, pupils and their senior staff for the teaching and learning of their pupils. TAs, HLTAs and cover supervisors are not qualified, trained or paid or enabled to be accountable – teachers write reports and assessments and take parents' consultation evenings. There are few schools that enable TAs to participate in these. TAs and HLTAs may inform the outcomes, but cannot and should not take responsibility for them.

But teachers should not just be told the facts baldly as I have set them out, but should be enabled to work with the TA. The line manager or headteacher should work with the teacher to ensure everyone's interest in improving the quality of experience for pupils. This is best served by partnership and collaboration. WR was not just about releasing teachers from the classroom but also about raising standards. Given a lead, appropriate guidance, training and good relationships with the class teacher, TAs can assist, using all of the skills of teaching in its generic meaning, with mutual agreement about boundaries. TAs definitely do teach, but do not take the responsibility for the direction and organisation of the learning.

Teachers have been accused by some TAs of pursuing their own targets, and forgetting that TAs may also have targets to achieve. There is ever the need for teachers to recognise the professionalism of their TA colleagues while preserving their own.

Working with teachers in the classroom

Teachers and managers, therefore, need not only to look carefully at the characteristics of their TAs, their performance management and development and the whole-school support of them but how the best use can be made of TAs' and teachers' time. During the twentieth century no teachers were trained to work with other adults and had to make it up as they went along.

Most ITT institutions are doing this now and involving local staff to assist. The local SCITT course in my area has used an Advanced Skills Teacher and an HLTA to run an 'effective use of TAs' course for their trainees. They covered things they wished some of their teachers had been told. Their course contained:

◆ a discussion on effective deployment – telling them not to assume TAs or LSAs know all about SEN;
◆ the need to develop respect for all adults in the room;
◆ planning together – principles of lesson planning;
◆ how a TA can support starters/plenaries and the bits in the middle;
◆ using TAs for assessment – e.g. concept mapping.

They used a DVD they had made in a lesson and asked the trainee teachers 'What would you do?'.

The more teachers involve TAs the more they will have a productive learning environment.

TAs can provide personal support and companionship, the extra pair of eyes, ears and hands, which relieve the stress. Spending time on planning for and working with TAs can assist in all three of these areas. They can provide assistance in the short-term tasks, adding to the adult energy resource and enabling debate and reflection in even a short feedback time. Teachers frequently refer to the TAs' support of themselves, making comments such as, 'It's a terrific burden off my shoulders'. Teachers talk of emotional as well as practical help during inspections, and of being able to share the joys of a breakthrough in an area of learning for a particular pupil. Primary schools use TAs as whole-class support much more frequently than secondary schools. Ofsted reported that secondary schools mainly employ assistants in class to support pupils with SEN or doing specialist jobs outside the classroom. 'Few secondary teachers share their planning with teaching assistants or provide guidance for them on how best to support pupils' (Ofsted 2005). A recent edition of the secondary DfES magazine *Teachers* has described the more generalised support a TA can give, which means there is no stigma attached to getting help from a TA (Davey 2007: 8, 9). The article emphasises the need for effective planning and agreed use of TAs' non-pupil contact time. It gives three tips: (1) communication at all levels; (2) full involvement of the TAs in the whole-school; and (3) students being made aware that all adults are interested in them and their development.

Circle time, however, is not something to leave to an untrained TA. The TA can become a participant in the circle to help set an example and, properly trained in how to manage such situations, enable more sensitive topics to be discussed as there will be a person present who can counsel any pupils disturbed by their own feelings. Some schools deliberately get TAs trained in circle time techniques or counselling skills, in order that they can be of use in any emotionally charged situation.

The TAs need to know what to do throughout the lesson, and throughout any informal times in other areas of the school as well. They will need specific training in the techniques and language used to support or control challenging pupils, and practise skills which support whatever the philosophy or policy is in the school. If they are working with disturbed children or children who are on identified SEN stages for problems with behaviour, the SENCO and class teachers need to be involved to ensure a consistent approach.

Because teachers have not often in the past been trained to work with additional adults in the classroom, they sometimes find that planning work for them, managing them as well as the pupils, and taking account of their views merely adds yet another burden to the workload. But, where a partnership develops between a teacher and the TAs who work with him or her, the strengths of the TAs can complement those of the teachers to raise standards and alleviate the workload and the stress. TAs assist in the teaching programme of the class under the guidance of a qualified teacher. The NOS values and principles recognise the importance of this relationship:

Working in partnership with the teacher:

It is the teacher whose curriculum and lesson planning and day-to-day direction set the framework within which teaching/classroom assistants work. The teaching/classroom assistant works under the direction of the teacher, whether in the whole class or on their own with an individual or a small group of pupils. Teaching/classroom assistants, therefore, need to be fully briefed about the teacher's plans and intentions for teaching and learning and her/his contribution to these. Ideally, teaching/classroom assistants will be involved by teachers in their planning and preparation of the work.

(LGNTO 2001: 5)

Ofsted found that, apart from the other ways in which TAs support teachers, the quality of teaching of the teacher actually goes up when they are accompanied by TA support.

The Ofsted report regarding TAs gives the following list of strategies HMI observed where TAs help pupils to learn better:

In whole class teaching . . .

◆ minimising distractions to the whole class by dealing with individual welfare issues and behaviour problems
◆ keeping individual pupils on task by prompting their responses
◆ repeating or rephrasing questions asked by the teacher
◆ providing additional or alternative explanations for individual pupils
◆ providing specialist support, for example, for hearing-impaired pupils
◆ observing and noting reactions and contributions of the pupils so that the more passive members of the class can later receive extra attention
◆ enabling less confident pupils, or those of lower ability or with SEN, to make contributions to the lesson.

During group or independent work, teaching assistants help pupils to learn better by:

◆ providing support for an individual or a group of pupils which enables them to tackle tasks that would otherwise be beyond them
◆ giving more individual explanations of a task than would be possible with the whole class
◆ giving feedback on the pupils' learning to the teacher so that he or she can adjust the challenge or pace of learning in later lessons
◆ giving pupils immediate relevant feedback on their work.

(Ofsted 2002: 11)

The following skills of teaching can be observed when watching a TA at work:

◆ Planning and preparation
◆ Performance
◆ Exposition – giving instructions, directions, explaining, using the correct language (naming things)

- ◆ Questioning facts, ideas or worth
- ◆ Challenging, pacing, motivating – increasing amount which could be done; extending ideas, encouraging thinking or imagination, using appropriate praise (verbal or smiles)
- ◆ Intervention and non intervention – promoting active learning
- ◆ Working with groups or individuals or a whole class
- ◆ Supporting practical work
- ◆ Resource management – organising and suggesting methods in and out of lessons
- ◆ Multitasking
- ◆ Supporting practical work
- ◆ Assessment activities – observing, feedback and reporting

(Watkinson 2003a: 20)

Working with teachers out of the classroom – the role of assistant SENCO

Where senior TAs or HLTAs are taking on a management role for a team of TAs, it relieves a teacher, often the deputy head or the SENCO, of line management responsibilities. As subject coordinators for ICT or music, again they are relieving teachers of a job rather than working in partnership with them. However, in one particular role, which in the very title indicates partnership, they are taking on responsibilities; that of assistant SENCO. There has been some concern about this role, especially in one or two schools where the TAs have actually been named as *the* SENCO. Complaining teachers and heads have quoted the Code of Practice as indicating that this post must be filled by a qualified teacher. In fact, the Code of Practice says 'In practice the division of day-to-day responsibilities is a matter for individual schools, to be decided in the light of a school's circumstances and size, priorities and ethos' (DfES 2001). It defines the SENCO as 'a member of staff of a school or early education setting who has responsibility for coordinating SEN provision within that school' (p. 206). The Code does say that it is inappropriate to have other curriculum responsibilities, that they are likely to be a member of the senior management team/senior leadership team (SMT/SLT) as it is seen as equivalent to a subject coordinator role in primary schools and head of faculty department or year in a secondary school. Also note that in October 2006 the DfES published a response to a Select Committee report on SEN: 'We share their view as to their (SENCOs) importance and believe that the person taking the lead responsibility should be a teacher and a member of the senior leadership team in the school.' They also propose after consultation and amendments to the Education Bill to introduce new regulations concerning SENCOs. Such is the importance attached to the role and the description of the responsibilities that it is unlikely that an unqualified TA could have all the knowledge and understanding to fulfil it.

TAs may be qualified in areas other than teaching, for instance social work, or a foundation degree with a specialism in SEN or possessing various SEN diplomas. The Code also speaks of having an SEN team although one member of staff must have being a SENCO as a specific responsibility. It reminds readers that provision is a matter for the school *as a whole* and the statutory duties lie with the governing body and the LA. So, having a senior TA or HLTA as assistant SENCO seems to make a great deal of sense but not a TA as SENCO itself.

A chapter in *Primary teaching assistants* describes such a role (Wallace 2005). Two such assistants, one primary and one secondary, recently gave a workshop at an HLTA conference in Devon describing their role. Operating as assistant SENCOs they carry out the more administrative side of the role. The size of the schools and, thus, the SEN register, means that the secondary SENCO assistant is more of a full-time job while the primary assistant SENCO has to fit her role around a more general TA/HLTA role. Boxes 10.1 and 10.2 and Figures 10.1, 10.2 and 10.3 give some indication of the range of activities of the post and the support such a post gives the SENCO.

Partnership

The way in which the TAs perform is very dependent on the quality of the relationship with the teacher and the time that is made available to them outside the pupil contact time. 'Essential elements in building a good relationship appeared to be: clear expectations from the teacher which enabled a sense of mutual responsibility to be fostered, and the teacher's desire to be proactive in building the working relationship' (Thornton and Hedges 2006). A good teacher is always aware of the learning needs of his or her class, and adapts their teaching programme to match those needs. These needs might reflect the ways in which the pupils learn, or might be a case of adjusting to physical, emotional, social, cultural or spiritual differences. In all the approaches to classroom organisation, teaching and learning the teacher must communicate as much as possible with the TA in order that they can share tasks and understand what each can contribute.

School example

One infant school head said: 'The teachers accept that the LSAs know more about some of the children, they are the experts on that child. They can write things about that child and enjoy their work because of this knowledge and contribution – but – they know they do not have the final responsibility. The teachers are careful not to let the LSA feel that ultimate responsibility. This is especially true when LSAs are dealing with children with physical needs. Because of the feelings that this can engender, there are several LSAs to cope so that the responsibility does not weigh them down. The LSA came from the nursery with one child and then on to the junior schools. She shared time between the two schools. She had the confidence to work with him and we respect that.'

It is this partnership that is going to make personalised learning work. A teacher cannot do it on their own. With the extra eyes and ears and contributions of a TA each child's needs can more easily be noted and addressed. But it is a two-way process. The teacher needs to determine how much the TA should know about individual pupils. K. Weddell, a retired EP, reported that when he was an LSA:

Box 10.1 A job description of a primary school assistant SENCO

POST DETAILS

TITLE   HLTA (supporting teaching and
                       learning) / Inclusion Assistant

SCHOOL   Lifton Community Primary School

LINE MANAGER   Inclusion Leader

GRADE   Level 4

PURPOSE OF JOB

- To complement the professional work of teachers by taking responsibility for agreed learning activities under an agreed system of supervision. This may involve planning, preparing and delivering learning activities for individuals/groups or short term for whole classes and monitoring pupils and assessing, recording and reporting of pupils achievement, progress and development.

- To support the Inclusion Leader with admin, liaison and the management of other teaching assistants including the allocation and monitoring of work, appraisal and training.

- To represent Teaching Assistants on the senior management team (SMT)

SUPERVISION ARRANGEMENTS

Work under the direction of the head teacher, inclusion leader, teaching and learning leader and class teachers.

MAJOR RESPONSIBILITIES

To work under an agreed system of supervision/management to deliver learning and to be a specialist knowledge resource by:

- Leading the planning cycle and delivering lessons to individuals, groups for Reading Discovery (KS1 and KS2), guided reading (KS2) and Sherborne movement
- Occasionally covering whole classes delivering lessons
- Supporting the inclusion leader with admin, liaison and strategic planning
- Managing the work and deployment of other TAs

DUTIES

Support the assigned teacher by:

- Organising and managing an appropriate learning environment and resources
- Within an agreed system of supervision, planning challenging teaching and learning objectives and evaluating and adjusting lessons/work plans as appropriate
- Monitoring and evaluating pupil responses to learning activities through a range of assessment and monitoring strategies against pre-determined learning objectives
- Providing objective and accurate feedback and reports as required on pupil achievement, progress and other matters, ensuring the availability of appropriate evidence
- Recording progress and achievement in lessons/activities systematically and providing evidence of range and level of progress and attainment
- Working within an established discipline policy to anticipate and manage behaviour constructively, promoting self control and independence
- Supporting the role of parents in pupils' learning and contributing to/leading meetings with parents to provide constructive feedback on pupil progress/achievement etc.
- Administering and assessing/marking tests and invigilating exams/tests
- Producing lesson plans, worksheets, plans etc.

Supporting pupils by:

- Assessing the needs of pupils and using detailed knowledge and specialist skills to support pupils' learning
- Establishing productive working relationships with pupils, acting as a role model and setting high expectations for behaviour and learning
- Promoting the inclusion and acceptance of all pupils within the classroom
- Supporting pupils consistently whilst recognising and responding to their individual needs
- Promoting independence and employing strategies to recognise and reward achievement of self-reliance
- Providing feedback to pupils in relation to progress and achievement

Support the curriculum by:

- Delivering learning activities to pupils within agreed systems of supervision, adjusting activities according to pupil responses/needs
- Delivering local and national learning strategies and making effective use of opportunities provided by other learning activities to support the development of pupils' skills
- Using ICT effectively to support learning activities, develop pupils' competence and independence in its use
- Selecting and preparing resources necessary to lead learning activities, taking account of pupils' interests and language and cultural backgrounds

Support the school by:

- Complying with assisting the development of policies and procedures relating to child protection, health, safety and security, confidentiality and data protection, and reporting all concerns to an appropriate person

- Being aware of and supporting difference and ensuring all pupils have equal access to opportunities to learn and develop
- Contributing to the overall ethos/work/aims of the school
- Establishing constructive relationships and communicating with other agencies/professionals, in liaison with the teacher, to support achievement and progress of pupils
- Delivering out of school learning activities within guidelines established by the school
- Contributing to the identification and execution of appropriate out of school learning activities which consolidate and extend work carried out in class

Support the Inclusion Leader by:

- Undertaking routine admin duties (arranging meetings, assisting with annual reviews etc)
- Liaising with outside agencies and taking the initiative as appropriate to develop appropriate multi-agency approaches to supporting pupils
- Supporting the strategic planning (action planning, deployment of staff and resources)
- Advising on appropriate deployment and use of specialist aid/resources/equipment
- Contributing to the termly report to Governors
- Supporting student teachers (induction and briefing)
- Attending meetings in the absence of the Inclusion Leader
- Ensuring appropriate special arrangements for SATS are in place
- Maintaining and updating a list of pupils at SA, SA+ and with statements
- Undertaking assessment of pupils to identify appropriate support
- Assisting with PLASC records
- Being knowledgeable of up to date research and inclusion issues
- Supporting the development and implementation of IEPs

To Undertake Line Management Responsibilities Where Appropriate by:

- Managing other teaching assistants
- Liaising between managers/teaching staff and teaching assistants
- Holding regular team meetings with managed staff
- Representing teaching assistants at teaching staff/management/other appropriate meetings
- Undertaking recruitment/induction/appraisal/training/mentoring for other teaching assistants

Date: ....

Signatures: Manager...

                   Postholder...

Box 10.2 A job description of a secondary school assistant SENCO

POST DETAILS

TITLE   Assistant Senco

LINE MANAGER   Assistant Head Learning Support (SENCO)

GRADE   Scale 6

PURPOSE OF JOB

To assist the work of the Senco in the strategic direction of the department, teaching and learning and managing resources. The Assistant Senco is expected to assist in the management of the Learning Support Team as well as working closely with students, parents/carers, other staff and outside agencies to identify, assess and plan to meet the needs of students with special educational needs. A key part of the role is the management of learning intervention programmes; ensuring pupils make good progress and effectively managing Access Arrangements.

MAJOR RESPONSIBILITIES

- Assist in drawing up SEN policy and implementation of SEN development plan.
- Regularly provide feedback to Senco on systems in place to identify and meet the needs of pupils with SEN/disabilities.
- Manage Access Arrangements (AA) effectively within the school, identifying pupils qualifying for AA, organising and co-ordinating the administration, ensuring effective supervision of AA in examinations and tests.
- Assist in the management of Learning Support team.
- Assist in the evaluation of SEN provision.
- Assist Senco in analysis of National, Local and School data.
- Promotion of the inclusion of pupils with SEN in mainstream classes.

Teaching and Learning

- Under agreed systems, assess pupils, identify SEN and review students' progress.
- Assist with the review process (including the Annual Statement review), developing and implementing Individual Education Plans (IEPs)
- Within an agreed system of supervision, deliver intervention programmes to individuals, groups or classes, assessing need, planning and delivering, monitoring and evaluating progress.
- Meet parents and outside agencies to discuss student needs, targets, action and progress and contribute to/lead the meetings.
- Collect and circulate specialist advice to relevant people.
- Take responsibility for the co-ordination of primary liaison tasks to ensure that students with SEN/disabilities successfully transfer from KS2 to KS3.

- Provide guidance to staff relating to policies concerning child protection, health, safety and security, confidentiality and data protection, and report all concerns to an appropriate person.

Managing Resources

- Advise Senco on staffing and resource needs within the LS team.
- Organise and co-ordinate the deployment of learning resources effectively, including ICT.
- Give Senco feedback on the effectiveness of resources.
- Maintain existing resources and liaise with Senco about developing new resources.
- Use accommodation to create a stimulating learning environment for the teaching and learning of interventions.

Leading and Managing Staff

- Line manage teaching assistants effectively.
- Observe and appraise TAs, to help them identify their training needs.
- Provide guidance in professional development.
- Be involved in providing training for TAs.
- Induct new TAs and give support.
- Assisting with recruitment and interviewing new staff.
- Ensure there is adequate cover for absent Learning Support staff.
- Write student profiles and provide information to all staff.
- Liaise between managers/teaching staff and teaching assistants.
- Chair cross faculty SEN meeting.
- Hold regular team meetings with managed staff.
- Management of break and lunchtime.
- Represent Learning Support team at teaching staff, management/other appropriate meetings.
- Recognise own strengths and areas of expertise and use these to lead, advise and support others.

Date:...

Signatures:

Manager:..

Post holder:...

STRATEGIC DIRECTION:	TEACHING & LEARNING	LEADING & MANAGING STAFF	MANAGING RESOURCES
▪ Assist in drawing up policy & take responsibility for implementation for areas within the Learning Support Development Plan ▪ Regularly provide feedback to SENCO on systems in place to identify & meet the needs of SEN pupils ▪ Assist SENCO in analysis & interpretation of National, Local & School's data ▪ Assist in evaluation of SEN provision	▪ Under agreed systems, assess pupils, identify SEN & review pupils' progress ▪ Under the supervision/management of SENCO, deliver intervention programmes to individuals, groups or classes, assessing need, planning, delivering, monitoring & evaluating progress ▪ Meet parents outside agencies & governors to discuss student needs, targets, action & progress & to develop effective partnerships ▪ To assist with the Annual Statement Review process ▪ Collect & circulate specialist advice to relevant people including student profiles ▪ Liaise with primary schools about pupils with SEN to ensure that there is good continuity in terms of support & progression in learning when pupils with SEN transfer ▪ To take responsibility for identification of students qualifying for access arrangements for examinations throughout the school & for the preparation of the appropriate assessments	▪ Line manage teaching assistants ▪ Observe & appraise TAs, to help them identify their training needs ▪ Provide guidance in professional development ▪ Be involved in providing training for TAs ▪ Induct new TAs & give support ▪ Assisting with recruitment & interviewing new staff ▪ Assistance in the construction & update of the Learning Support Timetable including allocation of LSA's duties ▪ Management of break & lunchtime supervision ▪ Assistance with Departmental Briefings/Meetings	▪ Advise SENCO on staffing & resource needs within the LS team ▪ Organise & co-ordinate the deployment of learning resources, including ICT ▪ Give SENCO feedback on the effectiveness of resources ▪ Maintain existing resources & liaise with SENCO about developing new resources ▪ Use accommodation to create an effective & stimulating environment for the teaching & learning of SEN interventions

Figure 10.1 The key tasks of a secondary school assistant SENCO

Monday 29th January 2007	9.30am – 11.00am	SS Annual Review (Transitional)
	9.45am	CATs Team work with 2 x LSAs– Organise
	11.30am – 1.00pm	AD Meeting with Parents/CATS/EdPsych
	1.00pm	Working lunch with Educational Psychologist
	1.45pm – 3.15pm	SF Annual Review (Transitional)
Tuesday 30th January 2007	9.00am – 10.30am	Student Referral Meeting
	10.30am – 12 Noon	Admin Time
	12.05pm P4	LSA Observation – AM 7K Tech D10
	1.40pm P5	LSA Annual Appraisal GH
	2.30pm P6	Meeting AM Asst H/T and JW Asst SENCO
	5.00pm – 6.30pm	SEN Options Evening – Library
Wednesday 31st January 2007	9.00am	MS Year 13 Free writing assessment by laptop (20 mins)
	9.30am – 10.45am	JB – Annual Review (Transitional)
	11.15am P3	Grade 2 Meeting – AM/JW
	12.05pm – 12.55pm	LSA Observation SD 8K RE K10
	P5 & P6	Meeting with KH – Vocational Studies Co-ordinator
Thursday 1st February 2007	P1, 2, 3	Assessments of Yr9's for Access Arrangements SATs
	P4	Meeting with JB Head of English re: Interventions/links with department – AM/JW
	1.45pm P5	Meeting – AM/JW Parents of Yr10 student with OCD
	3.20pm – 4.15pm	Meeting with RT ICT Teacher re: Yr10 Aspergers student - differentiation issues
Friday 2nd February 2007	9.00am – 12 Noon	Out at Great Moor House HLTA Conference Planning
	1.40pm – 4.15pm	Admin Time } Finalising/marking assmts Deciding who to apply E/T Preparing Applications for Amanuensis Access Arrangements – SATs

Figure 10.2 A week in the life of a secondary school assistant SENCO

it can be quite difficult to get specific information about what the teacher finds a child can and cannot do – and under what conditions. It is usually more difficult to obtain information about what a child can do than about where the child is failing. There is a similar problem about discovering the particular situations in which a child performs better than in others, so as to get an idea about teaching approaches.

(Weddell 2001: 92)

In the past, TAs learnt by watching the teacher, hopefully following the actions of a good role model. But, rarely were instructions explicit concerning the learning outcome required. This has changed with the emphasis on learning intentions in the strategy materials and the demand from inspection procedures that teachers' planning be written down. This explicit planning has helped the TA, but they

Autumn Term September	• Integration of New Year 7's. • Student Profiles to be prepared and distributed on all SA+, Statements and high priorities. • Group Reading Test on all Year 7's and marking. • Prioritise students for intervention.
October	• Access arrangements for Years 10 and 11 – Assess students and prepare applications. • Deadline for January modules applications by 31/10/07. • Observe LSAs in the classroom.
November	• Annual Appraisals of LSAs and target setting. • Conduct tours of SEN prospective parents and meetings. •
December	• Complete annual appraisal process and put forward to Headteacher.

Spring Term January	• Commence Annual Review Process:
	  Overview sheets to teachers
	  Book appointments
	  Commence Reviews
	• SEN Options Evening.

February	• Assess Year 9's and prepare applications for Access Arrangements for SATs. • Deadline for applications Access Arrangements for GCSE Summer exams. • Access Arrangements session Year 11's, scribes/readers/word processors. • Year 11 Mocks fortnight. Exam timetabling, invigilation, cover.
March	• Time management/Revision sessions for Year 11 GCSE's. • Deadline for completion of Annual Reviews 31/3/07 to CSET.
Summer Term April	• Commence Primary Liaison Visits to all schools with SEN transfers. • Prepare GCSE SEN timetable, rooming, invigilation and cover of LSAs. • Prepare SATs SEN timetable, rooming, invigilation and cover of LSAs. • Access Arrangements/Time Management Sessions Year 9's for SATs.
May	• Year 9 SATs. • Year 11 GCSEs May – 3rd week June. • Follow up visits to primaries, put in place transition plans.
June	• Small group induction visits. • Pen pictures of Year 6's to SLT.
July	• Year 10 modular exams. • Year 6 induction days. • Sports day – allocation of staff. • All information on Year 6's to tutors and LSAs.
August	• Timetabling of LSAs.
PLUS	Throughout the year: **Staffing** Advertise, select for interview, interviews and induction of new LSAs, Committee Meetings – Chair half termly SEN Committee Meetings. Set agendas, co-ordinate and facilitate Educational Psychologist meetings. Set up training opportunities for LSAs. Organise NPDs for Learning Support Department.

Figure 10.3 A year's calendar of events for a secondary school assistant SENCO

still need explicit guidance on how the teacher wants them to operate in the classroom. An observable trait of teachers and TAs is their ability to multitask. This, along with the relative mobility of TAs, compared with the teachers, means they can become a 'flexible friend' in the classroom, a 'gofer' in times of emergency, anything an extra pair of hands can do.

If relationships are good between the teacher and the TA it enables the TA to ask questions without fear, and the teacher to ask for changes in practice without upsetting the TA.

The *Good practice guide* (DfES 2000) has a whole section on creating partnerships with teachers on pages 24 to 27. It has a paragraph on each of the following:

1 differentiating the roles of teacher and TA;
2 ensuring teacher participation in planning;

3 creating a climate that encourages high-quality TA input;
4 developing feedback mechanisms;
5 dealing with behaviour management issues under teacher guidance;
6 ensuring TAs are informed of the learning needs and any behaviour difficulties of children with SEN;
7 including TAs in IEP reviews;
8 inviting TAs to staff meetings;
9 including TAs in the staffroom;
10 including TAs in written communications;
11 recognising the legal responsibilities of TAs;
12 encouraging reviews of the classroom relationships.

Exploring the teacher–TA partnership

Joint questionnaires as described in Chapter 6 to find the perceptions of the TA role by each 'side' can be helpful here. If TAs work in close partnership with one teacher they can share their replies with each other and see where the similarities and differences lie. The closer the partnership the closer the similarity will be. It is important that the school staff are ready for such an exercise and are wanting to look at their own practice and relationships – not always an easy situation to achieve. Do establish ground rules of purpose, confidentiality and use of results before you start such an investigation. The whole of Balshaw's book *Help in the classroom* (1999) is based on the assumption that once the climate for development is right teachers and TAs together can investigate how to improve their joint practice through various exercises in collaboration.

THINKING POINTS

Questions to ask both parties can be about:
The main aims of the school
Each other's roles – whether each knows what the other does both in their classroom and elsewhere in the schools
What their partner's experience and qualifications are for doing what they do
What feelings they have about their respective roles
The partnership
◆ What they think is happening
◆ What they get out of it
◆ What makes it work well and whether it could be improved and how
Any professional development and support given by the school
◆ Changes they might like to make
What expectations should they have for the future?
◆ What aspects of the TA's role they are most happy with
◆ What aspects are they least happy with?
Other comments

(Watkinson 2003a: 123, 124)

Lacey explored the whole issue of teacher–TA partnership in a chapter in her book about many kinds of partnerships. She gave some useful audit suggestions if partners are trying to address particular issues such as finding time to talk together, an essential element of partnership. She concludes the chapter:

> The partnership between teachers and assistants that are effective, have to struggle in the face of many adversities. When they work, the partners are supportive of each other and of children. They have sufficient time to plan and evaluate how best to work as well as efficient systems for communication. . . . This partnership appears to be built on mutual respect and trust, support of each other and a shared understanding of how to meet pupils' learning needs. It is underpinned by clear lines of communication, commitment to provide planning time and the security of a permanent job supported by a career structure and relevant training. Nothing less is sufficient.
>
> (Lacey 2001: 112)

Later in the book she gives a list of certain systems and strategies to promote partnership, based on work with many kinds of partners. It recognises that even where two people want to improve a relationship there are other constraints within any organisation. It needs attention to:

◆ management systems;
◆ management support;
◆ flexible time management;
◆ leadership;
◆ communication;
◆ common focus;
◆ shared learning; and
◆ team building.

She also suggested that schools or other services need to look at three levels if they wish to sort out their priorities – strategic, operational and fieldwork levels.

Boundaries

One of the things that have to be established between each teacher and TA working with them are the boundaries of the professional relationship. Each teacher has their own way of working and will need time to explore what their expectations are with TAs. When things are not talked about misunderstandings can arise or it takes much longer to establish how to work together. Lacey (1999) concluded that when considering inclusion at classroom level, it was vital that there were 'clarity of roles and responsibilities' and 'collaboration between teachers and LSAs, including time to plan and work together' (p. 33).

If a teacher is having a new TA, the following might be the questions in the TA's mind, and it is worth them spending time just clarifying the answers to them.

THINKING POINTS

What do you particularly want me to do?
What do I do if a pupil in your room asks to go to the toilet?
Can I write in any pupils' books?
What contact with parents or carers do you expect of the TA?
Do you want me to attend consultation evenings?
Do I take part in SEN reviews?
Can I do anything at the request of a parent such as change a child's reading book or search for lost equipment?
Can I tidy the rooms? Your desks? The resources area?
Is there anything you do not want me to do?

(Watkinson 2002a: 63)

Teachers need to make the most of another pair of hands:

◆   when following the strategies;
◆   because shared experiences give more opportunities for enjoyment and creativity;
◆   because it will enable more personalised learning for pupils;
◆   because the TA might be a mine of information about individual needs;
◆   to help other learners learn how to learn;
◆   to promote higher order thinking skills;
◆   to enable more open-ended questioning, investigation and exploration;
◆   to ensure a greater breadth of curriculum.

Supporting teaching and learning

The school will have already decided what their approach is to teaching and learning and many schools have established policies for just this area, and hopefully all teachers and TAs will have copies of this.

School example

Sarah Webber, an HLTA, has made this her area for her foundation degree study. She used a staff questionnaire to ask what areas needed to be covered by a TA policy. She has 'been developing a TA policy with the teaching and learning leader to clarify many areas of the TA role which are at present unclear due to the sheer diversity and changing nature of responsibilities'. In doing this she is now contributing to the teaching and learning policy itself as she 'felt TAs were much more at the core of teaching and learning than the policy suggested'. This contribution will result in some alterations to the policy.

A teaching and learning policy will address areas such as:

◆ differentiation – mixed ability, setting, and support for SEN;
◆ pupil involvement in active learning strategies;
◆ investigative/problem solving approaches to be used;
◆ written work – presentation and who marks what in what way;
◆ oral work – appropriate questioning skills;
◆ pupils' study skills.

Defining teaching and learning is complex, and has been the focus of much research. Watkins and Mortimore (1999) defined pedagogy (teaching) as 'any conscious activity by one person designed to enhance learning in another' (p. 3). It does not matter whether you read *Essential teaching skills* (Kyriacou 1998), *Effective teaching* (Dunne and Wragg 1994), look at the inspection frmaework in the Ofsted handbook (Ofsted 2003) or the *Values and principles underpinning the NOS* (LGNTO 2001), they all describe the teaching activities that TAs undertake.

The current regulations define 'specified teaching work' as follows:

a planning and preparing lessons and courses for pupils;
b delivering lessons to pupils;
c assessing the development, progress and attainment of pupils;
d reporting on the development, progress and attainment of pupils; and
e marking the work of pupils

but admit that 'these statements do not convey the degree of challenge and complexity of different learning situations'.

(DfES 2003: 20)

As TAs teach then any teaching and learning policy must include the work of TAs, let alone the contribution of HLTAs who may be taking classes without any other being present and where the learning is progressing.

Planning and preparation

It is so important that teachers share their planning with TAs in some way: TAs must know the teacher's curriculum objectives for the lesson. Teachers can decide to have separate plans for the TA, or photocopy their planning where the TA role is spelt out but they must have some kind of system for the TAs to have oversight of the planning before the lesson. How otherwise can they be expected to know what to do, why they are doing it and how the teacher wants it done. While formats or notebooks can save time and are useful for everyday working, it is imperative that you provide paid time for the TAs and teachers to plan together. Until they make a relationship and discuss the forthcoming lesson(s) there will be no joint progress. It is no economy to omit this. Too many HLTAs are 'doing cover' for emergency purposes, and picking up the planning as they go to the lesson or even finding it on the teacher's desk. When this happens, they are operating as cover supervisors and cannot properly advance the learning of the pupils. Too many TAs are wasting time, skill and potential without planning time. This is true in secondary as well as primary. A strange adult or even more than one appearing in a lesson can be a distraction, and they can only be used as glorified minders.

There is much to be gained from involving TAs in long-term and medium-term planning as well as the short-term planning for individual lessons. Provision for children with SEN can be discussed when looking at medium-term plans. TAs more often come from the locality than their teacher partners and contribute ideas of people to invite in, or local trips to make to enhance the enjoyment of the proposed curriculum. This kind of expertise is also useful in the long-term planning. TAs, particularly HLTAs, will have ideas on resources, placing pupils with peers, or not, and also get an idea of what the school wishes to concentrate on in the coming year.

It is also important that you enable the TA to have preparation time, both to prepare things for the teacher and to make their own preparations for what is expected of them. TAs need paid time to do this, especially if they are to relieve the teacher of some of the tasks that teachers should not routinely be expected to do. TAs can make work cards and work sheets given a prototype, make and mend equipment and books, or sort and organise classroom resources and equipment. Some equipment preparation and maintenance should be part of the pupils' tasks, and the distinctions need to be clarified for the TA. Even small children can and should clear up after themselves. TAs can help the pupils help themselves, with sufficient time allowed in the lesson for such activities. They can be encouraged to carry a few sharp pencils, a pencil sharpener and spare pens. If they are to use audiovisual equipment or a new software program on a computer, they need time to make sure it all works before the lesson, where to go for technical help or spare bits. New TAs might not have used projectors, PowerPoint or interactive whiteboards before, you or the class teacher should check.

Cronin and Bold (2005) have a useful chapter in *Working with support in the classroom* where they discuss what they believe are the three crucial issues which a classroom teacher must consider to ensure effective learning for pupils: communication, competence and confidence. Their chapter is about mathematical learning, where many adults admit lack of confidence, largely because of their own terrible experiences at school. TAs are usually much more confident with literacy activities but the issues discussed in this chapter can happen with any subject area. The authors suggest that teachers must be proactive in helping their TAs, which can happen most easily when sharing planning and feedback. Common misconceptions need to be aired and defused, the most recent developments in the subject shared, and ideas of what questions can be asked suggested. It puts the onus on the teacher, but the results are well worth it.

When evaluating the impact of TAs on the Further Literacy Support programme it was found that there was a reduction in efficacy in the second year (DfES 2005a). It is suggested that this might be due to reduced consultation between the teachers and TAs – a salutary thought.

Delivery

Performance

TAs will watch the various teachers with whom they work and see how they approach their teaching. Teaching is a performance, an act. Acting demands courage, forethought and practice, as does teaching. TAs may need comments on the way they use their ICT with pupils. Newer TAs lack confidence. Words, gestures and stance when asking pupils to do something need to assure them adults mean what they say, TAs must be encouraged to show sufficient authority to operate effectively. Their speech needs to be clear, grammatically correct, and with a confident but not loud, tone of voice. They might need to practise this. They might need to be trained in the use of gestures for the subtle behaviour management that can be achieved without a word, such as signalling 'turn it down' while maintaining eye contact. A TA sitting looking bored will signal to pupils that the lesson is boring – it might be, but the TA must act as if interested.

Exposition

Most teachers and lecturers have tried practising at home before a new lesson, and the TAs can be told of the benefit of such experiences. The development of 'critical friendships' between teachers and TAs where tips can be passed on frequently in an amicable way without waiting for an annual appraisal or a formal training session will pay dividends. The following checklist in Box 10.3 might be useful to give to TAs.

Questioning and challenging

One of the most important ways in which TAs can help children to learn, achieve and think is to question for themselves. Questions encourage thought and ideas, and, as pupils get older, enable them to ask questions themselves. Education is about imparting knowledge, for without it there is no context for understanding and any questioning is superficial; but without questioning, how can we be sure we understand, or make any progress. TAs need to understand about open and closed questions, particularly as teachers often use closed questions in whole-class situations to increase participation and a TA with a small group might have the time and opportunity to use open questions. The actual asking of the questions needs just the same kind of clarity, eye contact, and structure as an exposition. Questioning needs practice, like the other skills.

   Teachers could also ask a TA to collect the pupils' questions or take note who answers the teacher's questions with a tick grid with names on one side and columns just to note who answers, or who never even tries.

Intervention and non-intervention

TAs may need to be helped with this very important area, yet most seem to have an instinctive feel about allowing pupils to do what they can for themselves. *TAs are not there to do the pupils' work for them*, but they might need to interpret, scribe, repeat instructions, give an example. Both the pupil and the TA should be clear as to the purpose of the TA. The class teacher might need to monitor this, particularly being vigilant over marking any written work from the pupils, asking whose work is it? If there is a problem, the teacher must say so and not hope the problem will go away with time. The way learning takes place, the need for active participation and independence on behalf of the learner, will soon be understood by the TA, who will welcome any discussion on such matters. Basic learning psychology should be part of any TA course and usually fascinates TAs.

Box 10.3 Exposition guidance for a TA

Try and put your ideas in a logical sequence, and if possible note the key points. Try to have a beginning, middle and end, if it is prepared.

Find the right words, speak clearly, watch the tone and inflections in your voice.

Be sure of what you need to say or do – not too many 'ums' and 'ers'.

Try and involve the pupils. Even the television presenters try to do this, even without a live audience. Just watch a Blue Peter presenter - their eyes, their pace, their pauses. It all looks 'off the cuff', but is the result of practice.

Get the pupils' attention, maintain eye contact when you can. Use appropriate gestures. Explain what you are going to do or cover, and what the pupils should get out of it – or learn.

Try and get their interest from the start. Find out what they already know in the area if you have time, as this provides the scaffolding for the learning you are trying to promote. Where you can, link what you are saying to other lessons they have had in the same area, or what the teacher is particularly wanting to do. Even if you are working with pupils with SEN, try to make what you are doing relate to what the rest of the class are doing to allow them to keep up.
Emphasise the important bits. You may have to adapt as you go along, so be sensitive to the way in which the pupils are reacting to you and what you are saying. This will help you decide the next step, or how large a jump you can make in assuming understanding.

Use examples or analogies, objects or pictures, maps, diagrams, sounds, anything to create curiosity, motivate or add interest. Have a 'here is one I made earlier' item ready if that is relevant.

Draw or put key words down as you go along, you may even get to use the blackboard, whiteboard or overhead projector. Make sure you have paper, pencils, pens or chalk if you are going to need them. Do not get up to get things, this is an ideal opportunity for any pupils to lose interest and some to become disruptive.

Try and get feedback, and promote discussion, again if you have time. Did they understand what you were talking about? Dialogue keeps them both awake and participating. Respond to them.

Try to leave time to get one pupil to recall what you have been saying to another pupil. This helps them clarify their mind as well as give you an idea how well they have taken things in.

Summarise at the end.

[Watkinson 2002a pp. 54,55]

Listening

TAs might need help in understanding that listening to pupils is a very valuable way to spend time. Eighty per cent of time in school can be the teacher or TA giving out, with pupils actively participating for only 20 per cent of the time. Again, one of the opportunities of having a TA in the room is to give the pupils the opportunity of a listening ear.

TAs at first might need to be encouraged to leave their 'charges' to get on on their own for some learning strategies, or some tasks. Once the pupils understand what they have to do, and have the tools to do it, they must be allowed to work as unaided as possible. This might mean the teacher ensuring that the TA is mobile, and can offer support to other pupils, or has other classroom tasks with which to busy themselves.

The skill of the TA is to know when to intervene and when to stand back, and offering help appropriately when requested needs to be cultivated if it is not instinctive. This might mean looking at some of the classroom strategies for pupils' support as a whole. Primary teachers, working on their own, still find it quicker sometimes to give a child the correct spelling, to give the answer to a mathematical problem, rather than check a 'try'. They do not allow sufficient 'thinking' time. Having a TA to oversee such strategies should help active and independent learning.

Learners need language and social interaction to aid them, another area in which the TA can support, but keep the talk on the subject of the lesson not about last night's soap on television, the forthcoming football match or my mum's latest boyfriend. Monitoring group work for the teacher and reporting back can be a most useful added dimension to the lesson.

Practical work

TAs can work with a group, organise resources or equipment, use some explaining and tuition, question and observe what is going on. The pupils will be active, mobile and need to be as autonomous as possible. For these activities it is important that TAs are aware of all the Health and Safety procedures involved. For assisting in a subject such as secondary science this might well mean you have to set up a training session for the TA or TAs involved, to ensure they understand the principles of risk assessment and the safe ways of dealing with Bunsen burners, chemicals, glass, microbes and radioactive substances, all used in school laboratories.

There might be some activities for which the teacher needs to check the knowledge and skills of the TA, such as using measuring instruments correctly, understanding the level of accuracy that is required and the units to be used. Sometimes, in science tasks, pupils believe they have to find the answer, when actually the teacher's objective is to give them experience of certain equipment, or find a way to test, that can be repeated. In art, the emphasis by the pupil, again, might be on the end product, and whether or not they can achieve what is required, or something to satisfy themselves, whereas the teacher's objective has been to explore a variety of media, to find their potential for some other purpose entirely. It is essential that the TA knows the purpose of the task, they can then use appropriate questions to help the pupils think.

Any school ground rule of safety for active or practical group work must be discussed before any such activity.

Assessment activities: development, attainment and progress

All the time teachers work with pupils they inwardly make small judgements. Those with QTS recognise this as informal formative assessment. TAs will also judge but at first without training to realise what they are seeing. As they increase in understanding of how learning takes place, of the needs of pupils and the content of the curriculum, they will be increasingly useful in helping teachers in making more formal formative assessments. The feedback from TAs to the pupils can be part of the personalisation of the teaching process, supporting an individual's learning, but feedback to the teacher can be as important as the in-class support they are providing to the pupils. Teachers need to make arrangements to obtain this. Part of the planning activity should be to include how the feedback will take place as well as what kind of assessments the TA is to make. It will only be by prior discussion with the TA that both will know what to look for and what to communicate. The 'assessment for learning' strategies being proposed by government are really nothing new, but a vocalisation of the instinctive activity of a good teacher, enabling them to influence their teaching over the short or longer term. Assessment for learning focuses on progress not just attainment which is the focus of the testing and data collection which has received so much attention. The personalisation agenda is not just about SEN or identifying the gifted and talented but about all children, those often neglected in the middle.

Teachers need to ensure the TA understands the lesson objectives and what that will look like in outcomes for the class or group concerned: agreeing success criteria before a lesson will help enormously. Spending a little time looking together at pupils' work and commenting on progress, achievement and levelling would be a great training activity for TAs who will have little understanding of expectations otherwise. TAs will need more than discussion, some kind of deliberate training in some activities if any kind of levelling is wanted. Figure 10.4 shows where TAs have been trained what to look for in a Foundation stage class. They photograph events and with the teacher display some of the results.

Formal assessment activities such as undertaking levelled tasks or monitoring SATs activities really do need some structured input from the teacher as to what is required. Some of the strategy materials, designed for TA use, have their own assessment materials in them. Hopefully, if the TA is using them, their training explained their purpose and proper use. The ideas of 'more frequent tests – but shorter, better focused, "when ready" and lighter touch' proposals will be much more practicable if TAs can be involved but this will need both planning and training (DfES 2006b).

Feedback can be much more informal than the planning process, just a note on the planning sheet and handed back to the teacher will help. Task completion, levels of attention, verbal contributions of the individual or group can be most informative, but TAs will need guidance as to what exactly the teacher is looking for, if it is at all specific. This is where involvement with IEP formation and target setting is so helpful. Appropriate feedback to the pupils as well as to the teacher is also an essential part of personalised learning. Discussion at the planning level means that the TA can be helpful in return after the event. 'Post it' notes are invaluable and can be attached to pupils' work, the teacher's desk or planning sheets. Sometimes just a verbal comment at the end of a lesson before the TA and teacher separate, in the corridor on the way to the staffroom or even in the car

Figure 10.4 Photographic observations for the Foundation stage assessments

park on the way home can help the teacher plan the next step for the pupils with whom the TA has been working. In one school, the TAs themselves devised a separate written feedback system that would have some consistency for the teachers. Another school had a diary system for noting improvement and problem recording. TAs also use teachers' assessment forms after training and guidance, which can be ticked when things were achieved.

TAs are now widely used to input data into ICT programs for tracking progress. However, some kind of check as to the level of accuracy of the data should be made from time to time, as you would with anyone doing such a task.

TAs are the most cost-effective resource you have to ensure assessment for learning, to inform planning and provision mapping for planning additional interventions.

Marking

TAs have long been used for marking simple test sheets such as spelling tests or mental arithmetic, but even here the style and accuracy should be checked with the teacher before the task is undertaken. For any external test marking you should be very sure of their competence and understanding of the task. Where marking more ordinary school work is concerned, it will be a matter of judgement and training to ensure that the TA understands the purpose of the marking, the style and anything relevant on the school policy. HLTAs taking lessons will mark the work they have set, and should understand about being constructive, forward looking, not correcting every spelling, using a red pen or whatever the teacher and the school policy require.

In general

Some teachers do have problems with working with TAs. It might help senior managers to look at the following list when talking things over with a teacher who is having trouble. The ideas came from a chapter on partnership of teachers with nursery nurses (Jones 2005: 96–9).

THINKING POINTS

So why are there problems?
Personality differences
Training differences
Past experience of difficulties
Lack of trust
Lack of support from other staff/head/manager
Poor communication
Lack of consultation
Sharing the class with someone else
Not living up to expectations
Being less experienced than the assistant even if more qualified

Even in schools where all the systems, structures, strategies and philosophy are in place, and standards and expectations are high, time does not stand still. People change and can develop, all staff can be assisted in this process by managers.

Some of you may find Vincett *et al.*'s book *Teachers and assistants working together* useful (Vincett *et al.* 2005). It describes a research project undertaken in Essex where they experimented with various models of working together to support SEN. They looked at what they called room management, zoning and reflective teamwork. In the first the teacher is static and the TA works wherever there appears to be a need for support. In zoning, they split up the room geographically. Both of these models require an understanding prior to the lesson of how the pair will operate. The third requires regular meeting between lessons to reflect on what went well and what didn't and why. Taking what has been said about the importance of sharing understanding, planning together and communication, it is very understandable that the third model produces the best outcomes. But, it does depend on the school funding paid joint time together. The second part of Vincett *et al.*'s book contains lots of CPD activities exploring these models.

In the words of one teacher: 'It is worth the extra time and thought to get help like this.'

Chapter 11

Concluding thoughts

The effective school

The moves towards self-evaluation, the school effectiveness research movement and recognising that change is a fact of life, to be planned for not coped with, have moved the focus from the management to the leadership of an organisation. The image of the headteacher, cosily settled for life in a stable school, a pillar of the local community revered by staff, parents and children has long gone. Not only do schools have to plan for change, but part of their curriculum must be to help children and young people learn to live with and use change. Thomas and Webb (1998) describe an effective school as being:

> recognised to be one where all members are included and have a stake, not simply one which achieves high scores on academic criteria ... reducing inequality ... is about providing the chance to share in the common wealth of the school and its culture.
>
> (pp. 8, 9)

The teaching assistants are but one section of the support staff whose value is at last being recognised.

They are, however, the support staff group closest to the teaching and learning in the classroom. If teaching and learning are at the 'heart of school improvement ... real, lasting change can only come from what teachers and learning assistants do consistently in classrooms and other learning areas of the schools' (Brighouse and Woods 1999: 83). Brighouse and Woods go on to describe the development of teaching and learning climate with 'staff taking individual and collective responsibility to improve on their previous best'. Hopefully this book has helped towards developing the partnerships, inclusive practices and shared understanding that lead to a better quality of experience for all concerned. Brighouse and Woods describe ten factors which:

> if adopted would help to improve all schools:
>
> 1 an agreed policy about the practice of teaching and learning

2 a teaching and learning staffroom
3 collaborative teaching planning and assessment
4 the effective use of resources
5 monitoring and evaluation/collective review
6 professional development
7 action research
8 community involvement in the learning school
9 curriculum enrichment and extension
10 the celebration of teaching and learning.

(p. 85)

When these contributions are added to the research findings of Farrell *et al.* (1999) about TAs whose

general findings . . . suggest that effective practice:

◆ fosters the **participation** of pupils in the social and academic processes of the school;
◆ seeks to enable pupils to become more **independent learners**;
◆ helps to **raise standards** for all pupils (p. 4, their bold font),

it can be seen that working to improve the work with TAs, recognising them as professionals in their own right, can be a real move towards enhancing the education in your school and hopefully raising standards.

Professionalisation of the role of the TA

Until TAs and other support staff are considered professionals in their own right, and treated as such – with appropriate pay and conditions, CPD, performance management and respect from all classroom teachers – they will not be fully used and will continue to be exploited.

Morris (2001) talked of six characteristics being present in a modern profession. She then detailed how that can bolster the teaching profession. These characteristics could also be used to support the case for a profession in teaching assistance for the great majority of TAs (probably about 80 per cent) who are not aspiring to be teachers. I have taken each of her points and outlined how TAs could progress to also being a modern profession.

A *High standards at key levels of the profession, including entry and leadership, set nationally and regulated by a strong professional body*: For TAs, the HLTAs standards and the NOS are already in existence, with nationally recognised qualifications including NVQs. No entry qualifications are yet established. The HLTA status is still confused with a qualification, Foundation degrees are well established though. There is no independent national council, association or regulatory body for TAs. The General Teaching Council has taken a long time coming, and becoming established and recognised. HLTAs are registered with the DfES, could all TAs? Would a General TA Council be an answer? With the TDA, it could debate standards, operate the register, consider disciplinary matters if necessary and provide professional advice as well as be a voice in the public and political arena. Currently all is in the hands of the TDA and the DCFS.

B   *A body of knowledge about what works best and why, with regular training and development of opportunities so that members of the profession are always up to date*: The development of a pedagogy for TAs, to include teaching and learning theory and practice, curriculum knowledge and understanding, child development, SEN, etc., is well under way. The DfES Induction materials include a module on teaching and learning. The body of literature and research is growing and the development of foundation degrees has encouraged this as can be seen from the lists in Chapter 8.

The general pedagogic principles outlined by Ireson and Hallam (1999) were drawn up after they undertook various literature searches. These could well be adapted to make a set of principles for TAs.

It appears beneficial if teachers:

◆   are clear about their aims and share them with learners
◆   plan, organise and manage their teaching effectively
◆   try to formulate the highest expectations about the potential capabilities of learners within a general context of inclusivity
◆   provide learning tasks which will challenge and interest and which are aligned to appropriate assessment procedures
◆   seek to relate academic learning to other forms of learning and promote 'boundary crossing' skills
◆   make explicit the rules and at times, the hidden conventions of all learning institutions so that all learners become aware of ways in which they will be judged
◆   include an understanding of metacognition in their objectives so that all learners can benefit from this knowledge and – as they advance through their learning careers – take increasing responsibility for their own learning
◆   motivate and enthuse learners.

(Ireson and Hallam 1999: 230)

C   *Efficient organisation and management of complementary staff to support best professional practice*: The *Good practice guide* and the associated research done by Balshaw and Farrell (2002) have made a great start in supporting schools in their management strategies. Again a bibliography is growing.

D   *Effective use of leading edge technology to support best professional practice*: TAs have to negotiate access to resources and technology to give learning support. Now that teachers are not supposed to do the photocopying or laminating or similar administrative jobs, access to such facilities is much easier. Access to resource ideas, their own professional development and training to support ICT in pupils, needs space within the school. Rarely are TAs supplied with the same resources as teachers. Some HLTAs have laptops, but most have to access intranets through a common staffroom standalone computer.

E *Incentives and rewards for excellence, including through pay structures*: While case studies of effective use of TAs are increasing, it is hard to get concrete evidence of costs and meaningful performance-related pay. Facilitation of WR was widely disseminated with plenty of case studies available on the internet. But, real examples of creative budgeting are still hard to come by. Just handing out lump sums is no answer, nor is generally increased funding. School leaders and managers must play fair with their support staff, valuing them personally and financially as well as deploying and supporting them appropriately for the needs of the school. As mentioned earlier, the whole pay scene for TAs has been confused by the difficulties with some authorities in job evaluation and implementing single status awards. The difference between differing LAs has not helped either. We will have to await the outcome of this summer's DfES consultation on the matter. National pay scales would be another step to national recognition.

F *Relentless focus on what is in the best interests of those who use the service – in education, pupils and parents – backed by clear and effective arrangements for accountability and of measuring performance and outcomes*: What is the TA accountability to governors and parents for their responsibilities in your school? Does the TA effectiveness form part of your SEF? The philosophy behind this book supports the need for school vision with distributed leadership, stakeholder involvement and reflective partnerships, effective school self-review systems, ways of looking at the affective effectiveness of TAs, raising teacher morale by providing additional staff expertise, maintaining inclusive practices, promoting pupils self-esteem and independence, and the celebration of good practice.

TAs also need a voice of their own, just like the nurses, technicians and librarians. While the teacher unions, Unison the local government union and the GMB union, are voicing support for the TAs, none speak primarily for them, yet it is these organisations that are speaking for TAs in the DCFS and with employers. The TAs themselves are not represented. The bi-monthly magazine for TAs, *Learning Support*, is gaining readership. The most difficult problem for TAs is communication, not only inside but also with the world outside the school. Try checking your own distribution system in school for materials likely to interest TAs. Few circulars or fliers seem to get through to the TAs themselves. The development of senior TAs and HLTAs should begin to address this as administrative staff now have a named person to pass information on to. This goes for electronic communications as well as paper ones. All senior managers will recognise this problem as the DCFS themselves only send out e-mails with lists or access to things such as *Spectrum* and schools are expected to pick up the pieces for themselves.

There are TA groups around the country but they seem to meet informally, largely where senior managers or heads have encouraged them, offered to fund refreshments, circulated notices around the local communication systems and offered the school's hospitality. As leaders you can encourage such meetings and groups, and also encourage them to take the next step, and form a properly constituted TA association. TAs are perfectly capable of running such groups, and these could quickly grow, as with parents' and governors' groups to a representative national association. The PreSchool Learning Alliance grew from a letter in the *Guardian* newspaper in 1961 from Brenda Crowe, perhaps the TA movement will soon grow its own association.

Learning schools

TAs are not just an add-on to cope with SEN, they should be seen as a valuable part of a whole-school team if the ethos of the school needs to be that of a learning school, where all staff and other stakeholders are learners. Fullan (1991) talked of 'institutional development' and 'interactive professionalism' (p. 349) when discussing change in institutions. He also warns 'There are no short cuts, and there is no substitute for directly engaging in improvement projects with others. Like most complex endeavours, in order to get better at change we have to practice it on purpose' (p. 350).

All the above talk of effectiveness, using outside initiatives, of innovation, of improving all possible, indicates change – change in systems but also change in attitudes. Fullan (1991) describes taking one innovation at a time as 'firefighting and faddism' (p. 349). It seems WR has fallen into just this category, once done it does not have to be evaluated or reviewed.

There are cries of initiative overload, 'allow us to sort our own problems out – we are the professionals'. The freedom of the 1960s brought exciting education for a few but confusion and lack of opportunity for others. We have needed the legal entitlement to a curriculum and help with planning and ideas but it has brought us almost back to the Gradgrind days of rote learning, rows of children, silence and object lessons with year-based organisation. The challenge is to

◆ get the balance right;
◆ personalise the learning;
◆ support the disadvantaged;
◆ enthuse the disaffected;
◆ stretch the able;
◆ realise the potential of all staff.

It means being flexible, adapting, thinking the unthinkable. It means seeing where ICT fits in without it taking over. Even with the development of ICT there will always be the need for people, for personal interventions, guidance, help, encouragement and shared joy in success for all learners – pupils or adults. Noss and Pachler (1999) are convinced that teachers' professional judgement will still be needed in an ICT-rich learning environment: 'providing "scaffolding" . . . to maximise the effectiveness of the contribution of ICT to the learning process' (p. 206). Children are suffering from too much time spent in front of a screen and too little time interacting with people – be they parents teachers or peers. They need the real world around them as distinct from virtual worlds.

It means considering people's and pupils' feelings, emotional, social and spiritual needs as well as SEN. No one, pupil or staff, should feel neglected and no one should be exploited. Some schools have had a radical rethink on the way their school is run and staffed. Learning never stops. The ECM agenda and extended school initiatives will encourage schools to share their buildings and equipment but it takes people to act as learning facilitators. The role of teachers is already becoming that of a learning consultant, with a team of teaching and learning assistants, all themselves part of the learning organisation.

There is always a need for an open mind, a rethink, reflection on what is, has been and what might be.

Systemic thinking [Senge's Fifth Discipline] in practice is nothing more or less than a directed process of critical reflective inquiry looking into the nature of a situation and the relevance of possible different ways of handling the situation (including systems archytypes). It is a process that guides people to their own appreciation of matters of direct concern and how they might deal with them.

(Flood 1999: 73)

Flood recognises that we cannot know it all, or know what is going to happen to us. He has three paradoxes which might encourage you as you undertake yet more thinking:

◆ We will not struggle to manage over things – we will manage within the unmanageable.
◆ We will not battle to organise the totality – we will organise within the unorganisable.
◆ We will not simply know things – but we will know of the unknowable.

Systemic thinking in 'organisation and management' in essence is about being:

◆ ethically alert
◆ critically reflective
◆ appreciating issues and dilemmas that we face,
◆ exploring possible choices for action.

(Flood 1999: 194)

In conclusion

The ideas behind the WR, to get schools to take a step aside to consider the deployment of their most expensive resource – people – was great, but has largely come and gone with few schools having a radical rethink. Hopefully some of the ideas in this book will enable schools to regularly review and reflect; consider, consult and plan; enhance, encourage or change and celebrate. Not only does the school benefit, especially the pupils, but, also, an increasing number of adults will be appreciated, grow in personal stature and reach their potential or beyond.

Appendix 1

A list of the new National Occupational Standards units for those **Supporting teaching and learning in schools** which can be found in full on the ukstandards.org website.

The new units at level 2

Mandatory – 5 units

1 Provide support for learning activities
2 Support children's development
3 Help keep children safe
4 Contribute to positive relationships
5 Provide effective support for your colleagues

Optional units (Select 2)

6 Support literacy and numeracy activities
7 Support the use of information and communication technology for teaching and learning
8 Use information and communication technology to support pupils' learning
9 Observe and report on pupil performance
10 Support children's play and learning
11 Contribute to supporting bilingual/multilingual pupils
12 Support a child with disabilities or special educational needs
13 Contribute to moving and handling individuals
14 Support individuals during therapy sessions
15 Support children and young people's play
16 Provide displays
17 Invigilate tests and examinations

The new units at level 3

Mandatory (6 units)

3 Help keep children safe
18 Support pupils' learning activities
19 Promote positive behaviour
20 Develop and promote positive relationships
21 Support the development and effectiveness of work teams
22 Reflect on and develop practice

Optional units (Select any 4 units from groups A-E but no more than 2 units from group E)

Group A Supporting pupils' learning

8 Use information and communication technology to support children's learning
23 Plan, deliver and evaluate teaching and learning activities under the direction of a teacher
24 Contribute to the planning and evaluation of teaching and learning activities
25 Support literacy development
26 Support numeracy development
27 Support implementation of the early years curriculum
28 Support teaching and learning in a curriculum area
29 Observe and promote pupil performance and development
30 Contribute to assessment for learning
31 Prepare and maintain the learning environment
32 Promote the transfer of learning from outdoor experiences

Group B Meeting additional support needs

33 Provide literacy and numeracy support to enable pupils to access the wider curriculum
34 Support gifted and talented pupils
35 Support bilingual/multilingual pupils
36 Provide bilingual/multilingual support for teaching and learning
37 Contribute to the prevention and management of challenging behaviour in children and young people
38 Support children with disabilities or special educational needs and their families
39 Support pupils with communication and interaction needs
40 Support pupils with cognition and learning needs
41 Support pupils with behaviour, emotional and social development needs
42 Support pupils with sensory and/or physical needs
43 Assist in the administration of medicine
44 Work with children and young people with additional requirements to meet their personal support needs

Group C Providing pastoral support

45 Promote children's wellbeing and resilience
46 Work with young people to safeguard their welfare
47 Enable young people to be active citizens
48 Support young people in tackling problems and taking action
49 Support children and young people during transitions in their lives
50 Facilitate children and young peoples' learning and development through mentoring
51 Contribute to improving attendance
52 Support children and families through home visiting

Group D Supporting the wider work of the school

16 Provide displays
17 Invigilate tests and examinations
53 Lead an extra curricular activity
54 Plan and support self directed play
55 Contribute to maintaining pupils records
56 Monitor and maintain curriculum resources
57 Organise cover for absent colleagues
58 Organise and supervise travel
59 Escort and supervise pupils on educational visits and out-of-school activities
60 Liaise with parents, carers and families
61 Provide information to aid policy formation and the improvement of practices and provision

Group E Working with colleagues (no more than 2 units allowed from this group)

62 Develop and maintain working relationships with other practitioners
63 Provide leadership in your team
   OR
64 Provide leadership in your area of responsibility
65 Allocate and check work in your team
66 Lead and motivate volunteers
67 Provide learning opportunities for colleagues
68 Support learners by mentoring in the workplace
69 Support competence achieved in the workplace

Appendix 2

The Standards for Higher Level Teaching Assistants (HLTAs) as approved by ministers in June 2007

Those awarded HLTA status must meet all of the following standards:

Professional attributes

Those awarded HLTA must demonstrate, through their practice that they:

1 Have high expectations of children and young people with a commitment to helping them fulfil their potential
2 Establish fair, respectful, trusting supportive and constructive relationships with children and young people
3 Demonstrate the positive values, attitudes and behaviour they expect from children and young people
4 Communicate effectively and sensitively with children, young people, colleagues, parents and carers
5 Recognise and respect the contribution that parents and carers can make to the development and well-being of children and young people
6 Demonstrate a commitment to collaborative and cooperative working with colleagues
7 Improve their own knowledge and practice including responding to advice and feedback

Professional knowledge and understanding

Those awarded HLTA must demonstrate, through their practice that they:

8 Understand the key factors that affect children and young peoples' learning and progress
9 Know how to contribute to effective personalised provision by taking practical account of diversity

10 Have sufficient understanding of their area(s) of expertise to support the development, learning and progress of children and young people

11 Have achieved a nationally recognised qualification at level 2 or above in English/literacy and Mathematics/numeracy

12 Know how to use ICT to support their professional activities

13 Know how statutory and non statutory frameworks for the school curriculum relate to the age and ability ranges of the learners they support

14 Understand the objectives, content and intended outcomes for the learning activities in which they are involved

15 Know how to support learners in accessing the curriculum in accordance with the special educational needs (SEN) code of practice and disabilities legislation

16 Know how other frameworks, that support the development and well-being of children and young people, impact upon their practice

Professional skills

Teaching and learning activities must take place under the direction of a teacher and in accordance with arrangements made by the headteacher of the school

Planning and expectations

Those awarded HLTA must demonstrate, through their practice that they:

17 Use their area(s) of expertise to contribute to the planning and preparation of learning activities

18 Use their area(s) of expertise to plan their role in learning activities

19 Devise clearly structure activities that interest and motivate learners and advance their learning

20 Plan how they will support the inclusion of the children and young people in the learning activities

21 Contribute to the selection and preparation of resources suitable for children and young people's interests and abilities

Monitoring and assessment

Those awarded HLTA must demonstrate, through their practice that they:

22 Monitor learners' responses to activities and modify the approach accordingly

23 Monitor learners' progress in order to provide focussed support and feedback

24 Support the evaluation of learners' progress using a range of assessment techniques

25 Contribute to maintaining and analysing records of learners' progress

Teaching and learning activities

Those awarded HLTA must demonstrate, through their practice that they:

26 Use effective strategies to promote positive behaviour

27 Recognise and respond appropriately to situations that challenge equality of opportunity

28 Use their ICT skills to advance learning
29 Advance learning when working with individuals
30 Advance learning when working with small groups
31 Advance learning when working with whole classes without the presence of the assigned teacher
32 Organise and manage learning activities in ways which keep learners safe
33 Direct the work, where relevant, of other adults in supporting learning

Bibliography

Alfrey, C. (ed.) (2004) *Understanding children's learning.* London: David Fulton Publishers.

Anon. (2007a) 'Teachers TV more popular with TAs than teachers'. *Learning Support* (12), 6.

Anon. (2007b) 'What's on in talk2learn', (pp. Website chatroom). Nottingham: National College for School Leadership.

ATL, DfES, GMB, NAHT, NASUWT, NEOST, PAT, SHA, TGWU, UNISON and WAG (2003) 'Raising standards and tackling workload: a national agreement'. London: DfES.

Balshaw, M. (1991) *Help in the classroom.* London: David Fulton Publishers.

—— (1999) *Help in the classroom.* (2nd edn). London: David Fulton Publishers.

—— and Farrell, P. (2002) *Teaching assistants: practical strategies for effective classroom support.* London: David Fulton Publishers.

Ben-Peretz, M.S.S. and Kupermitz, H. (1999) 'The teachers' lounge and its role in improving learning environments in schools'. In H.J. Freiberg (ed.) *School climate.* London and Philadelphia: Falmer Press.

Birkett, V. (2004) *How to support and manage teaching assistants.* Cambridge: LDA with Findel Education.

Blatchford, P., Martin, C., Moriarty, V., Bassett, P. and Goldstein, H. (2002) 'Pupils adult ratio differences and educational progress over reception and Key Stage 1' (Research). London: DfES and the London Institute of Education.

——, Bassett, P., Brown, P., Martin, C., Russell, A., Webster, R. and Haywood, N. (2006) 'The deployment and impact of support staff in schools' (Research report RR 776). London: Institute of Education, University of London and DfES.

——, Bassett, P., Brown, P., Martin, C., Russell, A. and Webster, R. (2007) 'Deployment and impact of support staff in schools' (Research Report RROOS). London: Institute of Education, University of London and DCSF.

Bold, C. (ed.) (2004) *Supporting learning and teaching.* London: David Fulton Publishers.

Brighouse, T. and Woods, D. (1999) *How to improve your school.* London and New York: Routledge.

Brown, G. and Wragg, E.C. (1993) *Questioning.* London and New York: Routledge.

Cable, C. and Eyres, I. (eds) (2005) *Primary teaching assistants – curriculum in context.* London: David Fulton Publishers in association with The Open University.

Campbell, A. and Fairbairn, G. (eds) (2005) *Working with support in the classroom.* London, Thousand Oaks, CA and New Delhi: Paul Chapman Publishing.

Collarbone, P. and Billingham, M. (1998) 'Leadership and our schools' (Bulletin). London: Institute of Education.

Crane, M. (2002) 'Winning hearts and minds: leadership and performance management'. National College of School Leadership.

Cronin, S. and Bold, C. (2005) 'Partners in mathematical learning'. In A. Campbell and G. Fairbairn (eds) *Working with support in the classroom*. London, Thousand Oaks, CA and New Delhi: Paul Chapman Publishing.

Davey, A. (2007) 'Hitting the spot'. *Secondary Teachers*, January (48), 8–9.

DES (1978) *The Warnock Report*. London: Department of Education and Science.

DfEE (1998) 'Teachers meeting the challenge of change' (Green paper). London: DfEE.

—— (1999) *The National Curriculum – handbook for primary teachers in England; Key stages 1 and 2*. London: DfES and the Qualifications and Assessment Authority.

DfES (2000) *Working with teaching assistants – a good practice guide*. (DfES 0148/2000 ed.). London: DfES.

—— (2001) *Special Educational Needs Code of Practice*. London: DfES.

—— (2002) 'Time for standards: reforming the school workforce'. (Proposals DfES/0751/2002). London: DfES.

—— (2003) 'The education (Specified work and registration) (England) regulations 2003'. London: DfES.

—— (2004a) 'Advanced skills teachers working with support staff – report of conference held in November 2003' (DfES/0147/2004). London: DfES.

—— (2004b) 'Excellence and enjoyment: a strategy for primary schools' (Advice DfES/0377/2003). London: DfES.

—— (2005a) 'National evaluation of the NLS further literacy support programme: follow up study 2003–4'. Available at: www.standards.dfes.gov.uk/primary/features/inclusion/nls_fls (accessed 12 April 2007).

—— (2005b) 'The effective management of teaching assistants to improve standards in literacy and mathematics'. London: DfES with SureStart.

—— (2006a) '2020 vision – Report of the Teaching and Learning in 2020 review group' (Review group report PPOAK/D16/1206/53). London: DfES.

—— (2006b) 'Making good progress – how can we help every pupil to make good progress at school?' Consultation. London: DfES.

—— (2006c) 'Safeguarding children and safer recruitment in education' (04217-2006BKT-EN). London: DfES.

—— and TTA (2003) Standards for Higher Level Teaching Assistants – Consultation document April 2003 (Consultation). London: DfES and TTA.

Dunne, E. and Bennett, N. (1994) *Talking and learning in groups*. London and New York: Routledge.

Dunne, R. and Wragg, T. (1994) *Effective teaching*. London and New York: Routledge.

Easton, C., Edmonds, S., Kendall, L., Lee, B., Pye, D. and Whitby, K. (2003) 'Tracking the progress of Investors in People in schools' (RR406). Slough: National Foundation for Education Research.

ECC (2002) 'Performance management review scheme'. Notes of guidance and model policy for schools. Chelmsford: Essex County Council.

Farrell, P., Balshaw, M. and Polat, F. (1999) 'The management, role and training of learning support assistants' (Research report RR161). London: DfEE.

FAS (1998) 'The use of support staff in schools – a research report on Grant-Maintained schools'. York: Funding Agency for Schools.

Flood, R.L. (1999) *Rethinking the Fifth Discipline*. London and New York: Routledge.

Fox, G. (1998) *A handbook for Learning Support Assistants*. London: David Fulton Publishers.

Freiberg, H.J. and Stein, T.A. (1999) 'Measuring, improving and sustaining healthy learning environments'. In H.J. Freiberg (ed.) *School climate* (pp. 11–29). London and Philadelphia: Falmer Press.

Fullan, M.G. (1991) The new meaning of educational change. (2nd edn). London: Cassell Educational.

Gardner, H. (1983) *Frames of mind: the theory of multiple intelligences.* New York: Basic Books.

George, J. and Hunt, M. (2003) *Appointing and managing learning support assistants.* London: David Fulton Publishers.

Goleman, D. (1996) *Emotional intelligence.* London: Bloomsbury Publishing.

Haigh, G. (1996) 'To boldly go beyond washing the paintpots'. *Times Educational Supplement*: Primary Update, p. 21.

Hall, G.E. and George, A.A. (1999) 'The impact of principal change facilitator style on school and classroom culture'. In H.J. Freiberg (ed.) *School climate.* London and Philadelphia: Falmer Press.

Hancock, R. and Collins, J. (eds) (2005) *Primary teaching assistants.* London: David Fulton Publishers in association with The Open University.

Harding, J. and Meldon-Smith, L. (1996) *How to make observations and assessments.* London: Hodder & Stoughton.

Hargreaves, D.H. and Hopkins, D. (1991) *The empowered school.* London: Cassell Education.

Hayes, D. (2000) *The handbook for newly qualified teachers – meeting the standards in primary and middle schools.* London: David Fulton Publishers.

Hodgson, A. and Kambouri, M. (1999) 'Adults as lifelong learners: the role of pedagogy in the new policy context'. In P. Mortimore (ed.) *Understanding pedagogy and its impact on learning* (pp. 175–92). London, Thousand Oaks, CA and New Delhi: Paul Chapman Publishing.

Hryniewicz, L. (2004) *Teaching assistants – the complete handbook.* Ely: Adamson Publishing.

IiP (2005) Measure your improvements – Investors in People in schools and colleges. London: Investors in People UK.

Ireson, J.M.P. and Hallam, S. (1999) 'The common strands of pedagogy and their implications'. In P. Mortimore (ed.) *Understanding pedagogy and its impact on learning.* London, Thousand Oaks, CA and New Delhi: Paul Chapman Publishing/Sage Publications.

Johnson, P. (2007) 'Skills development session – chairing meetings', (notes for a training session for chairs of committees of Essex Wildlife Trust).

Jones, A.-M. (2005) 'The teacher and the nursery nurse: building the partnership'. In A. Campbell and G. Fairbairn (eds) *Working with support in the classroom.* London, Thousand Oaks, CA and New Delhi: Paul Chapman Publishing.

Jones, M. (2003) 'What makes a good school?' *New Era in Education*, 84(1).

Kerry, T. (2001) *Working with support staff – their roles and effective management in schools.* Harlow: Pearson Education.

—— and Mayes, A.S. (1995) *Issues in mentoring.* London and New York: Routledge in association with the Open University.

Kyriacou, C. (1997) *Effective teaching in schools: theory and practice.* (2nd edn). Cheltenham: Stanley Thornes (Publishers).

—— (1998) *Essential teaching skills.* (2nd edn). Cheltenham: Nelson Thornes.

Lacey, P. (1999) *On a wing and a prayer.* MENCAP.

—— (2001) *Support partnerships.* London: David Fulton Publishers.

Lee, B. (2002) 'Teaching assistants in schools: the current state of play' (LGA research report 34). Slough: National Foundations for Educational Research and Local Government Association Research.

LGNTO (2001) 'Teaching/classroom assistants National Occupational Standards'. London: Local Government National Training Organisation.

Lorenz, S. (1998) *Effective in-class support.* London: David Fulton Publishers.

Macbeath, J. (1999) *Schools must speak for themselves – the case for school self evaluation*. London and New York: Routledge.

——, Boyd, B.J.R. and Bell, S. (1996) *Schools speak for themselves*. National Union of Teachers for the University of Strathclyde.

MacGilchrist, B., Myers, K. and Reed, J. (1997) *The intelligent school*. London: Paul Chapman Publishing.

Morris, E. (2001) 'Professionalism and trust' (Speech to Social Market Foundation). London: DfES.

Mortimore, P., Mortimore, J. and Thomas, H. (1994) *Managing associate staff – innovation in primary and secondary schools*. London: Paul Chapman Publishing.

——, ——, ——, Cairns, R. and Taggart, B. (1992) 'The innovative uses of non-teaching staff in primary and secondary schools project' (Final report). London: Institute of Education University of London and Department for Education.

——, Sammons, P., Stoll, L., Lewis, D. and Ecob, R. (1988) *School matters*. Wells: Open Books Publishing.

NJC (2003) 'School support staff: the way forward'. London: Employers Organisation for the National Joint Council for Local Government Services.

Noss, R. and Pachler, N. (1999) 'The challenge of new technologies: doing old things in a new way, or doing new things?' In P. Mortimore (ed.) *Understanding pedagogy and its impact on learning* (pp. 195–211). London, Thousand Oaks, CA and New Delhi: Paul Chapman Publishing.

O'Brien, T. and Garner, P. (2001) *Untold stories – Learning Support Assistants and their work*. Stoke on Trent and Sterling, VA: Trentham Books.

Ofsted (2002) 'Teaching assistants in primary schools: an evaluation of the quality and impact of their work' (HMI 434). London: Ofsted.

—— (2003a) *Handbook for inspecting nursery and primary schools*. (May 2003 edn Vol. HMI 1359). London: Ofsted.

—— (2003b) 'Leadership and management: managing the school workforce' (HMI 1764). London: Ofsted.

—— (2005) 'Remodelling the school workforce' (Report HMI 2596). London: Ofsted.

O'Neill, J.M.D. and Glover, D. (1994) *Managing human resources in school and college*. EMDU University of Leicester/Longman.

Plowden, B. (1967) 'Children and their primary schools' (A report of the Central Advisory Council for Education England Vol. 1 Report HMSO).

Pollard, A. (2002a) *Reflective teaching – effective and evidence-informed professional practice*. London and New York: Continuum.

—— (ed.) (2002b) *Readings for reflective teaching*. London and New York: Continuum.

PricewaterhouseCoopers (2001) 'Teacher workload study' (Draft final report). PricewaterhouseCoopers.

—— (2007) 'Independent study into school leadership: main report' (Research Report RR818A). London: DfES.

QCA (1998) 'Draft framework for qualifications and training in early years education, childcare and playwork sector – Annexe 3'. London: Qualifications and Curriculum Authority.

Rose, C. (2001) 'Carole's story: looking back'. In T. O' Brien and P. Garner (eds) *Untold stories – Learning Support Assistants and their work* (pp. 71–82). Stoke on Trent and Sterling, VA: Trentham Books.

Rudduck, J., Brown, N. and Hendy, L. (2006) 'Personalised learning and pupil voice – The East Sussex project'. London: DfES with Innovation and the CfBT Education Trust.

Sammons, P.H.J. and Mortimore, P. (1995) *Key characteristics of effective schools*. London: Ofsted.

Sauvé, Bell, and Associates (2003) 'Functional map for the provision of learning mentor services – final version'. London: DfES.

Senge, P.M. (1990) *The fifth discipline*. London, Sydney, Auckland, Parktown: Century Business.

——, Cambron-McCabe, N., Lucas, T., Smith, B., Dutton, J. and Kleiner, A. (2000) *Schools that learn*. London and Yarmouth, ME: Nicholas Brealey Publishing.

Smith, P., Whitby, K. and Sharp, C. (2004) 'The employment and deployment of teaching assistants'. Slough: National Foundation for Educational Research.

Swann, W. and Loxley, A. (1998) 'The impact of school-based training on classroom assistants in primary schools'. *Research Papers in Education*, 13, pp. 141–60.

TDA (2005) *Career development framework for school support staff – guidance handbook*. London: Training and Development Agency for schools.

—— (2006a) *Teaching assistant file – primary induction*. London: Training and Development Agency.

—— (2006b) *Teaching assistant file – secondary induction*. London: Training and Development Agency.

—— (2007a) Draft revised standards for Higher Level Teaching Assistants (February 2007), [PDF]. Training and Development Agency.

—— (2007b) 'Remodelling: proven change process', www.remodelling.org/remodelling/managingchange. London: Training and Development Agency for Schools.

—— (2007c) 'National occupational standards for suppporting teaching and learning in schools', www.ukstandards.org.

TES (2007a) 'Support staff to gain their own pay structure'. *Times Educational Supplement*, 25 May, pp. 11.

—— (2007b) 'Ask a teacher'. *Times Educational Supplement*, 2 March, pp. 63.

Thomas, G.W.D. and Webb, J. (1998) *The making of the inclusive school*. London and New York: Routledge.

Thornton, M. and Hedges, C. (2006) 'The active engagement of teaching assistants in teaching and learning' (summary for the Teacher Research Conference 2006). London: DfES – National Teacher Research Panel.

TTA (2004) *Guidance to the standards – meeting the professional standards for the award of higher level teaching assistant status*. London: Teacher Training Agency.

Tyrer, R., Gunn, S., Lee, C., Parker, M., Pittman, M. and Townsend, M. (2004) *A toolkit for the effective teaching assistant*. London, Thousand Oaks, CA and New Delhi: Paul Chapman Publishing.

Vincett, K., Cremin, H. and Thomas, G. (2005) *Teachers and assistants working together*. Maidenhead: Open University Press.

Wallace, S. (2005) 'Being a SENCO's assistant'. In R. Hancock and J. Collins (eds) *Primary teaching assistants* (pp. 38–42). London: David Fulton Publishers in association with The Open University.

Watkins, C. and Mortimore, P. (1999) 'Pedagogy: what do we know?' In P. Mortimore (ed.) *Understanding pedagogy and its impact on learning*. London, Thousand Oaks, CA and New Delhi: Paul Chapman Publishing/Sage Publications.

Watkinson, A. (1998a) 'Supporting learning and assisting teaching: 1'. *Topic* National foundation for Educational Research, 19 (Spring).

—— (1998b) 'Supporting learning and assisting teaching: 2'. *Topic* National foundation for Educational Research, 20 (Autumn).

—— (2002a) *Assisting learning and supporting teaching*. London: David Fulton Publishers.

—— (2002b) 'When is a teacher not a teacher? When she is a teaching assistant'. *Education 3-13*, 30, pp. 58–65.

—— (2003a) *Managing teaching assistants – a guide for headteachers, managers and teachers*. London: Routledge Falmer.

—— (2003b) *The essential guide for competent teaching assistants – meeting the National Occupational Standards at Level 2.* London: David Fulton Publishers.

—— (2003c) *The essential guide for experienced teaching assistants – meeting the National Occupational Standards at level 3.* London: David Fulton Publishers.

—— (2005) *Professional values and practice: the essential guide for Higher Level Teaching Assistants.* London: David Fulton Publishers.

—— (2006) *Learning and teaching – the essential guide for Higher Level Teaching Assistants.* London: David Fulton Publishers.

Weddell, K. (2001) 'Klaus' story: the experience of a retired professor of special need education'. In T. O'Brien and P. Garner (eds) *Untold stories – Learning Support Assistants and their work* (pp. 89–96). Stoke on Trent and Sterling, VA: Trentham Books.

West-Burnham, J. (2004) 'Building leadership capacity – helping leaders learn' (PDF). National College for School Leadership.

—— and Ireson, J. (2006) 'Leadership development and personal effectiveness'. National College of School Leadership.

Wragg, E.C. (1994) *An introduction to classroom observation.* London and New York: Routledge.

—— and Brown, G. (1993) *Explaining.* London and New York: Routledge.

Index